Go
for
it!

For
Sylvie and Katie,
and all other youngsters
in the business of growing
up,
and in memory of
Jock Barr,
who devoted his life
to helping young people.

Go
for
it!

MARTYN LEWIS'S
ESSENTIAL
GUIDE TO
OPPORTUNITIES
FOR YOUNG
PEOPLE

**1994
REVISED EDITION**

Foreword by
HRH
The Prince of Wales

Lennard Publishing
produced in association with
the Prince's Trust, Drive For Youth and
the Institute for Citizenship Studies

First edition published in 1993 by
Lennard Publishing
a division of Lennard Associates Ltd
Mackerye End, Harpenden
Herts AL5 5DR

Second revised edition 1994

© 1994 Martyn Lewis and Lennard Associates

ISBN 1 85291 119 0

British Library Cataloguing in Publication
Data is available

Cover design by Cooper Wilson
Text design by Forest Publication Services
Index program by Mark Stephenson
Index by Adam Stephenson

Printed and bound in Great Britain by
Butler and Tanner Ltd, Frome and London

CONTENTS

ACKNOWLEDGEMENT

I am most grateful to the companies and trusts listed below. Through their generous support a complimentary copy of this new edition will be distributed to every secondary school, college of further education and university.

The Andrew Mitchell Christian Charitable Trust
The Bernard Sunley Charitable Foundation
British Airways
British Telecom
Cadbury Schweppes
John Laing
Marks & Spencer
Midland Bank
Northern Foods
The Nour Foundation
The Post Office
PowerGen
Reuters

I am also grateful the following who have offered help in developing public awareness of the book and its message: Daily Express, Department of Employment, McDonald's Restaurants, Next, Pizza Express, The Sunday Times and Tate & Lyle.

ST. JAMES'S PALACE

For young people in Britain today the most important choices they have to make are those that shape their lives and their careers after they leave school. And those choices are often dependent on the people and organisations they approach for help and information.

Knowing who can offer the best advice – and how to get in touch with them – can be a time-consuming and difficult process for both youngsters and their parents. This comprehensive book offers a much-needed shortcut to the vast range of youth opportunities now available in Britain. The contacts on offer range from new challenges for helping character-building, to academic and other long-term career opportunities. And there is much to interest the disadvantaged and disabled too. With plans to update the book every year, it should become essential reading for Britain's young people – and all who care about them.

PREFACE

'Is there,' I asked, 'a book that comprehensively and easily offers up a first port of call for all young people wanting to explore the huge range of opportunities available to them as they approach the end of their time at school and move on through their late teens and early twenties?'

'Yes,' came the reply, 'there must be. We'll find it for you!'

They came back days later to admit, rather sheepishly, that they were wrong.

Incredibly, no such book existed.

It does now.

That was late 1990. I had just become Chairman of a small, but innovative, charity called Drive For Youth, whose dedicated team was pioneering a new and highly successful formula for re-motivating the young, long-term unemployed, and leading them on to jobs or further education. Such young people are solidly among those in our society who most need help and opportunity – that vital life-raft which, if delivered properly and effectively, will help not just them, but, in time, society too. I have been a director of Drive For Youth since its formation in 1986, and have never ceased to be amazed at the positive way young people on the cliff-edge of desperation, often on the fringes of drugs and crime, respond when offered the right encouragement. But, of course, the opportunity to respond to the Drive For Youth course was only available to **those who knew it existed**.

It set me wondering how young people from **all** walks of life, and with all kinds of needs, set about homing in on those organisations offering the opportunities and help they needed most. So, where was the book that pulled all this advice, contacts and information together? There wasn't one. Yes, several publications did serve certain groups in special ways, but the United Kingdom as a whole had no single, all-embracing guide to opportunities for young people, no book which was an easily accessible and straightforward 'bible' of opportunity. It was clearly time that we had one, and that this unbelievable omission from the lives of youngsters and their parents and helpers was rectified.

Coincidentally, I went to a meeting around that time with Tom Shebbeare, Director of the Prince's Trust. While waiting for a colleague to join us, I aired my thoughts on what was then called simply 'The Youth Handbook'. Tom's initial reaction – like mine – was incredulity that such a book did not already exist. He rapidly, and generously, offered to fund research, first to establish whether there really was a strong market for the kind of book I had in mind and secondly to carry out the time-consuming chore of tracking down and checking the details of the hundreds of organisations and publications that would have to be pulled together.

Enter Broadcasting Support Services, with a

team led by Tom McAuliffe, whose thorough research not only uncovered an overwhelming demand for the kind of guidebook we had in mind, but carried on to gather, in the most comprehensive way, the welter of material from which the book has been compiled.

So I am deeply grateful to Tom Shebbeare and his deputy at the Prince's Trust, Jock Barr, for their rapid – indeed, splendidly unbureaucratic – response to my idea, and to Tom McAuliffe and the BSS team for their huge, invaluable contribution to its execution. My deepest thanks go also to the book's many sponsors, recorded on page 4, whose generosity has delivered a copy free to the head of every secondary school in the country and all institutions of further and higher education, and ensured that its distribution in high street shopping places is considerably wider than would be possible through bookshops alone; to Adrian Stephenson and his team at Lennard for so readily seizing the opportunity to publish; to Bernard Donoghue, former Chairman of the British Youth Council, for casting a wise and experienced eye over the original text; to careers counsellor Grenville Jenkins for allowing me to use his expert advice on job interview techniques and CVs; to Stephen O'Brien and his colleagues at Business in the Community for opening doors to potential sponsors at the highest level; to Claire Sawford of The Creative Umbrella and Gina Sussens for help in reaching those sponsors and developing publicity and markets for the book; and to HRH The Prince of Wales for his interest, and words of encouragement that form the foreword.

The price of the 1994 edition remains unchanged at the lowest level possible – a mark of the continuing efforts to make it readily available to the maximum number of young people. As last year the royalties will be equally divided between Drive For Youth, the Prince's Trust and the Institute for Citizenship Studies – another, more indirect, way in which this book will help young people.

This 1994 edition of *Go for it!* honours the promise made last year to turn it into an annual publication. Every entry has been checked and updated where necessary – and some 50 additional organisations have been included taking the total number of entries to well over the 450 hundred mark. Despite this it is still possible that one or two opportunities have been left out; if so a letter to me at the BBC's Six O'clock News, BBC TV Centre, London W12 7RJ – or via the publishers, Lennard Publishing – will ensure that the omission is corrected in next year's edition.

Demand for *Go for it!* was extremely high last year – and if you or your friends have any difficulty obtaining copies from your local bookshop, you will find an order form on the last page of this book to enable you to obtain it direct from publishers (postage and packing free).

Finally a huge thank you to all of you – young

people, parents and teachers – who took the
trouble to write to say how useful you found last
year's edition. It is most encouraging and most
appreciated. To you – and those newcomers
discovering *Go for it!* for the first time in 1994
– good hunting! The first signpost to the right
opportunity for you is only a few pages away.

Martyn Lewis
London, March 1994

FINDING YOUR WAY AROUND

This book is designed to give everyone quick and easy access to the particular opportunity – or range of opportunities – they are seeking. It is divided into two main sections.

Part One: The Categories

This is the section you should turn to first if:
(a) you know the kind of opportunities you are looking for, but don't know the precise name of any organisation(s) involved
(b) you know the name of one organisation, but would like to know what other opportunities exist in the same area
(c) you don't have any clear idea of what you're after – but want to explore as briefly as possible the type of opportunities on offer without having to read the whole book
    There are 19 category headings:
Volunteering
Community Projects
Working Holidays
Summer Vacation
Gap Year Challenges
Expeditions
Adventure Challenges
Opportunities Abroad – a wide variety of activities in other countries including student and cultural exchanges

Arts and Crafts – this has three sections covering Music, Drama, and Other Activities

Sport and Leisure

Careers – this is divided into three sub-sections too:

(1) Business and Industry

(2) Further Education, Training and Vocational Training

(3) Higher Education and Universities

Fund-raising lists organisations offering financial help of various kinds

Political lists simply the names and addresses of the parties represented by MPs at Westminster (no more details, I'm afraid – you'll have to write for their manifestos!)

Special Needs deals with organisations whose sole purpose is to help people with physical or learning difficulties (as distinct from many other organisations which deal with a more general clientele, and whose ability to help people with special needs is indicated in their individual entries)

Extra-Curricular Activities hoovers up organisations you can join to pursue a particular interest, where the opportunity on offer combines learning with comradeship and a variety of on-going courses tailored to the particular vision and purpose of each organisation (e.g. Scouts, Girl Guides, Junior Astronomical Society)

Each of the 19 categories simply lists each relevant organisation in alphabetical order, along with the page number in Part Two where you will find its more detailed entry. If you have trouble identifying your particular interest with any of these main categories, I suggest you look for an entry in the extensive index at the back of the book.

Part Two: The Dictionary of Opportunity

This, the main body of the book, will be the first port of call for those who already know the precise name of the organisation they are looking for. It lists by name, in alphabetical order, hundreds of organisations and publications offering advice, opportunity and help of one kind or another. Each of these entries describes briefly the work of the organisation, and lists the appropriate address, telephone and fax number from which you can obtain further details. But to save wasting your time and to avoid unnecessary telephone bills, other important information is also included, where appropriate.

Look first for the **Age Range** to see if you are eligible to apply. The **Numbers Passing Through** each year will give you some idea of the size of the organisation. The size of the **Waiting List** will tell you how much competition there might be for places. The **Costs** – if there are any – will be indicated too. **Regions Serviced** will indicate the area covered by the organisation and where there are **Regional Offices** details are supplied. Instructions on **How to Contact** each organisation should be carefully followed. The **Special Needs Provision** will, in each case, tell you whether enquiries are welcome from people with physical or learning difficulties (in most cases they are), and will give further details if these are available.

Part Three: What to Go For and How to Apply

This section tells you how to assess your own particular skills through a questionnaire which will also help you discover what sort of activities are best for you. There is useful advice on how to complete a *Curriculum Vitae* (CV) and some examples of letters of application.

Part Four: Help!

This is a brief section which tells you how to contact the main organisations offering help and advice with a wide range of addictions such as drugs, alcoholism, smoking and gambling. Also listed are the telephone hot-lines that offer information on all kinds of welfare benefits, legal matters, Aids and other medical problems; helping hands for those in debt, those who have left home, those who are homeless, have been raped or been victims of other kinds of crime – or simply need a shoulder to cry on.

Finally, there is an extensive **index**. I suggest you look there for any activities, organisations or publications that you may not have identified in the main category listings in Part One. There is also an order form on the very last page in case you need any more copies of this book.

Part One

THE CATEGORIES

NOTE

All the entries in the pages that follow are based on information from the organisations and companies concerned. Every attempt has been made to ensure that this information is accurate at the time of publication. Prices and costs listed are the latest available but are always subject to change.

Categories

Adventure Challenges

Arts and Crafts – Drama

Arts and Crafts – Music

Arts and Crafts – Other

Careers – Business and Industry

Careers – Further Education, Training, Vocational Training

Careers – Higher Education

Community Projects

Expeditions

Extra-Curricular Activities

Fund-raising, Sources of Money

Gap Year Challenges

Opportunities Abroad

Politics

Special Needs

Sport and Leisure

Summer Vacation

Volunteering

Working Holidays

Part Two

THE
DICTIONARY
OF
OPPORTUNITY

ACTION GROUP FOR IRISH YOUTH
5-15 Cromer Street
London WC1H 8LS
Tel: 071 278 1665

The AGIY is a voluntary agency which aims to promote the interests and welfare of emigrant Irish youth in London. The AGIY services the London Irish Youth Forum and publishes reports, leaflets and information on issues which affect young Irish people coming to London.

ADVENTURE HOLIDAYS 1994 (publication)
Vacation Work Publications
9 Park End Street
Oxford OX1 1HJ
Tel: 0865 241978 Fax: 0865 790885

Book listing 440 organisations offering opportunities to meet the challenge of windsurfing, canoeing, hang-gliding, sailing and climbing, mountaineering, overland expeditions, or more unusual activities from husky sledging in the Arctic to wilderness survival in Sweden, wildlife watching to volunteering on a scientific expedition in Britain or any of 100 countries abroad. The book includes information on types of accommodation, instruction provided, plus prices of the holidays and any other previous experience or equipment needed. Special chapter on young people's holidays. ISBN 1 85458 105 8. Available through libraries, bookshops (price £5.95), or direct from the above address (price £7.45 inc. p&p).

ADVERTISING ASSOCIATION
Abford House
15 Wilton Road
London SW1V 1NJ
Tel: 071 828 2771

Advertising is fiercely competitive and largely a young person's profession. Most jobs are in agencies but some companies have their own advertising departments and opportunities also exist in market research, sales, film production etc. Jobs in advertising are roughly split into three main areas – Account Executives, Media Planners and Creative. Account Executives are the main point of contact between clients and the agency. Media planning involves the placing of advertisements in the most effective way. Jobs in the creative department include copywriters and art directors. Contact the Advertising Association for information on careers in advertising.

AFS INTERCULTURAL EDUCATIONAL PROGRAMMES (AFS/IEP)
Arden House
Wellington Street
Bingley
West Yorkshire BD16 2NB
Tel: 0274 560677 Fax: 0274 567675

AFS/IEP is the UK partner of AFS Intercultural Programmes, a large worldwide network offering exchange opportunities. IEP offers young people the opportunity not just to live with a family abroad, but to become part of it for a year, attending school, learning the language and making a whole new network of friends. Participants develop a greater independence and self-confidence by dealing with new situations. Support is given throughout the programme by the local AFS office, volunteers and the selected host family.

AGE RANGE:
15-18
NUMBERS PASSING THROUGH:
60 in the UK – 30,000 worldwide (IEP are aiming to expand future UK involvement)
HOW TO CONTACT:
Write or phone for information and an application form
REGIONS SERVICED:
UK
SPECIAL NEEDS PROVISION:
Each person is treated individually
COSTS/WAITING LISTS:
The full cost of participation on the year programme is £3,850. Financial help is available and applicants are encouraged to seek sponsorship. Applications for August departure should be in by 31 October and January/February departures need to apply by 31 August. Late applicants can be considered.

AIESEC
29-31 Cowper Street
London EC2H 4AP
Tel: 071 336 7937

AIESEC is an organisation which arranges course-related paid work placements for degree-level students in business studies. Each year they give 150 UK students the chance to work abroad. The idea is for the individuals to 'make a positive contribution to the participating organisation while gaining an insight into a different business environment and culture'.

AMNESTY INTERNATIONAL BRITISH SECTION (AI)
99 Rosebery Avenue
London EC1R 4RE
Tel: 071 814 6200 Fax: 071 833 1510

Amnesty International is a worldwide human rights movement independent of any government, political or religious ideology. Amnesty campaigns through its membership by the technique of letter-writing. Members write letters to the heads of governments, justice ministers or whoever Amnesty thinks is the appropriate person in authority requesting the immediate and unconditional release of a prisoner of conscience, an end to torture or a halt to an execution. You can join AI as an individual or as a member of a group affiliating to Amnesty – there are over 300 youth groups in the UK campaigning through Amnesty. Two magazines produced by Amnesty of interest to young people are *New Release* – the youth magazine of AI, and *Amnesty Student*.

REGIONAL ADDRESSES:
AI Regional Office, St Michael's Studio, Queen Street, Derby DE1 3DX
Tel: 0332 290852
AGE RANGE:
Any
NUMBERS PASSING THROUGH:
c 8,000
HOW TO CONTACT:
By letter
REGIONS SERVICED:
UK
COSTS/WAITING LISTS:
Membership costs from £6 upwards depending on status

ANGLO-AUSTRIAN SOCIETY (AAS)
46 Queen Anne's Gate
London SW1H 9AU
Tel: 071 222 0366 Fax: 071 233 0293

The AAS organises exchange holidays in Austria for 15-17 year-olds, language courses in Austria for young people aged 15+, German language courses in the UK and can arrange reduced-rate air fares to Austria.

AGE RANGE:
15+
NUMBERS PASSING THROUGH:
4,000 from UK and Austria
HOW TO CONTACT:
Telephone, fax or letter for information
REGIONS SERVICED:
UK
SPECIAL NEEDS PROVISION:
Enquiries welcome
COSTS/WAITING LISTS:
Exchanges cost from £250; German courses
in Austria from £500; German courses in UK
from £90. There is a trust fund which can
help people who could not otherwise afford
to participate – details from AAS

ANIMAL AID
7 Castle Street
Tonbridge
Kent TN9 1BH
Tel: 0732 364546 Fax: 0732 366533

The Animal Aid Youth Group is for young
people aged 11-18 who are concerned about
the plight of animals and who wish to do
something about it. They provide information,
support and campaign ideas on all aspects of
animal rights, including factory farming, animal
experiments, dissection, vegetarianism, hunting
and the fur trade and have established a network
of school groups.

AGE RANGE:
11-18
NUMBERS PASSING THROUGH:
c 4,500
HOW TO CONTACT:
Letter or telephone for advice and
information
REGIONS SERVICED:
UK and overseas
SPECIAL NEEDS PROVISION:
No specific provision, but enquiries welcome
COSTS/WAITING LISTS:
Membership of the youth group is £4 per
year. School group membership is £10.

ARCTURUS EXPEDITIONS
PO Box 850
Gartocharn
Alexandria
Dumbartonshire G83 8EL
Tel & Fax: 0389 83204

Arcturus Expeditions introduces all ages to the
wildlife and geography of the Arctic and Antarctic.
There are places on expeditions leaving from
February to October to such places as northern
Norway, Svalbard, Greenland, northern Canada,
Franz Josef Land and Novaya Zemlya and to the
Antarctic from November to February.

COSTS/WAITING LISTS:
£1,600-£6,500

ARMY CADET FORCE ASSOCIATION
(ACFA)
E Block
Duke of York's Headquarters
London SW3 4RR
Tel: 071 730 9733 Fax: 071 730 8264

A national voluntary youth organisation committed to developing confidence, self-discipline, self-respect and health in 13-18 year-olds, so that they can gain employment and take their place in society as responsible, contributing young citizens. It achieves this through a challenging, structured programme of military, adventurous, sporting and citizenship training under the guidance of youth leaders trained by the Army. It is an operating authority for the Duke of Edinburgh's Award Scheme. Training is recognised for NVQ awards. Although sponsored in part by the Army it is heavily dependent upon public financial support for the non-military side of the training.

REGIONAL ADDRESSES:
ACFA Scotland: Army Headquarters Scotland, PO Box 85, Edinburgh EH1 2YX
ACFA Northern Ireland: HQ N Ireland, BFPO 825
ACFA Wales: c/o Wales TAVRA, Centre Block, Maindy Barracks, Cardiff, CF4 3YE
Tel: 0222 220251
AGE RANGE:
13-18³/4

NUMBERS PASSING THROUGH:
40,000
HOW TO CONTACT:
By telephone, fax or letter for an information booklet
REGIONS SERVICED:
UK
SPECIAL NEEDS PROVISION:
No provision
COSTS/WAITING LISTS:
No costs or waiting lists

ARMY CAREERS

Information about careers in the Army can be obtained from the Army Careers Information Service (ACIS) – check the telephone directory under 'Army' for your nearest office. If you are still at school your careers department can arrange an interview with an Army Schools Liaison Officer. For information about officer careers contact Ministry of Defence, Officer Entry, DAR 1a, Empress State Building, Lillie Road, London SW6 1TR. For information about careers in the Women's Royal Army Corps (WRAC), contact Corps Recruiting and Liaison Officer, WRAC Centre, Queen Elizabeth Park, Guildford, Surrey GU2 6QH.

ART AND DESIGN ADMISSIONS REGISTRY
Penn House
9 Broad Street
Hereford HR4 9AP
Tel: 0432 266653

Applications for university and higher education college Art and Design courses are processed by the Art and Design Admissions Registry. They can provide information about the range of courses available, who offers them, and what you need to get on. Write for further details.

AGE RANGE:
Any
HOW TO CONTACT:
Write to above address
REGIONS SERVICED:
UK
COSTS:
£16 registration fee for UK and EC students; £33 for other students

ARTS COUNCIL
14 Great Peter Street
London SW1P 3NQ
Tel: 071 333 0100 Fax: 071 973 6590

The object of the Arts Council is to develop and improve the knowledge, understanding and practice of the arts, and to increase the accessibility of the arts to the public. It achieves this through a wide range of schemes which include providing financial support for arts organisations, artists, performers and others, and by offering subsidies to drama, opera and dance companies, orchestras and other arts organisations. The Arts Council is the umbrella organisation for arts in the UK. In the first instance you should contact your Regional Arts Board for information about assistance with your artistic venture – details from Arts Council.

HOW TO CONTACT:
Letter
REGIONS SERVICED:
UK

ARTS DEVELOPMENT ASSOCIATION (ADA)
The Arts Centre
Vane Terrace
Darlington
Co. Durham DL3 7AX
Tel: 0325 465930

The ADA supports arts activities at a local level through a range of services including advice and information, training courses, seminars, publications and conferences and publishes a bi-monthly magazine which includes news of youth arts activities.

AGE RANGE:
Any
NUMBERS PASSING THROUGH:

Approx. 500 young people
HOW TO CONTACT:
By letter for advice and information
REGIONS SERVICED:
UK
SPECIAL NEEDS PROVISION:
All events are held in accessible venues (often using signers) and some information is available on tape
COSTS/WAITING LISTS:
Details of costs available from ADA

ARTSWORK LTD (Artswork)
Television Centre
Southampton SO9 5HZ

Artswork is a national charity set up in 1987 to create and promote opportunities in the arts for young people (14-19 year-olds). Artswork links with regional television companies and currently operates in the north and south/south-east of England with plans to move into the west Midlands. Artswork supports projects in all art forms from photography, mime, dance, drama, art and fashion to rap or rock. Activities take place in a variety of venues; in schools, colleges, youth centres, arts centres, hospitals, parks and secure units.

REGIONAL ADDRESSES:
Artswork North, Tyne Tees Television, City Road, Newcastle-upon-Tyne NE1 2AL
Tel: 091 261 0181 (ext 2317)

Artswork South, Meridian Broadcasting,
Television Centre, Southampton SO9 5HZ
Tel: 0703 222555
AGE RANGE:
14-19
NUMBERS PASSING THROUGH:
c 30,000
HOW TO CONTACT:
Contact regional offices above
REGIONS SERVICED:
Meridian (south/south-east), Tyne Tees (north)
– and Central TV (west Midlands)
SPECIAL NEEDS PROVISION:
The policy of Artswork is to include young
people with special needs, disabilities or
learning difficulties into the mainstream of its
programme and also to initiate special
programmes for these groups
COSTS/WAITING LISTS:
Minimal or no cost. Projects happen at
various times throughout the year

ASSOCIATION FOR JEWISH YOUTH (AJY)
AJY House
128 East Lane
Wembley
Middlesex HA0 3NL
Tel: 081 908 4747 Fax: 081 904 4323

The AJY mainly services youth leaders and
youth workers. However, it can inform young
people of the services available to Jewish young
people, and try to represent their interests. The

AJY may have information about the availability of grants for particular purposes, and have developed an apprenticeship scheme for young people who want to become youth workers.

REGIONAL ADDRESSES:
Nicky Alliance Centre, Middleton Road, Manchester M8 6JY Tel: 061 740 6168
AGE RANGE:
Any
HOW TO CONTACT:
Letter or telephone to Head Office
REGIONS SERVICED:
Major Jewish communities in England
SPECIAL NEEDS PROVISION:
Installing loop system for people with hearing difficulties. Disabled access patchy but improving
COSTS/WAITING LISTS:
None

ASSOCIATION OF BRITISH TRAVEL AGENTS (ABTA)
National Training Board
Waterloo House
11-17 Chertsey Road
Woking
Surrey GU21 5AL
Tel: 0483 727321

ABTA supplies a wide range of information on many careers in travel and tourism, both at home and abroad, what courses to take, training opportunities, ways into the industry and career development. Details of youth training, correspondence courses and other aspects of work in the tourism industry are available on request.

ASSOCIATION OF COMMONWEALTH UNIVERSITIES (ACU)
John Foster House
36 Gordon Square
London WC1H 0PF
Tel: 071 387 8572 Fax: 071 387 2655

Provides information about Commonwealth universities – where they are, what courses are on offer, what entrance qualifications are needed, what the universities are like, and how to get in.

REGIONAL ADDRESSES:
All enquiries to Head Office
AGE RANGE:
Any
NUMBERS PASSING THROUGH:
c 8,000 enquiries per year
HOW TO CONTACT:
Letter, telephone, fax or personal visit to Publications and Information Division.
Reference library at above address open to the public Monday-Friday 9.30am-1pm and 2pm-5.30pm

REGIONS SERVICED:
UK
SPECIAL NEEDS PROVISION:
No special provision
COSTS/WAITING LISTS:
No cost for information services

ASSOCIATION OF GRADUATE CAREERS ADVISORY SERVICES MUTUAL AID SCHEME
Central Services Unit (CSU)
Armstrong House
Oxford Road
Manchester M1 7ED
Tel: 061 236 9816

This is an agreement amongst careers services in higher education whereby, for the first three years after graduation, you can usually use a nearby careers service if you find it difficult to get to the careers service of the institution from which you graduated. Under Mutual Aid you can normally use the information room at another careers service, and it may be possible to have a short discussion with with a duty advisor. Before visiting a careers service it is suggested that you make contact by telephone or letter to establish the extent of the assistance that you can expect and the opening times.

ASSOCIATION OF JEWISH SIXTH-FORMERS (AJ6)
128 East Lane
Wembley
Middlesex HA0 3NL
Tel: 081 904 4357

AJ6 works to prepare Jewish students for religious and political problems they may face on campus. It produces the *AJ6 Guide to College Life*, runs seminars on topics of Jewish interest, takes school assemblies, runs local meetings and regularly mails out the group's magazine. AJ6 runs four summer tours to Israel, organises social events and weekends, and organises a National Conference. Its emphasis is on fun and education for all Jewish fifth- and sixth-formers, regardless of religious or political affiliation.

AGE RANGE:
15-18
NUMBERS PASSING THROUGH:
c 1,000 members. c 1,500 use services
HOW TO CONTACT:
Telephone to Head Office
REGIONS SERVICED:
UK
SPECIAL NEEDS PROVISION:
Depending on needs, AJ6 does everything possible to ensure that everyone can participate

ASSOCIATION OF PHOTOGRAPHERS
9-10 Domingo Street
London EC1Y 0TA
Tel: 071 608 0598

A trade association for freelance photographers working in fashion, advertising and magazine photography. It runs regular Kodak-sponsored careers talks in London and Manchester. Contact above address for further details (see also the British Institute of Professional Photography).

ASTRID TRUST
9 Trinity Street
Weymouth DT4 8TW
Tel: 0305 761916 Fax: 0305 761887

The Astrid Trust was founded in 1985 to encourage, through challenge and adventure, the highest qualities in youth. As well as two long transatlantic voyages, Astrid offers shorter voyages and the opportunity to participate in the Cutty Sark Tall Ships race. Royal Yachting Association and Duke of Edinburgh qualifications can be obtained.

REGIONAL ADDRESSES:
Scotland: Alan J. Miller DSC, VRD, Dollerie Lodge, by Crieff, Perthshire, PH7 3NX
AGE RANGE:
17-25

NUMBERS PASSING THROUGH:
c 180
HOW TO CONTACT:
Telephone, letter or fax for brochures and an
application form
REGIONS SERVICED:
UK and rest of Europe
SPECIAL NEEDS PROVISION:
Enquiries welcome and each application is
dealt with individually
COSTS/WAITING LISTS:
3-month transatlantic voyages cost approx
£6,000 (including air fare) per head, and
participants are asked to contribute £4,150
towards the total, through fund-raising,
sponsorship, wages, parents etc. Additional
expenses include insurance and pocket
money. Occasionally the Trust can arrange
an interest-free loan

**AU PAIR AND NANNY'S GUIDE TO
WORKING ABROAD (publication)**
Vacation Work Publications
9 Park End Street
Oxford OX1 1HJ
Tel: 0865 241978 Fax: 0865 790885

Guide for those who wish to work abroad as
nannies, au pairs and mothers' helps. Topics
include making the decision to go, the training
and experience that are necessary, how to find
a job, preparation, the duties and rewards of the
work, coping with problems and so on. Contains

a directory listing full details of 144 agencies (including fees charged), and a country-by-country guide giving information on visas and other regulations, health and insurance, and the advantages and disadvantages of working in 20 different countries from Europe to North America. Includes some basic advice on how to make looking after children easier – cooking for children, first aid and children's ailments, recommended games etc.

ISBN 1 85458 087 6. Available through libraries, bookshops (price £8.95), or direct from the above address (price £10.45 inc. p&p).

AU PAIR IN AMERICA
Department GFI
37a Queen's Gate
London SW7 5HR
Tel: 071 581 7311 (24-hour) /7322
Fax: 071 581 7345

Au Pair in America provides opportunities for young people aged 18-25 with some childcare experience and ability to drive to spend 12 months living and working with an American host family as an au pair exchange visitor. A 13th month is allowed for independent travel.

REGIONAL ADDRESSES:
All contact is through the London office
AGE RANGE:
18-25

NUMBERS PASSING THROUGH:
c 3,000 participants each year
HOW TO CONTACT:
Telephone or fax with name, address and
telephone number for a brochure and
application form quoting department code as
per address
REGIONS SERVICED:
Western Europe
SPECIAL NEEDS PROVISION:
All enquiries considered individually
COSTS/WAITING LISTS:
Participants must leave a $500 good faith
deposit which is refunded on successful
completion. Applications should be made
several months in advance

AUPAIRCARE
101 Lorna Road
Hove
Sussex BN3 3EL
Tel: 0273 220261 Fax: 0273 220376

AuPairCare gives young British people, aged
18-25 with some childcare experience and able
to drive, the opportunity to work as an au pair
for a year in the USA with an American family.
AuPairCare provides return flights, visas, board
and lodging plus $100 per week pocket money
as well as the opportunity to experience the
American way of life.

AGE RANGE:
18-25

HOW TO CONTACT:
Telephone, letter or fax for brochure, information sheet and application form

REGIONS SERVICED:
UK and Republic of Ireland

SPECIAL NEEDS PROVISION:
No provision

COSTS/WAITING LISTS:
Prior to departure, applicants must leave a goodwill deposit of $500 which will be refunded upon completion of their 12-month stay in the USA. Apply minimum 3 months in advance of desired departure date

---

AU PAIRS – ITALY
46 The Rise
Sevenoaks
Kent TN13 1RJ
Tel: 0732 451522 Fax: 0732 451522

Au Pairs – Italy places au pairs, mothers' helps, nannies and governesses with families in Italy and Sicily. Monthly salaries up to approx. £800 with board and lodging provided. The usual length of stay is 6-12 months but summer jobs are available from June until September mainly for 3 months and occasionally for 1-2 months. Italian is not essential, but some experience with children, patience, cheerfulness, adaptability and a willingness to help where needed is essential.

AGE RANGE:
18+
NUMBERS PASSING THROUGH:
240 approximately
HOW TO CONTACT:
SAE for information sheet, an application
form and recent job list
REGIONS SERVICED:
UK
SPECIAL NEEDS PROVISION:
No provision
COSTS/WAITING LISTS:
There is an optional services charge covering
translation into Italian if required, advice
regarding passports, immigration
requirements and travel arrangements,
insurance, addresses of other au pairs in the
area and follow-up service. It is best to apply
1-2 months in advance

**AVRIL DANKWORTH NATIONAL
CHILDREN'S MUSIC CAMPS (NCMC)**
56 Station Road
Long Marston
Tring
Hertfordshire HP23 4QS
Tel: 0296 668485

NCMC aims to bring together young people of
all musical ability levels to share their enjoyment
of music in a social environment. There are four
1-week camps under canvas in the July/August

period. The first two are for young people aged 13 to 17, the others for 8-12 year-olds. A wide range of musical interests, experiences and activities is offered including vocal and instrumental sessions. The only criterion is a love of music and the timetable is tailored according to ability and interests.

AGE RANGE:
8-17
NUMBERS PASSING THROUGH:
Nearly 300 (140 aged 13-17 and 16 helpers aged 18-22)
HOW TO CONTACT:
By telephone, letter or in person
REGIONS SERVICED:
UK
SPECIAL NEEDS PROVISION:
No provision
COSTS/WAITING LISTS:
Course fee for 13-17 year-olds is £150 inclusive of tuition, food, loan of tent etc. Brochures go out in December for the following summer; applications must be made by mid-February. The camps are very popular and many applications have to be refused

AYUSA INTERNATIONAL
101 Lorna Road
Hove
Sussex BN3 3EL
Tel: 0273 220261 Fax: 0273 220376

AYUSA International offers students between 16 and 18 years old with at least four GCSEs (grade C or above) the opportunity of studying at an American high school for an academic year or semester (6 months). Students live with an American family during their stay and have the opportunity of experiencing the American way of life and culture.

AGE RANGE:
16-18
HOW TO CONTACT:
Telephone, fax or letter for brochure and registration form
REGIONS SERVICED:
UK and Republic of Ireland
SPECIAL NEEDS PROVISION:
No provision
COSTS/WAITING LISTS:
Programme fees are approximately £2,500. Students should apply 6-9 months in advance

BACKPACKERS CLUB
PO Box 381
Reading
Berkshire RG3 4RL
Tel: 0491 680684
(24-hour telephone service)

The Backpackers Club is an organisation which supports and promotes backpacking, whether you are a walker, cyclist, canoeist, or just interested in this way of life. Membership of the club offers access to an overseas backpacking travel information service, a postal lending library, a farm pitch directory, a long distance path site and pitch directory, the club magazine, a special camping equipment and personal effects insurance scheme, the Backpacking Advisory Service, and the opportunity to take part in regular backpacking weekends in various parts of the UK.

AGE RANGE:
Any
HOW TO CONTACT:
Letter to above address
REGIONS SERVICED:
UK/international
SPECIAL NEEDS PROVISION:
Enquiries welcome
COSTS/WAITING LISTS:
Membership up to 18years: £7 per year.
18+: £12 per year

BANKING INFORMATION SERVICE
Careers Department
6th Floor
10 Lombard Street
London EC3V 9AT
Tel: 071 626 9386

The Banking Information Service is the central source of help, advice and information about a career in high street banking. It produces information packages covering the wide variety of careers available including advice about gaining entry, getting employment and subsequent training and career development. It is also worthwhile writing to the banks themselves for information about their own recruitment drives and career opportunities.

BANSTEAD PLACE ACCESS CENTRE
Park Road
Banstead
Surrey SM7 3EE
Tel: 0737 356222

The Access Centre at Banstead Place identifies microtechnology for adults with physical, sensory or specific learning disabilities who need to access communication (spoken or written), study situations (e.g. at college), employment training or leisure and recreation opportunities for which the use of computers is appropriate or necessary. Seating, software, hardware, peripherals, aids and strategies are identified and evaluated during a day-long assessment (this can be modified to suit the client). Impartial recommendations of equipment are made based on considerable expertise with a wide range of disabilities. The centre is a member of the National Federation of Access Centres.

AGE RANGE:
16+
HOW TO CONTACT:
Telephone, letter or fax to the Co-ordinator for further information
REGIONS SERVICED:
Banstead Place services southern England but the National Federation has centres nationwide. Banstead Place will supply contact addresses
COSTS/WAITING LISTS:
Assessment fee is approx £30 per hour and is frequently met by social services, health authority, education authority or FEFC. Information on enquiry

---

BARCLAYS YOUTH ACTION AWARDS
(in association with Youth Clubs UK)
11 St Bride Street
London EC4A 4AS
Tel: 071 353 2366 Fax: 071 353 2369

Although individuals cannot apply to the Barclays Youth Action Scheme, it is worth

mentioning for the help it can provide. Groups of young people, up to the age of 24, can apply for grants of between £500 and £2,000 for projects which benefit their local community. Funds are for 12 months only and projects with short-term targets are therefore favoured. There are awards in each of the following categories:
Promoting health and fitness
Fostering creativity
Coping with change
Helping young people in trouble or at risk
Community participation
International awareness
Integrating people with a disability
Environmental youth work

AGE RANGE:
Up to 24
HOW TO CONTACT:
All applications must be made on the required form through Youth Clubs UK at the above address. Applicants must be voluntary groups and will be required to supply the name and address of an independent person in their community, as a referee
REGIONS SERVICED:
England, Wales, Scotland and Northern Ireland
SPECIAL NEEDS PROVISION:
Any eligible group can apply
COSTS/WAITING LISTS:
None

CLOSING DATE FOR APPLICATIONS:
31 March. Successful applicants should be
informed about mid-June

BLACK ENVIRONMENT NETWORK (BEN)
Regent's Wharf
8 All Saints Street
London N1 9RL
Tel: 071 713 6161 Fax: 071 713 6300

Young people who belong to an ethnic minority
group and want to do an environmental project
can receive advice and information on the
environment and apply for grants to carry out
projects, for example, the Ethnic Minorities
Award Scheme (EMAS). The leader of the
project should wherever possible be from an
ethnic minority as should as some of the
participants of the scheme.

AGE RANGE:
Any
HOW TO CONTACT:
Letter to Head Office for advice and contacts
REGIONS SERVICED:
UK
SPECIAL NEEDS PROVISION:
Enquiries welcome
COSTS/WAITING LISTS:
The service is free and applications for funding
should ideally be made 3-6 months in advance

BOYS' BRIGADE
Felden Lodge
Felden
Hemel Hempstead
Hertfordshire HP3 0BL
Tel: 0442 231681 Fax: 0442 235391

The Boys' Brigade offers a wide range of social and sporting activities. It offers opportunities for year-round activities, including helping the elderly or the disabled in the community, or participating in award schemes, such as the Duke of Edinburgh's Award, through activities such as camping, canoeing, life saving, arts and crafts. Camp sites, mountaineering clubs and outdoor centres throughout the UK provide a wealth of exciting opportunities. The Boys' Brigade is a Christian, uniformed association.

REGIONAL ADDRESSES:
Scotland: Carronvale House, Carronvale, Larbert, Stirlingshire FK5 3LH
Tel: 0324 562008
Northern Ireland: Rathmore House, 126 Glenarm Road, Larne, Co. Antrim BT40 1DZ
Tel: 0574 272794
Wales: 80 Woodville Road, Cathays, Cardiff CF2 4ED Tel: 0222 232052
AGE RANGE:
6-18
NUMBERS PASSING THROUGH:
100,000 members

HOW TO CONTACT:
By letter or telephone to regional office
REGIONS SERVICED:
UK
SPECIAL NEEDS PROVISION:
Enquiries welcome
COSTS/WAITING LISTS:
Subscriptions vary but average 30p a week.
There is a charge for uniform and for
additional activities such as camping/
expeditions etc.

BP PORTRAIT AWARD
National Portrait Gallery
St Martin's Place
London WC2H 0HE
Tel: 071 306 0055 Fax: 071 306 0056

The BP Portrait Award is an annual competition
aimed at encouraging young artists to take up
portraiture. The competition is judged from original
paintings with a first prize of £10,000, a second
prize of £4,000 and third prize of £2,000. An
exhibition of works selected from the entries is
held at the National Portrait Gallery and in the
past many artists who have had their work shown
have gained commissions as a result.

AGE RANGE:
18-40
NUMBERS PASSING THROUGH:
Over 700 entries in 1993

HOW TO CONTACT:
Write, with an SAE, for an application form
REGIONS SERVICED:
UK
SPECIAL NEEDS PROVISION:
Anyone can enter the competition
COSTS/WAITING LISTS:
£5 registration fee
CLOSING DATE FOR APPLICATIONS:
Early April

BRATHAY EXPLORATION GROUP
Brathay Hall
Ambleside
Cumbria LA22 0HP
Tel: 05394 33942

Brathay Exploration Group is a non-profit-making voluntary organisation and has been running expeditions, training courses and other events for over 40 years. The group can give you the chance to explore areas of the UK and far-flung places like China, Nepal, Norway, Iceland and the French Alps in a way which will increase your awareness and understanding of the natural environment and the people and cultures visited. You can become a member of the group without joining an expedition and the benefits include the opportunity to plan and run your own expedition using the group's expertise, equipment and facilities for a small fee; copies of the group's own magazine; the opportunity to stay in the members' hut on the Brathay Estate in the heart of the Lake District and to join in a range of members' events including the annual members' reunion at Brathay in October.

AGE RANGE:
15-27
NUMBERS PASSING THROUGH:
300 members. 100 take part in expeditions/ courses
HOW TO CONTACT:
By letter, telephone (24 hours) or in person for information and application form
REGIONS SERVICED:
UK
SPECIAL NEEDS PROVISION:
No specific provision. Each application dealt with individually
COSTS/WAITING LISTS:
Membership costs £13.50 and associate membership is £10.50. Individual expedition/course fees vary depending on destination Direct bursary grants are available to help with expedition/course fees, as well as advice on fund-raising

---

BREAKS FOR YOUNG BANDS (publication)
Omnibus Press
8-9 Frith Street
London W1V 5TZ
Tel: 071 434 0066 Fax: 071 439 2848

Breaks for Young Bands: The Step-by-Step Guide to Success in the Music Business is a practical self-help guide for young hopeful bands wanting to progress in the music industry. ISBN 0 711 90978 4. Price £5.95. Available from booksellers, through your local library or direct from the above address.

BREMEX TRAINING SCHEME (Bremex)
London Information Centre
18 Westbourne Park Villas
London W2 5EA
Tel: 071 229 9251

Through a range of action-packed training courses Bremex enables young men and women to develop their full potential, and to aim for high standards of achievement. They offer opportunities to enjoy and gain competence in expedition, mountaineering and outdoor pursuit techniques under tough conditions in the mountains of the UK. Instruction is given by experts on courses lasting either 3 months or 9 months part-time. Absolute beginners are welcomed, and will be given special help. In addition there are opportunities to develop leadership and group management skills, and members are encouraged to give voluntary service to the community where their expertise can be of value. Enquiries welcomed from anybody prepared to work hard, show enthusiasm, co-operate positively within a team and display stamina.

AGE RANGE:
16+
NUMBERS PASSING THROUGH:
c 100
HOW TO CONTACT:
Telephone or letter to above address for
information and/or leaflets
REGIONS SERVICED:
UK
SPECIAL NEEDS PROVISION:
Bremex courses make heavy demands on the
physical and mental qualities of members,
but Bremex will endeavour to accommodate
anybody prepared to pull their weight
COSTS/WAITING LISTS:
Initial course fees: £39 per month if in work;
£28 per month if in education, out of work
etc. No waiting lists for enrolment at present

BRITISH FEDERATION OF YOUNG CHOIRS (BFYC)
37 Frederick Street
Loughborough
Leicestershire LE11 3BH
Tel: 0509 211664 Fax: 0509 233749

The work of the BFYC is concerned with
encouraging young people to sing by organising
local, regional, national and international choral
events for young singers, supporting member
choirs with advice, information and grant aid
and encouraging links between young choirs in

Britain and their counterparts overseas. They can help you find out about local activities, keep you informed about events in this country and abroad and provide exciting opportunities to sing at large-scale choral events with orchestras and leading conductors.

AGE RANGE:
Any
NUMBERS PASSING THROUGH:
3,000 directly in 1991 – more indirectly through their teacher or choir leader
HOW TO CONTACT:
By telephone or letter to above address (BFYC request that your teacher, youth worker or conductor does the same) for more information, including details of local and international choral activities available
REGIONS SERVICED:
UK
SPECIAL NEEDS PROVISION:
All BYFC events are held in fully accessible venues
COSTS/WAITING LISTS:
Individual membership is £15; choir £30. Participation fees at choral events range from £5 per choir to £3 per head

BRITISH FILM INSTITUTE (BFI)
21 Stephen Street
London W1P 1PL
Tel: 071 255 1444 Fax: 071 436 7950

The British Film Institute exists to stimulate a wider public interest in the arts of film, video and television – all the techniques by which images are made to move. The BFI Library and Information Services Department houses the world's largest collection of information on film and television. BFI runs the Museum of the Moving Image (MOMI), and the National Film Theatre (NFT). Membership of the BFI is open to anyone over 16, and offers a range of special offers. Reductions on BFI Film and Television Handbook, subscriptions to BFI Reading Room and *Sight and Sound* magazine.

AGE RANGE:
Any. 16+ for membership
HOW TO CONTACT:
Telephone, letter or fax to above address for general information about BFI
REGIONS SERVICED:
UK
SPECIAL NEEDS PROVISION:
BFI is working on special needs provision in all areas of its work. Enquiries welcome
COSTS/WAITING LISTS:
Annual membership: £11.95. Other types of membership are also available. Contact BFI for more information

BRITISH INSTITUTE OF PROFESSIONAL PHOTOGRAPHY
Fox Talbot House
2 Amwell End
Ware
Hertfordshire SG12 9HN
Tel: 0920 464011

Professional photographers work in one or more specialist field. Regarded by some as the most glamorous of these are fashion, advertising and press photography, which are usually the hardest to break into, but the majority of professionals work in social photography which includes portraiture (usually in a studio) and weddings etc. There are also opportunities to work in fields such as industrial and commercial, scientific, medical or forensic photography, some of which involve using advanced techniques. For more information about a career in photography contact the above address.

BRITISH RED CROSS YOUTH
British Red Cross National HQ
9 Grosvenor Crescent
London SW1X 7EJ
Tel: 071 235 5454 Fax: 071 235 7447

As a member of the British Red Cross you can receive free training in areas such as first aid, survival skills, health and hygiene and childcare or learn the skills needed to care for a sick or handicapped relative at home or to be of service to the local community. Red Cross Youth often work alongside adult members helping with rescue operations, manning first aid posts and looking after disabled youngsters on specially arranged holidays, as well as being involved with fund-raising ventures. There are also opportunities for leadership and development training, various leisure activities and the chance to make new friends through the large Red Cross network.

REGIONAL ADDRESSES:
91 regional associations – details from HQ
AGE RANGE:
5-25
NUMBERS PASSING THROUGH:
c 25,000 members
HOW TO CONTACT:
By letter to above address for information and a local contact. Or check the telephone directory for your nearest branch
REGIONS SERVICED:
UK
SPECIAL NEEDS PROVISION:
Enquiries welcome
COSTS/WAITING LISTS:
Some clubs have a small weekly subscription

BRITISH SCHOOLS EXPLORING SOCIETY (BSES)
c/o Royal Geographical Society
1 Kensington Gore
London SW7 2AR
Tel: 071 584 0710 Fax: 071 581 7995

BSES was founded in 1932 by Commander George Murray Levick, a member of Captain Scott's last expedition, and exists to provide an opportunity for self-development and self-awareness for young people through meeting the challenges of a scientifically based expedition in harsh and hostile environments overseas. The expeditions have been to arctic and sub-arctic regions (e.g. Greenland, Iceland, Alaska) but the Society is experimenting with warmer climes. Each year expeditions are mounted for 6 weeks during the summer holidays, and 3- or 4-month long 'gap' year expeditions are also undertaken.

AGE RANGE:
16^1/$_2$-20 on 1st July of year of participation
NUMBERS PASSING THROUGH:
c 200
HOW TO CONTACT:
By letter with SAE for information, leaflets and application form
REGIONS SERVICED:
UK
SPECIAL NEEDS PROVISION:
Some provision but limited by the nature of the expeditions

COSTS/WAITING LISTS:
Cost of expeditions varies depending on the location. For example in 1992, a 6-week expedition to Iceland or Greenland cost approximately £1,800-£2,100, which covered travel, food, major equipment, share of sea-freight, briefing weekend in UK, insurance and administration. Expedition cost also gives entitlement to 5-year society membership. There are various ways of raising the money such as business sponsorship, from trusts and charities, part-time working etc. The Society can help with advice and information on how to go about fund-raising

---

BRITISH SPORTS ASSOCIATION FOR THE DISABLED (BSAD)
Solecast House
13/27 Brunswick Place
London N1 6DX
Tel: 071 490 4919 Fax: 071 383 7332

BSAD provides opportunities for young people with disabilities in a vast range of sports at all levels as well as advice on vacation employment, especially volunteer work, and information for school projects, exams etc.

REGIONAL ADDRESSES:
About 15 regional offices – addresses available from Head Office

AGE RANGE:
Any (junior championships in swimming,
athletics and basketball for under 18s)
HOW TO CONTACT:
Telephone the Regional Development Officer
at your local office (address available from
above) for advice, information and names of
other relevant contacts if required
REGIONS SERVICED:
UK
SPECIAL NEEDS PROVISION:
BSAD deals mainly with individuals with any
type of disability but is willing to provide
information and advice etc. to anyone
irrespective of ability
COSTS/WAITING LISTS:
No costs or waiting lists

BRITISH TRUST FOR CONSERVATION
VOLUNTEERS (BTCV)
36 St Mary's Street
Wallingford
Oxfordshire OX10 0EU
Tel: 0491 839766 Fax: 0941 839646

BTCV is the UK's largest practical conservation
charity, creating opportunities for over 62,000
volunteers each year to take practical action to
protect their local environment. BTCV runs
over 600 Natural Breaks and international
conservation working holidays throughout the
year. These offer the chance to meet people,

learn new skills and most importantly have a great time. Examples of holidays include a bat bonanza in the Pennines, to enhance roosting sites and learn about bat ecology; managing the heathland habitats of the lizards and sand-burrowing wasps of the Wirral nature reserves;creating footpaths in a seashore national park on Cape Cod and a tree-planting safari in the mountainous deserts of Andalucia.

REGIONAL ADDRESSES:
BTCV has a network of over 90 Field Offices throughout England, Wales and Northern Ireland. Each office organises a wide range of weekday, weekend and week-long environmental projects

AGE RANGE:
16+ for Natural Breaks. No age limit for local projects

NUMBERS PASSING THROUGH:
62,000 volunteers each year. 5,000 people take part in Natural Breaks and international conservation working holidays

HOW TO CONTACT:
For a free Natural Break or international conservation working holidays brochure phone 0491 824602. For details of your local BTCV projects contact BTCV's Information Office on 0491 839766

COSTS/WAITING LISTS:
BTCV Membership costs £12, concessions £6. Natural Breaks start from £29 a week inclusive of food and accommodation.

International conservation working holidays start at around £50 excluding travel. Early booking is recommended.

BRITISH UNIVERSITIES NORTH AMERICA CLUB (BUNAC)
16 Bowling Green Lane
London EC1R 0BD
Tel: 071 251 3472 Fax: 071 251 0251

BUNAC is a non-profit-making organisation which enables students and young people to travel and work in America, Canada and Australia through various programmes. The largest of these is 'BUNACAMP' which places people aged 19$\frac{1}{2}$-35 as counsellors on American children's summer camps to teach a wide variety of activities from mid-June to mid/end August and allows time to travel for up to 6 weeks afterwards. There are also general work and travel programmes mainly for students and 'gap-year' students in America, Canada and Australia.

REGIONAL ADDRESSES:
There are voluntary representatives at most university campuses
AGE RANGE:
Programmes are mainly aimed at university and gap-year students. However, BUNACAMP is open to anyone aged 19$\frac{1}{2}$-35
NUMBERS PASSING THROUGH:
9,000

HOW TO CONTACT:
Send your name and address on a postcard to
the London address requesting a 'Working
Adventures Abroad' brochure or telephone
with any enquiries
REGIONS SERVICED:
UK
SPECIAL NEEDS PROVISION:
Enquiries welcome
COSTS/WAITING LISTS:
Costs of the schemes vary but all programmes
are designed to be self-financing so
participants can recover the costs of travelling
abroad by working once they arrive

BRITISH YOUTH COUNCIL (BYC)
57 Chalton Street
London NW1 1HU
Tel: 071 387 7559 Fax: 071 383 3545

The British Youth Council is the umbrella body
for people aged 16-25 working to increase the
participation of young people at all levels of
political and public decision-making. With an
affiliated membership of more than 6 million
young people, it represents youth nationally
and internationally. BYC's primary aim is to
advance the interests and views of young people
and to enable them to play a more active part in
decisions that affect their lives. BYC is run by
young people. They come together at council
meetings to debate and discuss ideas and they
elect an executive to carry out policy decisions.

All the main voluntary youth organisations are a part of BYC, as are many local youth councils and political youth groups. Membership offers subscription to the bi-monthly *Youth Bulletin*, containing news and information concerning young people, articles by a range of people from politics and the youth service, and information on the activities of BYC. It also offers access to BYC's advice and information service and, above all, it offers the opportunity for you and your group to have a say in the major decisions that affect your lives.

BRITISH YOUTH OPERA (BYO)
South Bank University
103 Borough Road
London SE1 0AA
Tel: 071 815 6090 Fax: 071 815 8155

Every summer BYO provide specialist training opportunities for musicians, conductors, assistant designers/directors, stage crew etc. Under expert professional tuition, they rehearse two operas which are performed in London and on tour. Young people who apply should already be trained to a reasonably high standard (especially singers).

AGE RANGE:
Singers 22-30, instrumentalists 18-30
NUMBERS PASSING THROUGH:
Over 200

HOW TO CONTACT:
SAE with covering letter, or telephone for advice, information and leaflets
REGIONS SERVICED:
UK
SPECIAL NEEDS PROVISION:
Enquiries welcome
COSTS/WAITING LISTS:
Training courses are free of charge and students receive subsistence whilst they are on tour. For rehearsals in London students are expected to pay for their own accommodation/travel/living expenses etc.

BUSINESS AND TECHNOLOGY EDUCATION COUNCIL (BTEC)
Central House
Upper Woburn Place
London WC1H 0HH
Tel: 071 413 8400 Fax: 071 387 6068

BTEC offers work-related qualifications delivered by schools, colleges and universities in a wide range of subject areas, including agriculture, business and finance, caring, computing, construction, design, engineering, hotel and catering, leisure and sciences. You may study full-time or part-time. BTEC qualifications are recognised by employers and professional bodies. They also enable students to progress to degree courses. BTEC is working closely with the National Council for Vocational

Qualifications (NCVQ) to help develop the national framework of vocational qualifications through NVQs and GNVQs.

AGE RANGE:
16+

NUMBERS PASSING THROUGH:
Over 300,000 students enrolled on to BTEC programmes in 1992/93 and over 500,000 are studying with BTEC at any time

HOW TO CONTACT:
For information about these qualifications you can contact your local college or sixth form; universities; your local careers office; your Training and Enterprise Council (TEC)

REGIONS SERVICED:
England, Wales and Northern Ireland

SPECIAL NEEDS PROVISION:
May be arranged with the college where you wish to study

COSTS/WAITING LISTS:
BTEC information and leaflets are free. Programmes are usually free to full-time students under 19. Some full-time students over 19 have their fees paid by their Local Education Authorities and receive a grant. Part-time students may have their fees paid by their employers. Many courses are over-subscribed, so you will need to apply for a place as early as possible

BUSINESS IN THE COMMUNITY (BITC)
8 Stratton Street
London W1X 5FD
Tel: 071 629 1600 Fax: 071 629 1836

BITC is the umbrella organisation for the Local Enterprise Agency network and can direct young people to one of 300 agencies around the country who deal with youth enterprise.

REGIONAL ADDRESSES:
Details from above
AGE RANGE:
Any
HOW TO CONTACT:
Telephone or letter to the Information Officer at the above address
REGIONS SERVICED:
UK
SPECIAL NEEDS PROVISION:
Each case dealt with individually
COSTS/WAITING LISTS:
No costs

CAMBRIDGE OCCUPATIONAL ANALYSTS
Sparham
Norwich NR9 5AQ
Tel: 0362 88722 Fax: 0362 88733

Cambridge Occupational Analysts offer a range of careers and courses questionnaires for young people in the fifth and sixth form. The programmes are geared towards helping you make the best, and most carefully researched, decisions about what career to work towards, or what course to go for in higher or further education. Should you go on to do 'A' levels or a BTEC/SCOTVEC? How about a GNVQ or Access course? Should you be looking to further or higher education, or should you look at in-house training within a particular career? The print-outs do not make decisions for you. They will not give you easy answers. But they will help you make a sound choice. The tests aim to match your main interests, abilities and personal qualities with the ranges of careers or courses that are available to you. They are available on computer or on paper. Essentially they ask you to respond to a range of questions about whether you like maths, English, sciences, arts etc., whether you can work well under pressure, are a good communicator, a persuader, what interests you, what doesn't, what you are good at, what you are not, academic abilities, practical skills and so on to build up a detailed 'personal profile'. Your personal profile is then used to provide you with a detailed summary of your options for careers or courses. It will outline why a particular option might be right for you, and will explain why another preferred option may not be right. You are not bound by the findings of the test – the intention is to provide you with a clear picture of your skills, aptitudes and abilities, and to match and link these to suggested options for your future.

AGE RANGE:
Fifth and Sixth form pupils and students at
colleges of further education
HOW TO CONTACT:
Through careers teachers, Careers Offices or
contact the above address
REGIONS SERVICED:
UK

CAMP AMERICA
Department GFI
37a Queen's Gate
London SW7 5HR
Tel: 071 581 7373 Fax: 071 581 7377

Camp America is looking for young people to
work as youth leaders at American children's
summer camps. Preferably you will have skills
to teach activities such as sports, arts and crafts,
drama etc. You don't need to be an expert to
apply. Camp America provides free London-
New York return flight; pocket money; board
and lodging at camp; J1 cultural exchange visa
and time for independent travel after your 9-
week placement. Camp maintenance positions
and family companion placements also
available.

AGE RANGE:
18-35
NUMBERS PASSING THROUGH:
Approx 6,500 placements from 10,500
applications

HOW TO CONTACT:
By letter to Department GFI for advice,
information and application form
REGIONS SERVICED:
UK
SPECIAL NEEDS PROVISION:
No information available
COSTS/WAITING LISTS:
First deposit: £25, second deposit/insurance/
visa processing fee: £140

CAMPHILL VILLAGE TRUST
Delrow House
Hillfield Lane
Aldenham
Watford
Hertfordshire WD2 8DJ
Tel: 0923 856006 Fax: 0923 858035

The Camphill Village Trust runs eight
communities where adults with mental
handicaps can achieve richer, more meaningful
lives. Young people who would like to assist in
the running, upkeep and development of these
communities should contact Head Office for
more information about where the communities
are, and what you can do to help.

REGIONAL ADDRESSES:
The Trust runs village communities in
Aberdeen, North Yorkshire, Hertfordshire,
Gloucestershire, West Midlands, Cleveland
and Dumfries. Full details from Head Office

AGE RANGE:
Any
HOW TO CONTACT:
Letter, telephone to Head Office
REGIONS SERVICED:
UK
SPECIAL NEEDS PROVISION:
The village communities operate for the
benefit of people with special needs
COSTS/WAITING LISTS:
None for advice and information

CAMPING CLUB YOUTH (CCY)
Greenfields House
Westwood Way
Coventry CV4 8JH
Tel: 0203 694995 Fax: 0203 694886

Camping Club Youth aims to help and encourage
young people to camp in the correct and safest
way through instructional weekends as well as
'Fun and Adventure Weekends' enabling them
to pass the CCY test. Each member receives *The
Fundamentals of Good Camping* handbook,
written and published by the club.

REGIONAL ADDRESSES:
Contact through Head Office
AGE RANGE:
12-21
NUMBERS PASSING THROUGH:
2,000 members

HOW TO CONTACT:
Telephone, letter or fax to the membership
department at HQ for leaflets and an
application form
REGIONS SERVICED:
UK
SPECIAL NEEDS PROVISION:
Each case dealt with individually
COSTS/WAITING LISTS:
£3 annual subscription

CAMPING FOR THE DISABLED (CFD)
20 Burton Close
Telford
Shropshire TF4 2BX
Tel: 0743 761889/0952 507653/
0909 562430

CFD can give advice and information about
equipment, camping sites in the UK and abroad
with special facilities and other sources of help
for individuals and groups.

AGE RANGE:
Any
NUMBERS PASSING THROUGH:
200
HOW TO CONTACT:
Telephone or letter
REGIONS SERVICED:
UK
SPECIAL NEEDS PROVISION:
Mainly deals with disabled people

COSTS/WAITING LISTS:
Subscription is £2 per year for individuals and
£5 for a group

CAMPUS TRAVEL
52 Grosvenor Gardens
London SW1W 0AG
Tel: 071 730 3402 (European enquiries)
071 730 8111 (Worldwide enquiries)

Campus Travel specialises in student and youth
travel worldwide. They can offer students and
young people under 26 discount fares on
scheduled flights worldwide, low-cost flexible
charter flights to popular destinations, and
discount rail fares in Europe. They can provide
help and advice on a wide range of travel ideas.

REGIONAL ADDRESSES:
Outlets: Birmingham, Bradford, Brighton,
Bristol, Cambridge, Cardiff, Dundee,
Edinburgh, Glasgow, Leeds, Liverpool,
London, Manchester, Newcastle,
Nottingham, Oxford and Sheffield. Contact
Head Office for addresses
AGE RANGE:
Under 26
HOW TO CONTACT:
Telephone or in person to nearest branch
REGIONS SERVICED:
UK and worldwide
COSTS/WAITING LISTS:
No costs for information and advice

CANAL CAMPS
see WATERWAY RECOVERY GROUP

CAREER DEVELOPMENT LOANS (CDLs)

Career Development Loans are available throughout Great Britain to help individuals aged 18+ pay for vocational training to improve their job prospects. You can apply for a loan of between £300 and £5,000 to cover up to 80% of fees, plus other course support expenses – whether full-time, part-time or distance learning – lasting between 1 week and a year. The Employment Department, which runs CDLs, in conjunction with Barclays, the Co-operative and Clydesdale Banks, offer successful applicants a 'repayment holiday': no repayments are required during training and for up to three months afterwards, during which time the Department pays the interest on the loan. It's then up to you to repay the loan, plus any interest.

For further details and an application form call 0800 585 505 free of charge

CAREERS AND OCCUPATIONAL INFORMATION CENTRE (COIC)
PO Box 348
Bristol BS99 7FE
Tel: 0272 777199

The Careers and Occupational Information Centre (COIC) is a publishing house which produces a wide range of books, computer programs and videos on careers, education, training and work. Publications range from 50 booklets about specific job areas to books to help you make the most of your skills. Fashion? Design? Engineering? Tourism? Whatever job interests you, COIC can tell you more. Contemplating buying a motorbike or setting up home? COIC can steer you past the pitfalls. Contact COIC for a free list of publications.

CAREERS, EDUCATION AND TRAINING FOR AGRICULTURE AND THE COUNTRYSIDE (CETAC)
c/o Warwickshire Careers Service
10 Northgate Street
Warwick CV34 4SR

Contact CETAC for advice and information on education, training, voluntary work, careers for people with disabilities, careers in agriculture, horticulture, landscaping, forestry, veterinary work, gamekeeping, fish farming, organic farming, rural crafts, and other land-related industries. A wide range of free literature is available on receipt of a written request sent with a stamped addressed envelope.

CAREERS EUROPE
Ground Floor
Equity Chambers
40 Piccadilly
Bradford BD1 3NN

The creation of the single European market
means it is possible for UK citizens to work,
study or train within any of the European
Community member states. In order to take
advantage of the range of opportunities available
to young people, up-to-date accurate
information is required about each of the
countries and the opportunities within them.
Careers Europe was set up by a partnership
between the Employment Department and
Bradford Education Careers Service to provide
up-to-date information about Europe. Careers
Europe produces an information database as
well as written publications about the
opportunities within Europe.

AGE RANGE:
Any
HOW TO CONTACT:
Information is available via local careers
services or by letter to the above address
REGIONS SERVICED:
UK
COSTS/WAITING LIST:
Negotiable

CAREERS OFFICES

Careers Offices have details of local vacancies and training places for younger people. They have specialist knowledge about all sorts of jobs, courses and training, as well as knowing the local job market. They also have access to computer-based lists of vacancies. One way they can guide you is by compiling profiles to pinpoint your strengths and weaknesses – you may even find you have a hidden talent! For your nearest Careers Office, look in the telephone directory either under 'Careers Office' or under the local authority; alternatively ask at your local library.

CAREERS RESEARCH AND ADVISORY CENTRE (CRAC)
Sheraton House
Castle Park
Cambridge CB3 0AX
Tel: 0223 460277 Fax: 0223 311708

CRAC offers 'Insight into Management' courses to 16-19 year-old students, undergraduates and post-graduates. Students from a range of disciplines and individuals working in a wide variety of different organisations can gain experience of teamwork, analysing problems and decision-making under pressure. You will be encouraged to examine a wide range of career possibilities, discover what it is really like working in different management areas and gain a general understanding of business priorities and the world of work.

CRAC also offers a 5-day 'Insight into Management in Europe' course, designed to help you make career decisions as well as acquire some vital business skills. It will bring together students from other EC countries and involve managers from multi-national companies and EC institutions. This course aims to give you an insight into different management careers. In addition the course helps you to relate your own qualifications, strengths and experience to opportunities in a variety of companies and organisations.

CRAC/SERC Graduate Schools are organised to give you a taste of the challenges, issues and problems you will face in a career outside academia. The courses are designed for penultimate and final-year PhD students and run by managers from a wide range of jobs and environments.

AGE RANGE:

16-19 year-old students, undergraduates, European higher education students, PhD scientists and technologists

HOW TO CONTACT:

For information about 'Insight into Management' courses contact address above. CRAC mainly provides information through its publications, not through individual advice. For details of the range of careers

books/publications contact Hobsons
Publishing, Bateman Street, Cambridge CB2
1LZ   Tel: 0223 354551
REGIONS SERVICED:
UK and Europe
COSTS/WAITING LISTS:
Insight courses cost £35-£75; travel costs only
for graduate schools

CARRY THE CAN (CTC)
16 Woodrush Close
London SE14 6DJ
Tel: 081 692 0013

A new organisation set up for graffiti artists who
would like to channel their skills for the benefit
of the community around them. CTC aims to
make spaces available where graffiti artists can
perform and practise their art without causing
danger to themselves or offence to public and/
or property.

AGE RANGE:
Any
HOW TO CONTACT:
Letter or telephone for further information
REGIONS SERVICED:
UK
SPECIAL NEEDS PROVISION:
Enquiries welcome

CATHEDRAL CAMPS
16 Glebe Avenue
Flitwick
Bedfordshire MK45 1HS
Tel: 0525 716237

Volunteers do routine maintenance and simple conservation work on cathedrals and Christian buildings of architectural significance, carrying out both routine and sometimes more spectacular tasks under the guidance of craftsmen. Camps take place at different cathedrals between mid-July and early September and last for 1 week with volunteers working approximately 36 hours a week, 8.30am to 5pm each day. Food and accommodation are provided and volunteers sleep in the Cathedral hall or similar building. Each camp is run by a leader and two assistant leaders, and volunteers are asked to contribute to the social life of the camp and help with domestic duties on a rota basis. Projects qualify under the Duke of Edinburgh's Award Scheme.

REGIONAL ADDRESSES:
Booking Secretary/ Administrator:
Shelley Bent, 16 Glebe Avenue, Flitwick, Bedfordshire, MK45 1HS
AGE RANGE:
16-30
NUMBERS PASSING THROUGH:
700

HOW TO CONTACT:
By letter to Booking Secretary – at Flitwick
address above – for brochures and bookings
REGIONS SERVICED:
UK
SPECIAL NEEDS PROVISION:
People with special needs welcome on
camps; bursaries available
COSTS/WAITING LISTS:
The camp fee is £33. Local Education
Authorities occasionally give grants but this is
rare. Some bursaries are available from
Cathedral Camps in cases of hardship/
unemployment. Camps are usually over-
subscribed and you are advised to apply
early. Brochures for each year are available
in February

CATHOLIC YOUTH SERVICES (CYS)
39 Fitzjohn's Avenue
London NW3 5JT
Tel: 071 435 3596 Fax: 071 435 3596

CYS exists within the total Youth Service of
England and Wales to provide a distinctive
contribution to the growth and development of
young people based on the principles and
practice of the faith of the Catholic Church.

AGE RANGE:
Any
HOW TO CONTACT:
Letter or telephone to above address

REGIONS SERVICED:
England and Wales

CENTRAL BUREAU FOR EDUCATIONAL VISITS AND EXCHANGES
Seymour Mews House
Seymour Mews
London W1H 9PE
Tel: 071 486 5101 Fax: 071 935 5741

The Central Bureau is the UK national office responsible for information and advice on all forms of educational visits and exchanges; the development and administration of a wide range of curriculum-related pre-service and in-service exchange programmes; the linking of educational establishments and local education authorities with counterparts abroad and the organisation of meetings, workshops and conferences related to professional international experience. Its information and advisory services extend throughout the educational field.

REGIONAL ADDRESSES:
Scotland: 3 Bruntsfield Crescent, Edinburgh
EH10 4HD Tel: 031 447 8024
Fax: 031 452 8569
Northern Ireland: 16 Malone Road, Belfast
BT9 5BN Tel: 0232 664418
Fax: 0232 661275
AGE RANGE:
No specific age

HOW TO CONTACT:
By letter, telephone, fax or in person to your
nearest office for advice, information, leaflets,
reference books etc.
REGIONS SERVICED:
UK
SPECIAL NEEDS PROVISION:
The service can be used by anyone
COSTS/WAITING LISTS:
Costs include registration fees for some
schemes and travel costs depending on the
programme. Prices of publications vary.
Some funding is available from the
Department of Education and Science, the
Scottish Office Education Department and the
Department of Education for Northern Ireland

CENTRE FOR INFORMATION ON
LANGUAGE TEACHING AND RESEARCH
(CILT)
20 Bedfordbury
London WC2N 4LB
Tel: 071 379 5101 Information Resource
Centre 071 3799 5110 Fax: 071 379 5082

Careers in languages cover specialist fields such
as interpreting, translating and teaching. A
wide range of career opportunities also exists in
international trade, banking, business, the Civil
Service, local government, information and
library work, insurance, work in international
organisations, journalism, the media, secretarial

work, tourism and other areas, both for language specialists and for those with a language linked to the career of their choice. The range of languages in demand is ever-increasing, and includes European languages, Chinese and Japanese, the languages of South America (Spanish and Brazilian Portuguese), Arabic and community languages such as Urdu. There is a variety of information available on careers. Some of this may be held in school and college libraries and at local Careers Offices and public libraries. Most booklets are inexpensive and easily obtainable. CILT does not provide an advisory service on careers with languages, but publishes some relevant titles. For details of the titles available contact the above address.

CHALLENGE TO YOUTH
BP Oil UK Ltd
Community and Educational Affairs
Department
BP House
Breakspear Way
Hemel Hempstead
Hertfordshire HP2 4UL
Tel: 0442 225446 Fax: 0442 225919

The BP Challenge to Youth programme comprises a number of schemes and competitions which give you and your friends the opportunity to work as a team to come up with designs and to build practical objects to the benefit of the community or the environment. The purpose of the Challenges is 'to bridge the gap between the theory of the classroom and the practicality of the adult world'. Cash prizes are awarded to teams for working well as a team, for innovation and for the success of their designs. Current challenges include the 'Buildacar' competition which has proved such a success that it now takes place every two years. Other projects have involved using technology to solve the problems faced by the elderly in their homes, or to design and produce aids for the disabled. Starter packs, advice and other needs are provided throughout the duration of all projects. 'Challenges' change from year to year but they always involve design, technology, making decisions, achieving results and teamwork.

AGE RANGE:
5-19
HOW TO CONTACT:
Write to above address, through your school or youth group, for information and entry forms
REGIONS SERVICED:
UK
COSTS/WAITING LISTS:
Write to above address, through your school or youth group, for details of current competitions

CHARTERED ASSOCIATION OF CERTIFIED ACCOUNTANTS (ACCA)
Student Recruitment and Training
29 Lincoln's Inn Fields
London WC2A 3EE
Tel: 071 396 5800

Certified accountants may work in any of the three main fields of accountancy – public practice (accounting firms offering a range of accounting services), industry and commerce or the public sector (local or central government, or in publicly owned industries). Contact above for careers and courses information and advice.

REGIONS SERVICED:
England, Wales and Northern Ireland

CHARTERED INSTITUTE OF MARKETING
Moor Hall
Cookham
Maidenhead
Berkshire SL6 9QH

Marketing covers a wide range of occupations including market research, communications, sales, brand management, distribution, product development and sales promotion. The Chartered Institute of Marketing offers professional courses, i.e. the Certificate in Marketing, Certificate in Sales Mangement and the Diploma in Marketing, leading to membership of the Institute.

CHARTERED INSURANCE INSTITUTE (CII)
Careers Department
31 Hillcrest Road
South Woodford
London E18 2JP
Tel: 081 530 6243

A wide range of professional, administrative and clerical careers are available in insurance – as underwriter, broker, salesperson, claims official, clerk, surveyor and loss adjuster. For more information about starting out in or developing your career in insurance contact the CII. They produce a range of factsheets, leaflets and booklets covering all aspects of the insurance industry – entry requirements, courses and training opportunities, career development etc. – and will also deal with telephone enquiries. For details of your nearest branch contact the above address.

CHURCH OF ENGLAND YOUTH SERVICES
Board of Education
Church House
Great Smith Street
London SW1P 3NZ
Tel: 071 222 9011 (ext. 408)
Fax: 071 799 2714

The Church of England Youth Services promotes the education, spiritual and social development of young people between the ages of 14 and 25.

The Church's youth work is delivered mainly through volunteer youth workers. Support, advice, consultancy and training is offered through the network of Diocesan Youth Officers of whom there are approximately 60 in 43 dioceses. Diocesan Youth Workers can provide information about youth groups and events and activities around the country. In addition to the Diocesan youth network, training opportunities and resource production are provided by the four main Church of England agencies:

Church Youth Fellowship Association (CYFA)
Church Lads and Church Girls Brigade (CLCGB)
Girls Friendly Society (GFS)
Anglican Youth (AY)

Anne Foreman and Jonathan Roberts, the National Youth Officers at the above address, can put you in touch with Diocesan Youth Officers and/or any of the agencies.

CHURCH ORGAN SCHOOL
Scottish Amateur Music Association
PO Box 1085
Bearsden
Glasgow G61 4AP
Tel: 0360 60021

Young organists are invited to apply for the 1994 course which will be held at St Andrews University, Fife from 8-12 August. No special standard of playing is required.

AGE RANGE:
Any
NUMBERS PASSING THROUGH:
30
HOW TO CONTACT:
By telephone or letter for further information
REGIONS SERVICED:
UK but mainly Scotland
SPECIAL NEEDS PROVISION:
Special tuition at an advanced level available
COSTS/WAITING LISTS:
There is a course fee of £225 which includes
tuition, accommodation and the services of
professional musicians. Some local authority
grants may be available. Waiting lists can be
up to 6months preceding the next year's
course

CITIES IN SCHOOLS (CiS)
60-61 Trafalgar Square
London WC2N 5DS
Tel: 071 839 2899 Fax: 071 839 6186

If you have been turned off school you can get
some education and develop other skills by
joining a CiS project. We also aim to help you
build confidence and improve your image of
yourself. If you are interested in volunteering to
help other young people in a local project you
might be eligible for free training.

REGIONAL ADDRESSES:
CiS – Tower Hamlets: 91 Brick Lane,

London E1 6QN Tel: 071 247 9489
CiS – Gwent: c/o K Block, British Steel, Strip
Products, Llanwern Works, Newport, Gwent
NP9 0XN Tel: 0633 290011 (ext. 4441)

AGE RANGE:

Varies according to the project

NUMBERS PASSING THROUGH:

CiS projects are generally small, with larger
vacation programmes. More than 1,000
young people have been involved so far

HOW TO CONTACT:

Referrals normally come from schoolteachers
and youth agencies but it is possible for
young people to refer themselves on to a CiS
project. Contact numbers are above

COSTS/WAITING LISTS:

No costs. There are waiting lists in local CiS
areas. If there are places you will be invited
to join a project

CITY AND GUILDS (C&G)
76 Portland Place
London W1N 9AA
Tel: 071 278 2468 Fax: 071 436 7630

City and Guilds of London Institute, to give it its
full name, does not run courses itself. The
courses are offered in approved centres, such as
colleges of further education, training centres,
and companies etc. Most C&G courses are run
on a part-time day-release basis, but full-time
and evening courses are also available. In

general, there are no specified lengths of study nor minimum age or educational requirements for candidates. Courses are available in subjects as diverse as gamekeeping, floristry and tree surgery through to electrical and electronic engineering, and computer-aided draughting and design. You may take C&G courses in photography, fashion, languages, furniture craft, animal care, or in any one of hundreds of subjects offered. You might take a City and Guilds as you gain experience at work, and as part of learning your job and developing a career, or you might take one in the hope of gaining employment in the future. Holders of C&G Certificates have evidence that they have achieved a nationally recognised standard – a bonus when meeting new employers. City and Guilds also offers National Vocational Qualifications (NVQs) – see separate entry. Most C&G assessments and tests which are available in the UK are also available to candidates in about 85 countries around the world. For information about examinations available worldwide, contact Division 42, City and Guilds of London Institute, 46 Britannia Street, London WC1X 9RG. For information about C&G courses in your local area contact your nearest college of further education, your Local Education Authority or Careers Office. For a free City and Guilds 'List of Publications' or 'List of Subjects' write to Sales Section, City and Guilds of London Institute, 76 Portland Place, London W1N 4AA.

AGE RANGE:
14+
NUMBERS PASSING THROUGH:
2.3 million entrants for C&G awards every year
HOW TO CONTACT:
Letter, telephone, fax
REGIONS SERVICED:
UK

CITY TECHNOLOGY COLLEGES (CTCs)
The CTC Trust
15 Young Street
London W8 5EH
Tel: 071 376 2511 Fax: 071 938 1961

City Technology Colleges (CTCs) are sponsored by industry and maintain close links with local employers. They are secondary schools, normally catering for 11-18 year-olds, but they are particularly geared to helping young people continue their education by offering a variety of subjects at different levels in preparation for the world of work. They offer a wide variety of course options at 16+ including 'A' and 'AS' levels, International Baccalaureate, BTEC National and First Diplomas, and other vocational certificates such as City and Guilds, Institute of Linguists, RSA and National Vocational Qualifications.

REGIONAL ADDRESSES:
CTCs are presently open, or preparing to
open, in London (5), Derby, Corby,
Nottingham, Birmingham, Telford, Dartford,
Bristol, Middlesborough, Bradford and
Gateshead. There are plans for CTCs to be
set up in Preston and Lincoln.
AGE RANGE:
11-18 usually
NUMBERS PASSING THROUGH:
c 8,000 in 1993
HOW TO CONTACT:
Letter, telephone, fax to CTC Trust for details
of your local CTC

CIVIL SERVICE COMMISSION
Alencon Link
Basingstoke
Hampshire RG21 1JB
Tel: 0256 846560

The Civil Service comprises over 60 departments
and their executive agencies and is one of
Britain's largest employers with opportunities in
a very wide range of occupations. There are
opportunities for administrators (both in the UK
and Europe), scientists, engineers and other
professionals such as accountants, diplomatic
service officers, tax inspectors, actuaries,
economists, customs officers, government
communication trainees, health and safety
inspectors, press and publicity specialists, prison

service staff, psychologists, legal trainees, museum and gallery curators, factory and agricultural inspectors, librarians, immigration officers, IT specialists, research officers, linguists and statisticians.

The entry level is dependent upon a combination of qualifications, age and experience. Vacancies will be advertised in Jobcentres and via other media such as national, local and specialist press and to careers services, as appropriate. For more information on the work and opportunities available in individual government departments and agencies, please see your careers service.

COMETT
(Community Action Programme for
Education and Training in Technology)
COMETT Liaison Office
Department for Education
Sanctuary Buildings, Great Smith Street
London SW1P 3BT
Tel: 071 925 5254 Fax: 071 925 6985

The objectives of the EC COMETT Programme are to stimulate and develop co-operation between higher education institutions and industry in the field of education and training for technology. Initiatives include financial support for work placement of undergraduate and postgraduate students to industrial enterprises in other EC or EFTA countries for periods ranging from 3-12 months.

REGIONAL ADDRESSES:
Details available from above
AGE RANGE:
No strict limits other than normal university
age range
NUMBERS PASSING THROUGH:
c 1,000
HOW TO CONTACT:
Work placements arranged through university
– Enterprise Training Partnerships (UETPs).
Details of nearest UETP available from
European/External Relations Officers at
individual universities or contact COMETT
Liaison Office. Students must be registered
with a UK university and undertaking a
technology-related degree course
REGIONS SERVICED:
UK
COSTS/WAITING LISTS:
Applications are only accepted once a year
so there could be a long wait between initial
contact and receiving any grant

COMMISSION OF THE EUROPEAN COMMUNITIES

The Commission of the European Communities
can give information on all aspects of what it
means to live in a Member State of the EC. They
produce a range of literature – including
information about the right to work in Member
States, young people and europe, disabled
people in the community, mutual recognition

of diplomas and other professional qualifications, freedom of movement, and education and training initiatives and opportunities.

REGIONAL ADDRESSES:
England: 8 Storey's Gate, London SW1P 3AT
Tel: 071 973 1992
Scotland: 9 Alva Street, Edinburgh EH2 4PH
Tel: 031 225 2058
Wales: 4 Cathedral Street, Cardiff CF1 1SG
Tel: 0222 395489
Northern Ireland: 9-15 Bedford Street, Belfast
BT2 7EG Tel: 0232 240708

COMMITTEE OF SCOTTISH CLEARING BANKERS
19 Rutland Square
Edinburgh EH1 2DD
Tel: 031 229 1326

Can provide advice and information on all aspects of careers in high street banking in Scotland, from gaining entry to getting employment and developing your career.

COMMONWEALTH YOUTH EXCHANGE COUNCIL (CYEC)
7 Lion Yard
Tremadoc Road
London SW4 7NQ
Tel: 071 498 6151 Fax: 071 720 5403

CYEC can assist, through advice, information, publications and grant aid, the planning and financing of a youth exchange link between your group and partner groups overseas. Commonwealth Youth Exchange projects are a challenging and exciting way of sharing and learning about young people in the 50 member countries of the Commonwealth.

AGE RANGE:
16-25

NUMBERS PASSING THROUGH:
In 1992 CYEC gave financial support to 963 young people from 78 groups and advice and information to many more

HOW TO CONTACT:
Letter or telephone. Open to contact by either young people or youth organisations

REGIONS SERVICED:
UK

SPECIAL NEEDS PROVISION:
CYEC are open to all and they encourage participation of special needs groups in exchanges

COSTS/WAITING LISTS:
CYEC do not charge for services. Grants cover 20-25% of the total cost of an exchange. The remaining costs are raised by the individual group by sponsorship, fund-raising etc. Applications for financial support should be made about 12 months before the project takes place. Grant guidelines available on request and on receipt of SAE

COMMUNITY ACTION

Community Action is designed to help people who have been unemployed for over a year to get back to work. It offers an opportunity for part-time work of direct benefit to the local community, combined with practical help in looking for work. Community Action offers a wide range of opportunities, all of them voluntary. They may include caring, working in hospitals, the probation service, childcare, environmental work, recycling initiatives, or administration and research projects. Coomunity Action offers people an opportunity to get recent work experience lasting up to 6months. On completion all who participate will be given a completion certificate and reference. People who take part in Community Action will receive an allowance equivalent to their benefit entitlement plus £10. Contact your local Jobcentre for details.

COMMUNITY CIRCUS
43 Trueway Road
Leicester LE5 5UG
Tel: 0533 733503 Fax: 0533 855646

Community Circus is essentially a travelling circus school working mainly in inner cities offering training in street theatre skills and workshops in circus skills, clowning, face-painting, stilt-walking, juggling and much more.

The main difference compared to traditional circus is that the skills learned are for personal confidence, shared pleasure and shared events.

AGE RANGE:
Any
NUMBERS PASSING THROUGH:
c 6,000
HOW TO CONTACT:
By telephone for further information, as well as contacts with courses run by Fool Time – Britain's only circus school (see separate entry)
REGIONS SERVICED:
UK
SPECIAL NEEDS PROVISION:
Workshops dealing specifically with special needs
COSTS/WAITING LISTS:
Individual organisations usually pay for workshops

COMMUNITY LINKS
Canning Town Public Hall
105 Barking Road
London E16 4HQ
Tel: 071 473 2270 Fax: 071 473 6671

Community Links is a multi-purpose social action centre based in East London which encourages and enables groups and individuals to understand and tackle their own problems. Their Children's and Youth Work Programme includes a huge variety of activities – some specifically targeting young people with special needs, but all open to everyone. Young people are involved in running all that is done by Community Links and the organisation is entirely dependent upon the active involvement of more than 300 trained volunteers. The 1993 activity programme will include 120 holiday playschemes, 56 camping holidays, 16 regular after-school clubs (6 providing full care), 10 weekly groups working with 120 young people at risk of going into care, 12 children's Fun Days attracting over 60,000 children, information and advice services for over 750 young people, 16 weekly youth groups and an extensive range of seasonal activities. Community Links is constantly seeking new volunteers and participants.

AGE RANGE:
No limits
NUMBERS PASSING THROUGH:
7,000+ per year
HOW TO CONTACT:
Write to the above address

COMMUNITY SERVICE VOLUNTEERS (CSV)
237 Pentonville Road
London N1 9NJ
Tel: 071 278 6601 Fax: 071 837 9621

Community Service Volunteers invites all young people to experience the challenge, excitement and reward of helping people in need. Every year 3,000 volunteers work throughout the UK with elderly people, adults with disabilities, children who are handicapped, in care or in trouble, and homeless people. Volunteers work hard, have fun, and gain valuable experience. Volunteers work away from home, full-time, from 4 to 12 months and receive full board, lodging, and a weekly allowance. Applications are welcome throughout the year, and no previous experience or qualifications are needed.

AGE RANGE:
16-35
NUMBERS PASSING THROUGH:
3,000 each year
HOW TO CONTACT:
By phone or letter to address above
REGIONS SERVICED:
UK
COSTS/WAITING LISTS:
No costs involved for information or to take up placements. Usually takes 6 to 8weeks to place volunteers after application

---

COMPUTER PALS ACROSS THE WORLD (CPAW)
c/o John Meadows
Electronic Mail Box No TCD 004

CPAW is a worldwide organisation which promotes links and friendships between individuals of all nations by using the latest technology to put you in touch.

CONCORDIA (YSV) LTD
8 Brunswick Place
Hove BN3 1ET
Tel: 0273 772086 Fax: 0273 27284

Concordia offers volunteering opportunities in Europe on short-term community or environmental work projects involving young people from other countries.

AGE RANGE:
18-30
NUMBERS PASSING THROUGH:
250
HOW TO CONTACT:
Telephone or letter for leaflets and information
REGIONS SERVICED:
UK
SPECIAL NEEDS PROVISION:
No provision
COSTS/WAITING LISTS:
Enrolment fees are £16-£35, depending on the country involved. Volunteers are expected to pay their own travel costs.
Contact in spring when project details become available

CONNAUGHT EXECUTIVE CAREER SERVICES LTD
23 Savile Row
London W1X 1AG
Tel: 071 734 3879 Fax: 071 734 2620

Offers a Special Graduate Service including a two-hour assessment meeting with a Senior Counsellor with a psychometric test. This is followed within a week by a further meeting of at least one hour to assess the psychometric test report and to summarise the counsellor's opinion on your career options. There is also advice on how to set up a professional CV and guidelines for the setting up of a job search campaign, plus assistance on where to find names and addresses of prospective employers, institutions and organisations.

AGE RANGE:
Any
HOW TO CONTACT:
Regional offices in Birmingham, Cambridge, Winchester, Guildford and Warwick
(addresses/phone numbers available from main office)
COSTS/WAITING LISTS:
£300 + VAT

CONSERVATION VOLUNTEERS –
NORTHERN IRELAND (CVNI)
The Pavilion
Cherryvale Playing Fields
Ravenhill Road
Belfast BT6 0BZ
Tel: 0232 645169

An opportunity to be involved in practical conservation and to do something that makes a difference, such as tree-planting, creating habitats for wildlife, helping to save wildlife in rural areas etc., by taking part in a working holiday or weekend break with CVNI. There are also training courses available and you can become a member of CVNI either through school or as an individual.

AGE RANGE:
Any
NUMBERS PASSING THROUGH:
c 350
HOW TO CONTACT:
Contact individual area offices (addresses available from main office), preferably by SAE or by telephone
REGIONS SERVICED:
UK
SPECIAL NEEDS PROVISION:
Access to certain sites
COSTS/WAITING LISTS:
Annual membership is £10. No charge for any volunteer work

CONSERVATIVE PARTY

32 Smith Square
London SW1P 3HH
Tel: 071 222 9000

CONSTRUCTION INDUSTRY TRAINING BOARD (CITB)

Careers Advisory Service
Bircham Newton
King's Lynn
Norfolk PE31 6RH
Tel: 0553 776677

Careers advice and information is available on a wide range of construction activities. Our range of literature and videos cover over 60 different craft, technician, professional and management career opportunities.

CONTEMPORARY ART SOCIETY (CAS)

20 John Islip Street
London SW1P 4LL
Tel: 071 821 5323 Fax: 071 834 0228

Membership society which promotes contemporary art and helps acquire work by living artists for gift to public galleries.

CONTINENTAL CONNECTIONS
Cranford
Church End
Albury
Near Ware,
Hertfordshire SG11 2JG
Tel: 0279 771541 Fax: 0279 771541

Continental Connections is an organisation which arranges holiday exchanges between young people aged 13 to 18 who wish to improve their language ability in French, German or Spanish.   Young people are individually matched with others of similar age and interests for a period of up to two weeks in each country. The agency can also send young people as paying guests to families with or without tuition during their stay.

AGE RANGE:
13-18
NUMBERS PASSING THROUGH:
c 100
HOW TO CONTACT:
Telephone, SAE or fax for further information
REGIONS SERVICED:
UK with excellent contacts in Europe
SPECIAL NEEDS PROVISION:
No specific provision although an enthusiasm to learn a language and an ability to get on with host family is an added advantage
COSTS/WAITING LISTS:
The agency fee for 1994 is £125, which

included telephone and postage costs and the introduction to the foreign family. Contact Mrs Ann Sachs from September onwards for the following year. There are no waiting lists as such but early contact is advised to leave time for the right family to be found.

CO-OP YOUNG PEOPLE'S
FILM & VIDEO FESTIVAL
Member Relations Department
Co-operative Retail Services Ltd
29 Dantzic Street
Manchester M4 4BA
Tel: 061 958 1412 Fax: 061 832 7355

Entries for the film and video festival are invited from schools, colleges, youth groups etc. The emphasis is on groups of young people working together to produce an entry. The festival is held each year with national screenings taking place alternately at the National Film Theatre and Museum of the Moving Image in London and the National Museum of Film, Photography & Television in Bradford.

AGE RANGE:
Up to 21 (flexible if some members of the group are over 21)
HOW TO CONTACT:
Telephone or letter to above address
REGIONS SERVICED:
UK

COSTS/WAITING LISTS:
None

CO-OPERATION PROJECT
PO Box 28183
Washington DC
20038-8183
USA
Tel: 010 202 857 8037
Fax: 010 202 861 0621

The Co-operation Project is the joint work of non-governmental organisations dedicated to promoting multi-cultural perspectives on ecological and social issues. The three branches of the project, in Russia, Japan and the USA, collaborate in organising international citizen exchange programmes, including voluntary service work camps and nature expeditions, language exchange programmes and educational tours. The purpose of these exchanges is to introduce people from a wide variety of countries to the host country and its people, as well as to the positive and negative aspects of its social and economic systems, particularly their effects on ecology and human life.

AGE RANGE:
18+
NUMBERS PASSING THROUGH:
150
HOW TO CONTACT:
The best contact address for Great Britain is

in Holland : The Co-operation Project,
Foundation for Ecological Co-operation,
Postbus 13844, 2501 EV Den Haag, The
Netherlands. The main office in the west is
the Washington address above and you can
write to either for further information

REGIONS SERVICED:
Worldwide

SPECIAL NEEDS PROVISION:
No specific provision, but individuals are
encouraged to contact the project to see what
can be arranged

COSTS/WAITING LISTS:
Participants are responsible for their own
travel costs and there are participation and
membership fees – contact the Co-operation
Project for full details. Some help is available
for those unable to pay the full fees but funds
are currently quite limited

CO-OPERATIVE DEVELOPMENT AGENCIES

Co-operative Development Agencies can offer
free help and advice on setting up in business as
a co-operative covering all stages of development
from an initial idea through to viability testing,
raising capital and business planning. Details of
local offices are listed in the Yellow Pages under
'Local or Business Enterprise Agencies', or
contact the Industrial Common Ownership
Movement (see separate entry), who can advise
you of your nearest agency.

CORAL CAY CONSERVATION PROGRAMME
Tel: 081 669 0011

An opportunity to do some important reef survey work off Belize. Some diving tuition is available in the UK before departure (novices welcome) and there is an extensive training programme on arrival in Belize. You can take part for 1, 2 or 3 months and the project will run until 1995.

AGE RANGE:
18+
COSTS/WAITING LISTS:
£1,600-£3,000

COUNCIL FOR BRITISH ARCHAEOLOGY (CBA)
Bowes Morrell House
111 Walmgate
York YO1 2UA
Tel: 0904 671417 Fax: 0904 671384

The CBA is a registered charity dedicated to advancing the study and practice of archaeology and can provide information and advice on where to study and careers in archaeology. They also produce relevant factsheets, e.g. Getting Started in Archaeology, Archaeology in Higher Education, A Job in Archaeology. Membership of the CBA is open to individuals and institutions – most national, regional and local archaeological societies are affiliated to the CBA. Student membership of the CBA, available to all those in full-time education for £9.50 a year, brings a regular magazine, *British Archaeological News,* with its information supplement *CBA Briefing,* giving details of excavations and other projects looking for volunteers. The CBA Information Service will also answer questions on any aspect of British archaeology.

COUNCIL FOR ENVIRONMENTAL EDUCATION (CEE)
University of Reading
London Road
Reading RG1 5AQ
Tel: 0734 756061 Fax: 0734 756264

The CEE acts as a national focus, in England, Wales and Northern Ireland, encouraging and promoting an environmental approach to education. The CEE Youth Unit works directly with the youth services and environmental organisations, providing advice and training on the development of environmental youth work. The CEE Information Unit responds to requests for environmental information from young people, often by referring them to other appropriate organisations.

AGE RANGE:
Any

NUMBERS PASSING THROUGH:
c 500 requests for information from young
people each year
HOW TO CONTACT:
Send SAE for information and leaflets
REGIONS SERVICED:
UK
SPECIAL NEEDS PROVISION:
Information service is open to anyone
COSTS/WAITING LISTS:
None

COUNCIL FOR THE PROTECTION OF
RURAL ENGLAND (CPRE)
25 Buckingham Palace Road
London SW1W 0PP
Tel: 071 976 6433 Fax: 071 976 6373

CPRE campaigns for the better protection of the
countryside. If you want to become practically
involved in local conservation you can become
a member of CPRE and they will keep you
informed of all that is going on in your area.

REGIONAL ADDRESSES:
Approx. 44 regional offices. Contact address
above for details of your nearest branch
AGE RANGE:
Any
HOW TO CONTACT:
By letter to local branch. Information about
your nearest branch from address above –
phone, letter, fax

REGIONS SERVICED:
England only
SPECIAL NEEDS PROVISION:
Enquiries welcomed
COSTS/WAITING LISTS:
No costs for general information.
Membership costs £10 per year. No waiting lists

COUNCIL ON INTERNATIONAL EDUCATIONAL EXCHANGE (CIEE)
33 Seymour Place
London W1H 6AT
Tel: 071 706 3008 Fax: 071 724 8468

CIEE's University Enrolment Service offers young people, educated to at least 'A' level standard, the opportunity to take degree-level courses in many different subjects at US universities, and language and culture courses at European universities. All courses are run during the summer and are an excellent way of learning about and experiencing the US education system and culture, improving your language skills and adding to your CV. For an administrative fee CIEE will provide academic advice, process your enrolment and make accommodation and visa arrangements.

AGE RANGE:
Any
NUMBERS PASSING THROUGH:
25

HOW TO CONTACT:
By letter addressed to the particular
programme you are interested in
REGIONS SERVICED:
UK
SPECIAL NEEDS PROVISION:
CIEE aim to make their programmes as
accessible as possible
COSTS/WAITING LISTS:
USA administration fee: £85; France: £75.
Tuition and accommodation for two courses
costs £500-£1400, plus flight. Apply from
April and no later than 4 weeks before the
start of the course

CSU (PUBLICATIONS) LTD
Student Sales
Armstrong House
Oxford Road
Manchester M1 7ED
Tel: 061 236 9816 Fax: 061 236 8541

For higher education students and graduates
looking for help with career choice, details of
companies and their vacancies or postgraduate
opportunities the *Prospect* series of graduate
careers publications is the place to look.
Publications in the series include *Prospects*, the
annual careers services' guide to graduate
opportunities, and *Prospects Today*, a fortnightly
newsletter of immediate jobs for graduates.

AGE RANGE:
16+
HOW TO CONTACT:
All publications are available for reference in university and college careers centres or can be purchased directly from CSU. Write or phone for an order form
REGIONS SERVICED:
Publications cover opportunities in the UK and Eire
COSTS:
Price list sent out with order forms

CULTURAL AND EDUCATIONAL SERVICES ABROAD (CESA)
Western House
Malpas
Truro TR1 1SQ
Tel: 0872 225300 Fax: 0872 225400

CESA offers an information and advice service on language courses abroad, mainly within the European Community, but they also work with Colleges in China, Mexico, Russia and Japan. You can choose between taking a very intensive language course, or more of a 'holiday' course with lessons in the morning and plenty of free time to add to the enjoyment of your stay. 3months+ programmes allow students to study for the state-recognised Diplomas at various centres e.g. DELF and DALF qualifications in France and the Goethe Institute exams in

Germany. Once you have decided on a course,
CESA can make all the necessary arrangements
from reserving your place in the language school
to arranging whichever type of accommodation
you need for your stay.

AGE RANGE:
12+ – French and German courses only (all
linguistic levels). 16+ – all languages (all
linguistic levels)

NUMBERS PASSING THROUGH:
600 in 1993

HOW TO CONTACT:
By telephone or letter for details of courses
available

REGIONS SERVICED:
UK (CESA also advise and book courses for
students from USA, Europe and Hong Kong)

COSTS/WAITING LISTS:
Costs vary depending on country, length of
stay, time of the year and type of course, e.g.
two weeks in France, 20 hours of tuition and
half-board family accommodation costs
approx. £600. Travel costs are not included
in the course fees and most students make
their own arrangements but CESA is happy to
offer advice on travel options.
Waiting lists are not a problem as programmes
run throughout the year. However, be warned
July and August are very busy months and need
to be booked well in advance

CYCLISTS' TOURING CLUB (CTC)
Cotterell House
69 Meadrow
Godalming
Surrey GU7 3HS
Tel: 0483 417217 Fax: 0483 426994

The CTC is the governing body for recreational and utility cycling. It is the largest (and oldest – est. 1878) association for cyclists in the UK. Although primarily a membership organisation, the CTC does much work for all cyclists, whatever their age or ability. Cycling is an economical form of transport, it's healthy and it's fun. The CTC organises various events and operates through a large network of local groups with various special interest sections (young people, disabled etc.). There are volunteering opportunities in setting up and running local CTC clubs.

REGIONAL ADDRESSES:
70 regional district associations – details from HQ
AGE RANGE:
Any
HOW TO CONTACT:
Telephone, letter or fax for further information about membership
REGIONS SERVICED:
UK and overseas
SPECIAL NEEDS PROVISION:
CTC can provide facilities, e.g. blind and disabled tandems, ideas and information

COSTS/WAITING LISTS:
Under 18 annual membership: £12;
Full: £24; Unemployed : £12; Household
groups: £40

DEMOCRATIC UNIONIST PARTY
296 Albertsbridge Road
Belfast BT5 4GX
Tel: 0232 458597

DEPARTMENT FOR EDUCATION
Sanctuary Buildings
Great Smith Street
Westminster
London SW1P 3BT
Tel: 071 925 5000 Fax: 071 925 6000

The DFE can provide information and leaflets
on many aspects of education, e.g. grants and
loans for further education, options at 16 etc. as
well as on the many European Community
programmes available such as ERASMUS,
TEMPUS, COMETT etc. (see individual entries).

REGIONAL ADDRESSES:
Scottish Office Education Department, New
St Andrew's House, Edinburgh EH1 3SY
Tel: 031 556 8400
Department of Education – Northern Ireland,
Rathgael House, Balloo Road, Bangor, Co.
Down BT19 2PR Tel: 0247 270077

AGE RANGE:
Any

HOW TO CONTACT:
Telephone or letter for further information or leaflets depending on the nature of the enquiry

REGIONS SERVICED:
England and Wales – see above for Scotland and Northern Ireland

SPECIAL NEEDS PROVISION:
Information is available to everyone

COSTS/WAITING LISTS:
Most leaflets are free

THE DESIGN COUNCIL
28 Haymarket
London SW1Y 4SU
Tel: 071 839 8000

The Design Council can provide comprehensive information about all aspects of the design industry and can offer detailed information about ways of getting in and developing your career as a designer. They have a very large design bookshop and produce a range of booklets and factsheets covering courses and career development in design.

REGIONAL OFFICES:
Northern Ireland: Business Design Centre, 39 Corporation Street, Belfast BT1 3BA
Tel: 0232 238452

Scotland: Ca'd'Oro Building, 45 Gordon
Street, Glasgow G1 3LZ Tel: 041 221 6121
Wales: QED Centre, Main Avenue, Treforest
Estate, Treforest CF37 5YR Tel: 0443 841888

DEUTSCHER AKADEMISCHER AUSTAUSCHDIENST (DAAD)
(German Academic Exchange Service)
Kennedyallee 50
D-53175 Bonn
Germany
Tel: 010 49 228 882 455
Fax: 010 49 228 882 444

Applicants must be academic students enroled
at institutions of higher education or research
institutes with a good basic knowledge of the
German language. The three main schemes run
by DAAD are: scholarships for university summer
courses in Germany for undergraduate students;
annual scholarships for postgraduate students
for study in Germany; group study visits for
undergraduate or postgraduate visits to
Germany. DAAD also produce many leaflets
and booklets on the German educational system
including scholarships, funding, exchange
programmes etc.

REGIONAL ADDRESSES:
London Branch: 17 Bloomsbury Square,
London WC1A 2LP Tel: 071 404 4065
Fax: 071 430 2634

AGE RANGE:
Any
NUMBERS PASSING THROUGH:
In 1992 the DAAD provided funding for over 25,000 people worldwide for study research and training in Germany
HOW TO CONTACT:
Telephone, letter, fax or in person to the London office for information and an application form for funding schemes if eligible
REGIONS SERVICED:
UK (the service operates worldwide)
SPECIAL NEEDS PROVISION:
Enquiries welcome – the same provisions apply to all applicants
COSTS/WAITING LISTS:
Applications for funding should be made a year in advance

DIRECTORY OF COLLEGE ACCOMMODATIONS USA AND CANADA
(publication)
Vacation Work Publications
9 Park End Street
Oxford OX1 1HJ
Tel: 0865 241978 Fax: 0865 790885

Some 175 colleges and universities in the USA and Canada offer inexpensive (from $5 per night) but clean and comfortable accommodation to travellers. This directory gives all the information travellers need to stay on a campus, including the dates the accommodation is available, rates, facilities, restrictions and telephone numbers to contact. ISBN 0 87866 869 1. Available through libraries, bookshops (price £5.95), or direct from the above address (price £7.45 inc. p&p).

DIRECTORY OF JOBS AND CAREERS ABROAD (publication)
Vacation Work Publications
9 Park End Street
Oxford OX1 1HJ
Tel: 0865 241978 Fax: 0865 790885

A guide to permanent career opportunities abroad. Explains the most successful methods of finding work abroad for people of all walks of life, from the school leaver to the fully qualified professional. Gives facts on careers abroad for teachers, doctors, fitters, policemen, secretaries, printers, engineers, accountants, nurses, lawyers, computer operators, journalists and more. Lists the trades and professions most in demand in Europe, Australia, New Zealand, USA, Canada, and China giving details of the qualifications required and addresses to contact.
ISBN 85458 101 5. Available through libraries, bookshops (price £9.95), or direct from the above address (price £11.45 inc. p&p).

DIRECTORY OF SUMMER JOBS ABROAD
1994 (publication)
Vacation Work Publications
9 Park End Street
Oxford OX1 1HJ
Tel: 0865 241978 Fax: 0865 790885

30,000 varied vacancies listed at employers' request in over 40 different countries, including Germany, France, Spain, Switzerland, Scandinavia, Italy, Israel, Morocco, Greece etc. Jobs for couriers, sailing and scuba diving instructors, voluntary workers, overland expedition leaders, English teachers, secretaries, hiking tour managers, hotel workers, fruit pickers, villa staff etc. Full details of jobs offered, the period of work and wages are given, together with names and addresses of employers. Wages up to £1,000 per month. Special supplements on working with families and cheap travel. Facts about visas and work permits plus a section on health insurance and a chapter on winter jobs abroad.
ISBN 1 85458 101 5. Available through libraries, bookshops (price £7.95) or direct from the above address (price £9.45 inc. p&p).

**DIRECTORY OF SUMMER JOBS IN BRITAIN
1994 (publication)**
Vacation Work Publications
9 Park End Street
Oxford OX1 1HJ
Tel: 0865 241978 Fax: 0865 790885

30,000 vacancies listed at employers' request
in England, Scotland and Wales. Fruit and hop
picking, hotels, sports instruction, farming,
childcare, office work, holiday camps,
archaeological digs, riding centres, voluntary
work etc. The jobs vary in location from offices
in London, to fairgrounds, to remote Scottish
castles, and can pay as much as £220 per week.
Details of wages and hours, general conditions
of work, and qualifications required are given,
together with names and addresses of whom to
contact when applying. Also includes advice
on approaching an employer, and how to create
your own job.
ISBN 1 85458 103 1. Available through libraries,
bookshops (price £7.95) or direct from the
above address (price £9.45 inc. p&p).

DIRECTORY OF WORK AND STUDY IN DEVELOPING COUNTRIES (publication)
Vacation Work Publications
9 Park End Street
Oxford OX1 1HJ
Tel: 0865 241978 Fax: 0865 790885

A guide to employment, voluntary work, and academic opportunities in the Third World for those who wish to experience life there as more than a tourist. It lists thousands of opportunities for work or study with over 400 organisations in over 100 countries throughout the developing world as well as sources of further information. Both short- and long-term openings are covered in Africa, the Middle East, Asia, the Far East, the Pacific, Latin America, and the Caribbean.
ISBN 1 85458 029 9 Available in bookshops (price £7.95), through libraries or direct from the above address (price £9.45 inc. p&p).

DISABILITY EMPLOYMENT ADVISERS

DEAs can help if your chances of employment are affected by a disability. DEAs are specially trained staff experienced in placing disabled people in jobs. They can offer advice and support to anyone who has problems in finding or keeping work due to a disability, and can help identify suitable job opportunities or job placements on a trial basis. Contact DEAs through your local Jobcentre.

**DISABLED GRADUATES CAREERS
INFORMATION SERVICE (DGCIS)**
Panstar House
13-15 Swakeleys Road
Ickenham
Uxbridge UB10 8DF
Tel: 0734 318659

A database of around 700 employed graduates
together with their job profiles, disabilities and
how they overcame any problems.

DRAGONS INTERNATIONAL
The Old Vicarage
South Newington
Banbury
Oxon OX15 4JN
Tel: 0295 721717 Fax: 0295 721991

Dragons International is a commercial company
specialising in exchange holidays to France,
Germany and Spain and paying-guest visits to
France. They can also offer escorted travel to
France for those who already have an exchange
partner or host family and simply need to travel
there and back. Applicants for exchanges are
matched with a partner of similar age, interests
and background and the exchanges take place
at various times between April and September.
Supervised travel is provided throughout the
journey to France and passengers are collected
from 16 different meeting points in the UK.

AGE RANGE:
11-19
HOW TO CONTACT:
Write to the above address for further
information
REGIONS SERVICED:
UK
COSTS/WAITING LISTS:
The cost depends on the UK point of
departure and varies from about £150 to
£200. This includes the return fare,
supervised travel, matching of partners and
insurance. Early application is recommended
as applications are dealt with as received

DRIVE FOR YOUTH (DFY)
Celmi Centre
Llanegryn
Tywyn
Gwynedd LL36 9SA
Tel: 0654 710454 Fax: 0654 712326

Drive For Youth specialises in 22-week courses
for motivating the young, long-term
unemployed, and placing them in jobs or further
education. The success rate is among the
highest in the country. To qualify for acceptance
as a DFY Trainee, you need to have been out of
work for at least one year, and have a genuine
desire (however small!) to escape from the mess
which you feel your life has become. Our
intense career and development programme,
based at our own residential centre in the

Snowdonia National Park, includes outdoor pursuits with the emphasis on working as a team, personal counselling, community projects in Britain and abroad where you help others, and in-depth careers help and guidance. Completion of the course earns you a DFY Graduate's Diploma and a City and Guilds Certificate.

REGIONAL ADDRESSES:
London Office: c/o Coopers and Lybrand, Plumtree Court, London EC4A 4HT
AGE RANGE:
18-24
NUMBERS PASSING THROUGH:
240 a year
HOW TO CONTACT:
For information, advice, brochure and regular newsletter, telephone Celmi Training Centre or write (no stamp necessary) to:
Drive For Youth, FREEPOST, Celmi Training Centre, Llanegryn, Nr Tywyn, Gwynedd, Wales LL36 9SA
REGIONS SERVICED:
England, Scotland and Wales
SPECIAL NEEDS PROVISION:
Limited because of the nature of the course, but has proved possible in the past in some circumstances – please enquire
COSTS/WAITING LISTS:
There is no cost for the course, which is funded by business, charitable trusts and the government (through TECs and LECs).

Courses (6 a year) start from April to October. Apply January through September

THE DUKE OF EDINBURGH'S AWARD
Gulliver House
Madeira Walk
Windsor
Berks SL4 1EU
Tel: 0753 810753 Fax: 0753 810666

The Duke of Edinburgh's Award is for all young people, including those with special needs, between the ages of 14 and 25. It gives opportunities for personal achievements, adventure, community and social involvement and a widening of interests. There are three Awards – Bronze, for those over 14; Silver, for those over 15 and Gold, for those over 16. All Awards must be completed by the 25th birthday and started by the 23rd birthday. To qualify for an Award a young person must satisfy the requirements of the following four sections: Service, Expeditions, Skills and Physical Recreation. For the Gold Award, a young person must also undertake a Residential Project.

REGIONAL ADDRESSES:
Scotland: 69 Dublin Street, Edinburgh EH3 6NS Tel: 031 556 9097
Wales: Oak House, 12 The Bulwark, Brecon, Powys LD3 7AD Tel: 0874 3086
Northern Ireland: Northern Bank House, 109

Royal Avenue, Belfast BT1 1EW
Tel: 0232 232253
Local contacts available from Headquarters
AGE RANGE:
14-25
NUMBERS PASSING THROUGH:
87,000 new participants per year
HOW TO CONTACT:
By letter to Head Office or Regional Office
for leaflets, information and a local contact
REGIONS SERVICED:
UK
SPECIAL NEEDS PROVISION:
Programmes are usually sufficiently flexible to
require no special provision
COSTS/WAITING LISTS:
Entry fee is £7.50 for Bronze/Silver level and
£9.70 for Gold level. Other costs will vary
according to local circumstances and
activities chosen. Some funding may be
available from various sources such as Local
Education Authorities, Rotary Clubs etc. as
well as from individual fund-raising ventures.

DULUX COMMUNITY PROJECTS (DCP)
PO Box 343
London WC2E 3RJ

Each year ICI Paints, as sponsor of the Dulux
Community Projects Scheme, invites
applications for free supplies of paint for use
with worthwhile community projects. An
independent panel decides which of the projects

merits donations of paint and allocates supplies accordingly. Applications are accepted from voluntary groups or registered charities whose work benefits the community.

AGE RANGE:
Any
HOW TO CONTACT:
The dates of the scheme vary from year to year. However, applications are generally processed between Easter and mid-June of each year. For an application form send a large SAE to the above address, but only during the application period
REGIONS SERVICED:
UK
SPECIAL NEEDS PROVISION:
Any eligible community group can apply
COSTS/WAITING LISTS:
None

EARTH ACTION (FRIENDS OF THE EARTH YOUTH SECTION)
26-28 Underwood Street
London N1 7JQ
Tel: 071 490 1555 Fax: 071 490 0881

Earth Action is the youth section of Friends of the Earth and enables young people to become actively involved in campaigning on environmental issues. Local groups are based in schools and colleges, or in a local area, town or village, and together form a large network supported and co-ordinated nationally by the Earth Action Office. Local group activities could include anything from presenting a talk in school on tropical rainforests, writing to your MP, initiating a recycling scheme in your school, to getting out on the streets to inform the public on what is happening. Help for each campaign is provided by the Earth Action Office.

STOP PRESS
The activities of Earth Action ceased at the end of 1993, and young people are now encouraged to involve themselves directly with their local group of Friends of the Earth. Details can be obtained from the same Earth Action\/Friends of the Earth phone number as printed on the previous page

EARTHWATCH EUROPE
Belsyre Court
57 Woodstock Road
Oxford OX2 6HU
Tel: 0865 516366 Fax: 0865 311383

Earthwatch raises funds from the business community, trusts and individuals to enable them to give awards of financial aid to students over 16 and to teachers to participate on many of the environmental expeditions it sponsors. Further information on criteria, eligibility, how to apply etc. is available from Earthwatch Education Awards at the above address.

AGE RANGE:
16+
HOW TO CONTACT:
SAE to above address for an information packet
REGIONS SERVICED:
UK and Europe
SPECIAL NEEDS PROVISION:
Enquiries welcome
COSTS/WAITING LISTS:
Membership is £25. Most projects require participants to raise some funds for themselves and Earthwatch can give some advice on sponsorship and fund-raising

ECCTIS 2000
Fulton House
Jessop Avenue
Cheltenham
Gloucester GL50 3SH
Tel: 0242 518724 Fax: 0242 225914

ECCTIS is a government-owned, computerised course information service covering over 80,000 courses in all universities and colleges of further education. ECCTIS is available at nearly 3,500 access points in the UK, in schools, further and higher education colleges, Careers Offices and through TECs and LECs. ECCTIS is available at these centres either on personal computers using compact disc or as an on-line service. You will find ECCTIS quick and easy to use. ECCTIS can also be found at higher education and careers fairs.

In considering your choice of college or university course you may use the service directly or with the help of an adviser. ECCTIS gives you information on who offers courses on your chosen subject areas and location, the entry requirements and a description of what the course involves – whether it is a university degree or vocational course at a further education college – full-time or part-time. Whatever your starting point and interest there will be information on a course for you. ECCTIS gives you information on how to contact universities and colleges and how to apply for courses. The vocational qualifications which are accredited by NCVQ and awarded by BTEC, City and Guilds and RSA are explained together with their links to careers. During late August and throughout September ECCTIS 2000 provides information on vacancies on degree and HND courses. ECCTIS carries information on access courses to higher education for students without 'A' levels or equivalent qualifications.

AGE RANGE:
Courses for 16+ but you can start looking at 14
HOW TO CONTACT:
At your school, Careers Office, further education college, university, TEC/LEC or careers and higher education fairs
REGIONS SERVICED:
UK and overseas
SPECIAL NEEDS PROVISION:
Information available on college courses for students with special needs and facilities for the disabled at universities
COSTS/WAITING LISTS:
Free (institutions subscribe to the system)

EDUCATION YEARBOOK 1994
(publication)
Longman Group UK Ltd
6th Floor, Westgate House
The High
Harlow
Essex CM20 1YR
Tel: 0279 442601 Fax: 0279 444501

The Education Yearbook, published annually, is a comprehensive guide to all aspects of education and training. It contains several chapters of particular interest to young people such as information on higher, further and vocational education including universities and colleges, business, technical and management education, art and design, music, dance and drama colleges, and independent further education establishments. The Employment and Careers section contains details of Industrial Training Boards, the careers services, professional bodies and sponsored training and apprenticeships. Studying and travelling abroad are widely covered from details of exchange visits, voluntary service and working holidays to European organisations, European schools, the British Council and embassies and institutes providing further information on education and travel abroad. Copies are usually available for reference in public libraries, Careers Offices and schools. ISBN 0 582 09198 5.

EDUCATIONAL GRANTS ADVISORY SERVICE (EGAS)
Family Welfare Association
501-505 Kingsland Road
Dalston
London E8 4AU

EGAS advises students about non-statutory sources of financial help, specialising in advice about educational trust funds. They hold details about educational charities on a computerised database as well as information on government departments, educational and professional institutes and student welfare services, enabling them to provide an expert and up-to-date advice service on the complex world of educational funding.

AGE RANGE:
16+
NUMBERS PASSING THROUGH:
6,000+
HOW TO CONTACT:
By letter for advice and information
REGIONS SERVICED:
UK
SPECIAL NEEDS PROVISION:
EGAS tries to give priority to people from disadvantaged groups which includes people with disabilities
COSTS/WAITING LISTS:
Enquiries should be made as far in advance of the course starting as possible

---

EMPLOIS D'ETE EN FRANCE 1994
(publication)
Vacation Work Publications
9 Park End Street
Oxford OX1 1HJ
Tel: 0865 241978 Fax: 0865 790885

Book listing thousands of vacancies in France. Jobs include all the usual holiday resort opportunities from Brittany to the Côte d'Azur, for waiters and bar staff, sports instructors, receptionists, helpers in children's summer camps etc. The book includes special information for foreign students, with details of documents necessary to work in France – social security etc. Full details of wages and hours, qualifications needed and general conditions of work are given, plus names and addresses of companies, and who to contact.

ISBN 2 9504172 3 X Available through libraries, bookshops (price £7.95), or direct from the above address (price £9.45 inc. p&p)

EN FAMILLE OVERSEAS (EFO)
The Old Stables
60b Maltravers Street
Arundel
West Sussex BN18 9BG
Tel: 0903 883266 Fax: 0903 883582

EFO offers you the chance to get to know a foreign country and its people, to speak the language, and experience family life by arranging for you to stay with a host family, mainly in France but also in Germany, Italy and Spain. You will be treated as one of the family, taking part in all the family activities and meeting their friends and relations, making it an ideal way to improve your spoken language and make new friends. Special language holidays are also available which provide some form of tuition, ranging from classes at a language school through

to intensive language practice whilst staying
with a teacher's family.

AGE RANGE:
Any
NUMBERS PASSING THROUGH:
1,000
HOW TO CONTACT:
Telephone or SAE for advice and information
REGIONS SERVICED:
UK
SPECIAL NEEDS PROVISION:
No provision
COSTS/WAITING LISTS:
Fees are approx. £40. Host family weekly
charges in European countries approx. £165-
£230. Language courses cost from £452 for 2
weeks including accom-modation and
lessons. No waiting lists but 2 months' notice
of stay is preferred

ENDEAVOUR TRAINING LTD (Endeavour)
17a Glumangate
Chesterfield
Derbyshire S40 1TX
Tel: 0246 237201 Fax: 0246 203828

Young people can join a local group, take part
in follow-up and activity weekends, undertake
community work, help staff summer camps for
underprivileged children or hold local social
events and competitions. There are also
opportunities to take part in expeditions and

work projects both at home and overseas.

AGE RANGE:
16+

NUMBERS PASSING THROUGH:
500+ staff and volunteers working with
2,000-3,000 people every year

HOW TO CONTACT:
The Endeavour Association office, in
whatever manner is convenient – letter, fax,
phone etc. – for information and leaflets

REGIONS SERVICED:
UK

SPECIAL NEEDS PROVISION:
Enquiries welcome

COSTS/WAITING LISTS:
Membership fees: £3.50 unwaged; £7.50
employed; £10 family membership. All
courses are subsidised to take into account
personal circumstances. Most of the work
undertaken is funded by the Endeavour
Association. Endeavour is a National
Educational Charity

**ENGINEERING CAREERS INFORMATION
SERVICE (ECIS)**
Engineering Training Authority (EnTra)
Vector House
41 Clarendon Road
Watford
Hertfordshire WD1 1HS
Tel: 0923 238441 Fax: 0923 256086

Engineering covers such a vast range it is impossible to describe all the different fields in any detail here. Any form of manufacturing or production requires engineers from the design stage right through to the final product, whether it is an aeroplane, a washing machine, a computer or motorway. The list is endless and engineers usually specialise in one particular branch. ECIS can provide information on careers in the manufacturing branches of engineering. For more general information on the whole range of engineering careers write to ECIS at the above address or telephone free of charge on 0800 282167.

ENGLISH SPEAKING UNION (ESU)
Dartmouth House
37 Charles Street
London W1X 8AB
Tel: 071 493 3328 Fax: 071 495 6108

If you are an undergraduate or have just completed your 'A' levels you could spend your gap year at an independent school in Canada, USA or South America or work for a US Senator on Capitol Hill during your university vacation.

AGE RANGE:
No specific age range
NUMBERS PASSING THROUGH:
80

HOW TO CONTACT:
Send SAE to Education Department
REGIONS SERVICED:
UK
SPECIAL NEEDS PROVISION:
No special provision – enquiries welcome
COSTS/WAITING LISTS:
Costs will include flight and insurance
expenses plus some pocket money

ENVIRONMENT COUNCIL
31 Elizabeth Street
London SW1W 9RP
Tel: 071 824 8411 Fax: 071 730 9941

The Environment Council is a forum for
organisations and individuals working towards
a sustainable future. It is an independent charity,
made up of individuals from all walks of life, all
of whom have a common interest in
environmental issues, and a desire to make
progress happen. Membership brings a number
of benefits, including regular news of the latest
developments through periodical newsletters.
The EC's Information Programme produces a
range of directories such as *Who's Who in the
Environment*, *Directory of Environmental
Courses*, and a leaflet entitled *Careers in the
Environment*.

HOW TO CONTACT:
Telephone, letter or fax to above address for
general information. SAE required for leaflets

ERASMUS
(European Community Action Scheme for the Mobility of University Students)
UK Erasmus Student Grants Council
The University
Canterbury CT2 7PD
Tel: 0227 762712 Fax: 0227 762711

The ERASMUS scheme encourages the exchange of students in higher education and offers them the opportunity to study in another EC Member State, or EFTA territory, as part of their course. Grants are available, via your university, as a 'top-up' to other funding. These are not intended to cover the full costs of studying abroad.

AGE RANGE:
From second year of higher education
HOW TO CONTACT:
Write to above address for further general information, or contact your higher education institution about their involvement in particular subject areas. For information on ERASMUS programmes offered by UK higher education institutions please see *The UK Guide*, available from ISCO Publications, 12a-18a Princess Way, Camberley, Surrey GU15 3SP
REGIONS SERVICED:
UK

EURAUPAIR
17 Wheatfield Drive
Shifnal
Shropshire TF11 8HL
Tel: 0952 460733 Fax: 0952 588291

EurAupair is a programme initiated by ASSE International in order to give young Europeans a chance to spend a year as an au pair in America within a reliable and secure organization.

AGE RANGE:
18-24
HOW TO CONTACT:
Letter, telephone or fax to above address

EURO-ACADEMY
77A George Street
Croydon
Surrey CR0 1LD
Tel: 081 686 2363 Fax: 081 681 8850

Learn the language on location. Home stays and language courses in France, Austria, Germany, Spain, Italy and Portugal all year round for all levels and ages. Ideal for those about to take GCSEs or 'A' levels, gap-year students and undergraduates. Also available are vacation courses with leisure activities and sports options (tennis, riding, windsurfing etc.) with drawing and painting in Italy.

AGE RANGE:
16-27
NUMBERS PASSING THROUGH:
c 500 individuals and 300 travelling in groups
HOW TO CONTACT:
Telephone, letter, fax or in person for advice,
information and brochures
REGIONS SERVICED:
UK
SPECIAL NEEDS PROVISION:
Enquiries welcome
COSTS/WAITING LISTS:
Home stays cost from £210 (1 week) to £385
(2 weeks). Vacation courses from £605 to
£890 (2 weeks). French university summer
schools from £580 (3 weeks) to £945. Full
details in Euro-Academy brochure. Travel
grants for approved study visits are available
from LEAs – apply through school or college.
Information on scholarships for long-term study
abroad can be obtained from the cultural
section of the relevant embassy. Bookings
should ideally be made 2 to 3 months in
advance but can be accepted later

EURO BURO
52 Queen's Gardens
London W2 3AA
Tel: 071 724 5346 Fax: 071 221 3408

Euro Buro is an advice line that helps people to
find work in Europe and internationally. The

company which runs it also publishes the
monthly magazine *Jobs in Europe* (see separate
entry). Euro Buro also offers nearly 100 books
on working in Europe.

AGE RANGE:
All ages
HOW TO CONTACT:
Ring, write or fax

EUROPE – A MANUAL FOR HITCH-HIKERS
(publication)
Vacation Work Publications
9 Park End Street
Oxford OX1 1HJ
Tel: 0865 241978 Fax: 0865 790885

This manual covers the whole of Europe and
gives country-by-country information on
hitching techniques, route planning, sources of
free maps and attitudes towards hitch-hikers. It
includes a town guide of Europe's largest cities
and maps of the principal motorways which
reveal the best hitching points as well as cheap
and free ways of crossing the channel; reading
foreign number plates; hitch-hiking agencies;
the law; a hitch-hiking vocabulary in ten
languages and the best and worst places to hitch
in Europe.
ISBN 0 907638 28 7.   Available through
libraries, bookshops (price £4.95), or direct
from the above address (price £5.45 inc. p&p).

EUROPE: The Livewire Guide to Living and Working in the EC (publication)
Livewire Books For Teenagers
c/o The Women's Press
34 Great Sutton Street
London EC1V 0DX
Tel: 071 251 3007 (Sales)

A guide for the school leaver heading for work in Europe in 1993. It offers practical information on a range of areas including accommodation, employment and health services. Available through libraries, bookshops, or direct from the above address (price £4.50).

EUROPEAN COMMUNITY YOUTH ORCHESTRA (ECYO)
6a Pont Street
London SW1X 9EL
Tel: 071 235 7671/6641
Fax: 071 235 7370

The Youth Orchestra meets twice annually for a course of approximately 2 weeks, followed by a tour of 8-10 concerts either within Europe or elsewhere in the world. This is an opportunity to work with the world's leading conductors and to meet young people of all 12 EC countries. Applications are invited from orchestral musicians, post grade 8.

AGE RANGE:
14-23
NUMBERS PASSING THROUGH:
c 180
HOW TO CONTACT:
Telephone, letter or fax to Head Office for an application form
REGIONS SERVICED:
UK
SPECIAL NEEDS PROVISION:
No special provision but every effort would be made to include someone if possible
COSTS/WAITING LISTS:
Audition deadline is normally in October for the following year. Once the orchestra is chosen there is also a reserve list

---

EUROPEAN WORK EXPERIENCE PROJECT
Kipling House
43 Villiers Street
London WC2N 6NE
Tel: 071 839 6800

The EWE Project is funded by the European Commission and the UK government. It facilitates for schools/colleges and work experience exchange schemes for 16-19 year-old students between the UK and other EC member states. The object is to develop awareness in industrial, economic, language, European and social aspects. For further details contact the EWE Project Co-ordinator at the above address.

EXCEL AT INTERVIEWS (publication)
Hobsons Publishing
Bateman Street
Cambridge CB2 1LZ
Tel: 0223 354551 Fax: 0223 323154

A step-by-step guide to preparing yourself before coming face-to-face with an employer or college boss. Commissioned by the Careers and Research Advisory Centre, the book is aimed at the 16-20 age group and encourages young people to evaluate their strengths and weaknesses. It explores the essential work to be carried out before the interview, the interview itself and what needs to be done after the event. It also looks closely at body language, presentation skills, techniques for calming the nerves and dealing with those awkward questions.

EXPEDITION ADVISORY CENTRE
Royal Geographical Society
1 Kensington Gore
London SW7 2AR
Tel: 071 581 2057 Fax: 071 584 4447

The Expedition Advisory Centre can provide information, advice, training and publications for anyone planning or wishing to join a scientific or adventurous expedition overseas. This includes annual seminars in November on 'Planning a Small Expedition' and in May on

'Independent Travel'. The EAC at the Royal Geographical Society publishes various books of interest to young people thinking of becoming involved in an expedition or travel, either through a structured organisation such as Operation Raleigh, or independently:

Joining an Expedition: how to take advantage of the expedition opportunities offered by over 50 UK-based organisations, with fund-raising advice (price £5.00)

Fund-raising to Join an Expedition: a guide for those raising funds required to join ventures such as Operation Raleigh (price £1.50)

Sources of Information for Independent Travellers: where to get the best information on health, equipment, visas, insurance, maps etc. (price £5.00)

Expedition Planners Handbook and Directory for those organising adventurous and scientific projects overseas (price £12.95)

AGE RANGE:
Any
NUMBERS PASSING THROUGH:
10,000+ enquiries per year
HOW TO CONTACT:
By letter, telephone or fax for advice, information and publications
REGIONS SERVICED:
Worldwide
SPECIAL NEEDS PROVISION:
No specific provision

COSTS/WAITING LISTS:
Details of costs of publications, courses and
seminars available from above. Replies
usually within 21 days

EXPERIMENT IN INTERNATIONAL LIVING
(EIL)
'Otesaga'
West Malvern Road
Malvern
Worcestershire WR14 4EN
Tel: 0684 562577 Fax: 0684 562212

EIL is a non-profit-making, non-political and
non-religious organisation, existing to promote
international understanding, and has been
involved in international education and
exchange since 1932, working mainly through
the 'home stay' principle, sending and receiving
people to and from more than 50 countries
worldwide, either in groups or as individuals.
As well as its main programme of individual
home stays, EIL can arrange youth exchanges,
including Young Worker and Disabled and
Disadvantaged programmes with EEC and East
European countries, Language Acquisition
programmes in many countries and much more.
They can also arrange a 1-year Au Pair Home
Stay programme to the USA.

AGE RANGE:
18+

NUMBERS PASSING THROUGH:
Thousands over all programmes
HOW TO CONTACT:
For home stays, contact main office above by
letter or telephone. For Au Pair programme
contact CBR Au Pair, 63 Foregate Street,
Worcester WR1 1DX Tel: 0905 26671
REGIONS SERVICED:
UK
SPECIAL NEEDS PROVISION:
Specific programmes available
COSTS/WAITING LISTS:
Costs vary enormously depending on the type
of programme, the country visited and the
length of stay. Language courses tend to cost
more. 8 weeks' notice before departure is
required. Write or telephone for a
comprehensive brochure with full
information

FAIRBRIDGE
5 Westminster Bridge Road
London SE1 7XW
Tel: 071 928 1704 Fax: 071 928 6016

Fairbridge offers support with a taste of adventure
through outdoor activities (such as climbing,
abseiling, camping etc.), conservation and
community projects, sail training on a tall ship
and basic training in various job skills. You'll be
able to make new friends, do something different
and stretch yourself. Fairbridge will open up
new interests and give you constructive help in

finding a job. All training is under the supervision of qualified instructors.

REGIONAL ADDRESSES:
13 Team Centres around the UK. Details available from main office

AGE RANGE:
14-25

NUMBERS PASSING THROUGH:
c 7,300

HOW TO CONTACT:
Telephone, write or call in person to the nearest Team Centre

REGIONS SERVICED:
UK

SPECIAL NEEDS PROVISION:
Courses and activities are altered to cater for group and individual needs

COSTS/WAITING LISTS:
Course participants are asked to contribute £15 towards the running costs if they can afford it. Basic courses usually last 7-10 days. Waiting lists vary. Ideally, give as much notice as possible

---

**FEDERATION OF RECRUITMENT AND
EMPLOYMENT SERVICES LIMITED (FRES)**
36-38 Mortimer Street
London W1N 7RB
Tel: 071 323 4300

FRES is the association for the private recruitment industry in the UK. A number of FRES agencies specialise in employment opportunities in Europe and further afield. Such opportunities are usually for highly skilled applicants only. FRES also has specialist au pair agencies in membership, who are able to help those wishing to live abroad as part of a family.

HOW TO CONTACT:
Write to the above address to request a copy of the FRES Overseas List and enclose a £2 postal order plus SAE. There is no charge for the au pair list but please send SAE
REGIONS SERVICED:
UK

FESTIVAL WELFARE SERVICES (FWS)
61b Hornsey Road
London N7 6DG
Tel: 071 700 5754

FWS is a small charity whose main concern is to encourage festival organisers to make provisions for appropriate welfare services to be available on site. As a service to festival-goers, FWS produces a free, regularly updated list of festivals, starting in early April until early September, which they send out together with a copy of their free *Survival Guide*, full of advice and information on attending a festival. They also produce a range of publications on a variety of related subjects from organising a festival to advice on drugs and alcohol. For further information send a stamped addressed envelope (approx. 9" x 6.5") to the above address.

FILM AND TELEVISION LIGHTING APPRENTICE PROGRAMME FOR SCHOOL LEAVERS
c/o Training Services
City of Westminster College
Lancaster Road
London W11 1QT
Tel: 071 258 2888 Fax: 071 229 1025

A 4-year apprenticeship designed to equip young people with the knowledge and skills needed to become competent and qualified lighting technicians in the film and television industry. It is run in conjunction with companies within the film and television industry, and successful completion of the apprenticeship leads to a Diploma from the British Kinematograph, Sound and Television Society (BKSTS). Other youth training courses offered by City of Westminster College include Stage Electrics, Sound Engineering, Video, Photography, Graphics etc.

AGE RANGE:
16-18 only
HOW TO CONTACT:
Letter, telephone, fax to above address
REGIONS SERVICED:
UK

SPECIAL NEEDS PROVISION:
Enquiries welcome

FOOL TIME: CENTRE FOR CIRCUS SKILLS
AND PERFORMING ARTS
Britannia Road
Kingswood
Bristol BS15 2DA
Tel: 0272 478788 Fax: 0272 476354

Fool Time is Britain's leading training centre for
circus skills. Our curriculum is designed to
integrate the traditional physical skills of circus
with the dramatic quality and emotional interplay
of dance, movement and theatre. For further
details and our current prospectus please contact
the above address.

AGE RANGE:
Minimum 18
HOW TO CONTACT:
Telephone, letter, fax or in person for further
information
REGIONS SERVICED:
UK and international
COSTS/WAITING LISTS:
Please write for information on course fees
and audition dates. Ideally, apply 6 months
in advance

FORD CONSERVATION AWARDS
The Conservation Foundation
1 Kensington Gore
London SW7 2AR
Tel: 071 823 8842 Fax: 071 823 8791

The Ford Conservation Awards, now in their tenth year in Europe, are for conservation initiatives undertaken by individuals or community groups in 22 European countries. Projects that involve natural environment, national heritage and conservation engineering are all eligible. Entries will be judged by the Conservation Foundation panel, which will select the best project from every country. There will be a cash prize for the winner in each country, and the winner may be chosen to represent their country at the Ford European Conservation Awards Final.

AGE RANGE:
Any
HOW TO CONTACT:
Send SAE for further information
REGIONS SERVICED:
UK
SPECIAL NEEDS PROVISION:
No special provision but anyone can enter a project
COSTS/WAITING LISTS:
The closing date is usually around the beginning of September each year

FOREST SCHOOL CAMPS (FSC)
110 Burbage Road
London SE24 9HD

An FSC camp is an adventure giving a group of young people the opportunity to live in a remote place for a week or two, learning to live in harmony with themselves, with others and with their surroundings. A typical standing camp has about 65 young people and 20 leaders and lasts 2 weeks. Mobile camps (travelling on foot, cycle and canoe) are smaller. At 18, young people can train as leaders – apply to Head Office.

AGE RANGE:
6-17 (first-time camp members are not accepted after 15th birthday)
NUMBERS PASSING THROUGH:
1,300
HOW TO CONTACT:
By letter to: New Enquiries, Elaine Morton, 7 Park Crescent, London N3 2NL for a programme of camps
REGIONS SERVICED:
UK
SPECIAL NEEDS PROVISION:
10% of places are kept for young people with special needs. One camp is run for those with severe learning difficulties and a weekend for active young people with physical disabilities

COSTS/WAITING LISTS:
A 2-week camp (including escorted travel
from London main-line station) costs approx.
£170. Waiting list for some age-groups.
Programme is published in January and
prompt booking is recommended

FOYER FEDERATION FOR YOUTH
91 Brick Lane
London E1 6QN
Tel: 071 377 9789 Fax: 071 247 1633

Young people caught in the 'no job – no home'
trap in the UK can get help from Foyers, a new
scheme based on a very successful French
concept. Foyers are special hostels that provide
a secure home, together with advice about job-
hunting or skills training. Because the planned
network of Foyers is still in its early stages, the
Foyer Federation (spearheaded by GrandMet
and Shelter) has been set up to act as a central
information source. The length of stay provided
by the hostels is dependent on need, but will not
be longer than 2 years.

AGE RANGE:
16-25
HOW TO CONTACT:
Contact the above address by letter or phone
to find out about your nearest Foyer

FREEFONE ENTERPRISE
Tel: Freefone 0800 222999

Call the freefone number for details of your local Small Firms Centre. Small Firms Centres can provide free information and advice about business problems, and they can point you in the direction of other sources to help you get your business idea off the ground.

FRENCH LANGUAGE PROGRAMMES IN FRANCE
Challenge Educational Services
101 Lorna Road
Hove
Sussex BN3 3EL
Tel: 0273 220261 Fax: 0273 220376

Challenge Educational Services offer French language courses at various universities in France including the Sorbonne in Paris. Academic year, semester and summer courses available. Courses also available year-round at various venues including Easter and summer 'A' Level revision courses in Bordeaux.

University courses are ideal for gap-year students, offering French university life whilst studying French.

Programmes are comprehensive including board and lodging plus other benefits.

AGE RANGE:
University courses 18+; 'A' level revision 17+
HOW TO CONTACT:
Telephone, fax or letter for brochure and booking form
REGIONS SERVICED:
UK and Republic of Ireland
COSTS/WAITING LISTS:
Cost dependent on length of course and venue. Application at any time for short courses. 3 months in advance for university and 'A' level revision courses, though late bookings accepted dependent on availability

FRIENDS FOR THE YOUNG DEAF (FYD)
East Court Mansion Council Offices
College Lane
East Grinstead
West Sussex RH19 3LT
Tel: 0342 323444 Fax: 0342 410232

FYD organise an annual programme of projects and courses for deaf, hard of hearing and hearing young people. The intention is to encourage the personal development of individuals, to create opportunities for deaf children and young people to have fun and try out new experiences, and to help integrate deaf and hearing children and young people. Recent projects include conservation holidays, activity weekends, yachting fortnights, participating in sports festivals, and adventure weeks. FYD also offer training in leadership skills, fund-raising, many types of work experience, and in a number of other areas. Volunteers are always welcome to help out with the work of FYD.

REGIONAL ADDRESSES:
FYD Training Centre, Rooms 16 & 17, Ladywood Arts and Leisure Centre, Freeth Street, Ladywood, Birmingham
Tel: 021 454 4423 Fax: 021 454 4375
AGE RANGE:
7-25
NUMBERS PASSING THROUGH:
c 4,000
HOW TO CONTACT:
Letter, telephone or in person, for advice, information, leaflets and a list of forthcoming projects
REGIONS SERVICED:
UK
SPECIAL NEEDS PROVISION:
Communication facilitators/interpreters available for the deaf/ hard of hearing
COSTS/WAITING LISTS:
Costs for courses/projects/training vary. Some help may be available (further details from FYD)

FRIENDS OF THE EARTH SCOTLAND (FOE)
Bonnington Mill
72 Newhaven Road
Edinburgh EH6 5QG
Tel: 031 554 9977 Fax: 031 554 8656

FOE Scotland is independent of FOE (England and Wales) and works on the full range of environmental issues. Campaign topics include the ozone layer, tropical deforestation, recycling, transport, air pollution, superquarry development, contaminated land waste disposal and countryside issues. If you wish to find out more about, or become involved in environmental issues, contact FOE for further information.

REGIONAL ADDRESSES:
Several local, independent groups throughout Scotland
AGE RANGE:
Any
HOW TO CONTACT:
By letter (with SAE) for information and leaflets
REGIONS SERVICED:
Mainly Scotland
SPECIAL NEEDS PROVISION:
No special provision
COSTS/WAITING LISTS:
None

FRONTIER – THE SOCIETY FOR ENVIRONMENTAL EXPLORATION
77 Leonard Street
London EC2A 4QS
Tel: 071 613 2422 Fax: 071 613 2992

The Society is a non-profit-making company, established in 1989. Its objective is to provide an effective channel through which individuals can make a potent personal contribution to urgent research and conservation issues in developing countries. Anyone committed to taking an active part in environmental protection can join a Frontier project. Specific skills, such as scientific, mechanical or administrative, are useful but not essential as all work is supervised by qualified research scientists and Frontier staff. Great value is placed during selection on genuine enthusiasm for environmental issues and the capacity to tolerate a degree of hardship.

AGE RANGE:
Over 17 years
NUMBERS PASSING THROUGH:
150-200 per year
HOW TO CONTACT:
Send an SAE for information pack on projects and an application form
REGIONS SERVICED:
UK and worldwide
SPECIAL NEEDS PROVISION:
No special provision. Each case dealt with individually

COSTS/WAITING LISTS:
Participation in a 10-week expedition to
Africa would cost candidates approx. £2,400,
which covers all expenses such as air fare,
camp equipment, insurance, food,
transportation etc. Some examples of sources
of funds are: trusts; sponsorship from local
companies; places of higher education or
Local Education Authorities; personal fund-
raising projects. Candidates should
preferably apply 6 months in advance

FULBRIGHT COMMISSION (US-UK EDUCATIONAL COMMISSION)
62 Doughty Street
London WC1N 2LQ
Tel: 071 404 6880 Fax: 071 404 6834

The Fulbright Commission runs a programme of
educational and cultural exchanges with the
USA. A range of awards is available to fund
study at postgraduate level in the US in any
field. The Commission's Educational Advisory
Service (tel: 071 404 6994) deals with enquiries
on all aspects of US education and advises
students wishing to pursue their further
education in the United States.

AGE RANGE:
Any
ELIGIBILITY:
UK citizen holding or expecting to obtain
minimum 2:1 honours degree

HOW TO CONTACT:
Write with A4 size SAE for further information
REGIONS SERVICED:
UK
SPECIAL NEEDS PROVISION:
No special provision

FULLEMPLOY TRAINING
91 Brick Lane
London E1 6QN
Tel: 071 377 9536 Fax: 071 377 9858

A training organisation helping young people, mainly from minority ethnic communities, into work. Training is provided in many areas, and particularly in office skills and self-employment. Fullemploy may also be able to provide advice and access to equipment, and can provide on-going training and counselling for new businesses.

REGIONAL ADDRESSES:
Fullemploy Birmingham: 7th Floor, Bridge House, 63 Smallbrook, Queensway, Birmingham B5 4JP Tel: 021 643 1282 Fax: 021 616 1052
Fullemploy Gloucester: Fullemploy House, 33 St Michael's Square, Gloucester GL1 1HX Tel: 0452 310004 Fax: 0452 424435
Fullemploy Leeds: Unit 30, Chel Building, 26 Roundhay Road, Leeds LS7 1AB Tel: 0532 440602 Fax: 0532 446792

Fullemploy Sandwell: 43 High Street, West
Bromwich, B70 6PB Tel: 021 525 3464
Fullemploy Manchester: 3rd-5th Floor, Basil
House, 105-107 Portland Street, Manchester
M1 6DF Tel: 061 228 7481
Fax: 061 236 5450
Fullemploy Wales: Coptic House, 4-5 Mount
Stuart Square, Cardiff CF1 6EE
Tel: 0222 464445 Fax: 0222 484751
Contact Head Office for list of London
addresses

AGE RANGE:
18+

HOW TO CONTACT:
Letter, telephone, fax or in person for more
information

REGIONS SERVICED:
England and Wales

SPECIAL NEEDS PROVISION:
Enquiries welcome

COSTS/WAITING LISTS:
None for information

GAP ACTIVITY PROJECTS LTD (GAP)
44 Queen's Road
Reading
Berkshire RG1 4BB
Tel: 0734 594914 Fax: 0734 576634

GAP offers work opportunities overseas for
young people aged 18-19 in their gap year
between school and higher education or training.

Placements are usually for 6-9 months, thereby leaving time for travel. GAP operates in over 30 different countries and the type of work varies from teaching English as a foreign language through to conservation work and social/community work.

AGE RANGE:
School leavers aged 18-19
NUMBERS PASSING THROUGH:
1,000 placements out of 2,000 applications
HOW TO CONTACT:
Telephone, letter or fax for advice, information and an application form
REGIONS SERVICED:
UK
SPECIAL NEEDS PROVISION:
No provision
COSTS/WAITING LISTS:
£20 registration fee on application to cover administrative costs. On selection volunteers pay a GAP fee which is currently £375, and additional costs for insurance and medical requirements. A 1- or 2-week TEFL course (approx £100-£150) is required for English teaching. Once at the placement, volunteers receive free board and lodging and, in most cases, pocket money. Students need to apply as early as possible, during their last year at school, preferably in September or October. The closing date for applications is 1 February each year

THE GAP YEAR GUIDEBOOK (publication)
Peridot Press
2 Blenheim Crescent
London W11 1NN
Tel: 071 221 7404 Fax: 071 792 0833

A guide published in August each year when 'A' level results come out, and packed with facts and anecdotes for those who want to take a year off between 'A' levels and university. This book is best read by sixth-formers before they fill in their university entrance forms. It takes the student through UCAS form-filling and 'A' level retake procedures. It covers office skills and other training courses for gap-year jobs, and the 1994/95 edition gives gap-year opportunities at Britain's 100 biggest companies as well as pointing out organised work experience schemes. Overseas voluntary work organisations are included and their placements overseas are listed under country headings. There are travel tips and details of language courses and feedback from students runs right through the book.
ISBN 095187551 X. Available through libraries, bookshops or direct from the above address (price £7.75 inc. p&p).

GIRL GUIDES ASSOCIATION (GGA)
17-19 Buckingham Palace Road
London SW1W 0PT
Tel: 071 834 6242 Fax: 071 828 8317

The aim of guiding is to help girls and young women to develop emotionally, mentally, physically and spiritually so that they can make a positive contribution to their community and to the wider world. Guiding offers friendship and fun with a wide range of indoor and outdoor activities.

REGIONAL ADDRESSES:
Contact through Head Office
AGE RANGE:
Brownie Guides 7-10 years; Guides 10-14 years; Ranger Guides 14-18 years; Young Leaders 15-18 years
NUMBERS PASSING THROUGH:
c 750,000 members
HOW TO CONTACT:
Letter to HQ in London for further information
REGIONS SERVICED:
UK
SPECIAL NEEDS PROVISION:
Enquiries welcome
COSTS/WAITING LISTS:
Small annual subscription

GIRLS VENTURE CORPS AIR CADETS
(GVAC)
Redhill Aerodrome
Kings Mill Lane
South Nutfield
Redhill
Surrey RH1 5JY
Tel: 0737 823345

The GVAC offers a wide and challenging range of activities aimed at giving its members a broader outlook and greater sense of purpose. Activities include camping, canoeing, skiing, rifle-shooting, gliding, drill, drama and handicrafts as well as more unusual pursuits such as theory of aviation and air experience flights in small aircraft. Leadership and initiative training plays a major role and every aspect of the Duke of Edinburgh's Award Scheme is covered.

REGIONAL ADDRESSES:
Details from Head Office
AGE RANGE:
11-20
NUMBERS PASSING THROUGH:
2,000-3,000
HOW TO CONTACT:
Write to or phone Head Office for details of nearest unit
REGIONS SERVICED:
There are regional offices covering the majority of England

SPECIAL NEEDS PROVISION:
Enquiries welcome
COSTS/WAITING LISTS:
Costs include subscriptions, course and camp
fees and uniform

GRADUATE CAREERLINE
Tel: 041 553 4177 (Glasgow)
Wednesdays 5-8pm
or 0272 303149 (Bristol)
Thursdays 3-8pm

A national telephone careers advisory service
for UK graduates in the first 3 years after
graduation. It is based at the Universities of
Bristol and Strathclyde, staffed by professional
careers advisers, and funded by the Association
of Graduate Careers Advisory Services.

COSTS/WAITING LISTS:
You pay for the call– but the advice is free

GRANDMET TRUST
64-65 North Road
Brighton
East Sussex BN1 1YD
Tel: 0273 570170 Fax: 0273 682086

Grand Metropolitan is one of the UK's most
successful national companies. GrandMet Trust
is the part of the company that gives all kinds of
help to people in need. Its special concern is

with deprived inner-city areas where young people in particular want jobs and homes. The Trust can boost your job chances at one of its nationwide network of training centres where you can get the very best training in a huge range of skills. But the Trust doesn't stop at occupational training. The training teams offer moral support, expert advice on the sort of job you should be trying for and all the encouragement and help you need when you are applying for jobs.

REGIONAL ADDRESSES:
London, Midlands and North: 91 Brick Lane, London E1 6QN Tel: 071 247 5884 Fax: 071 377 8477
South: Suite 4, Thrift House, 12-15 Wellington Place, Hastings, East Sussex TN34 1NY Tel: 0424 718491 Fax: 0424 718519
Scotland: Olympic House, 142 Queen Street, Glasgow G1 3BU Tel: 041 204 4090 Fax: 041 204 2576
HOW TO CONTACT:
For the address and phone number of your nearest GrandMet Training Centre ask your Jobcentre, or contact the Trust's Head Office (address above) or your nearest regional office

GREENPEACE
Canonbury Villas
London N1 2PN
Tel: 071 354 5100 Fax: 071 696 0014/0012

Greenpeace is an international, independent environmental pressure group which acts against abuse of the natural world. Local support groups organise fund-raising activities, such as street collections and sponsored events. Occasionally they help with campaigns by lobbying MPs, organising petitions and generally publicising campaign issues. If you want to become involved write to the Public Information Office at the above address for details of your nearest Area Co-ordinator.

REGIONAL ADDRESSES:
200 local support groups – contact main office for details
AGE RANGE:
Any
HOW TO CONTACT:
Write to the Public Information Unit at the above address
REGIONS SERVICED:
UK
SPECIAL NEEDS PROVISION:
Enquiries welcome

GROUNDWORK FOUNDATION
85-87 Cornwall Street
Birmingham B3 3BY
Tel: 021 236 8565 Fax: 021 236 7356

Groundwork is a fast-growing national network working towards the restoration of landscapes and wildlife habitats, and towards the positive use of derelict and disused wasteland in and around Britain's towns and cities. Groundwork works in partnership with local communities, business and government and is happy to train and provide work experience for volunteers of all ages and abilities. If you want the opportunity to improve the environment in your area, contact the address above for more information.

REGIONAL ADDRESSES:
There are about 30 Groundwork Trust locations around the country – details from above address
AGE RANGE:
Any
HOW TO CONTACT:
Telephone or letter to above address for details of Groundwork Trust locations
REGIONS SERVICED:
Areas where Trusts operate
SPECIAL NEEDS PROVISION:
Provision varies between Trusts
COSTS/WAITING LISTS:
None

HAIRDRESSING TRAINING BOARD
3 Chequer Road
Doncaster DN1 2AA
Tel: 0302 342837 Fax: 0302 323381

The Hairdressing Training Board is the best first point of contact for information about careers in hairdressing. They produce a comprehensive career leaflet which outlines career opportunities within hairdressing.

HEALTH PROJECTS ABROAD (HPA)
HMS President
Victoria Embankment
London EC4Y 0HJ
Tel: 071 583 5725 Fax: 071 583 2840

HPA works in developing countries and offers a year-long programme which includes a selection weekend, 2 training/briefing weekends, 3 months abroad and a follow-up weekend. Volunteers face the challenge of raising money to help support the projects and will then spend 3 months working alongside the local people to help complete the projects, being involved in simple tasks such as assisting with construction and renovation work. There are 2 weeks at the end of each project for the volunteer to spend time travelling. HPA provides a support structure to help volunteers in their fund-raising, in preparing for their time abroad and to give support when they return.

AGE RANGE:
18-28
NUMBERS PASSING THROUGH:
Over 50 in 1993
HOW TO CONTACT:
Send SAE to above address or telephone for
further information
REGIONS SERVICED:
UK
SPECIAL NEEDS PROVISION:
Many of the projects are not suitable, but
each application is dealt with individually
COSTS/WAITING LISTS:
Each volunteer must raise £2,450 as a
contribution to their air fares, food,
accommodation and travel and to the cost of
running the projects. This includes the cost
of the HPA weekends. Examples of sources
of funding are the Prince's Trust, Rotary
Clubs, Local Councils, local businesses,
various trusts and grant-making bodies as
well as individual activities such as parachute
jumps, raffles, sponsored events etc.

HELP US HELP YOU (publication)
Duke of Edinburgh's Award
69 Dublin Street
Edinburgh EH3 6NS
Tel: 031 556 9097

Available from the Duke of Edinburgh's Award
scheme, *Help Us Help You* contains information

on voluntary work opportunities for young people. The directory is aimed specifically at Award participants but is also a useful source of information on organisations for any young person interested in volunteer work. Details are given of the type of work of each organisation and how to contact them.

HISPANIC AND LUSO BRAZILIAN COUNCIL
Canning House
2 Belgrave Square
London SW1X 8PJ
Tel: 071 235 2303 Fax: 071 235 3587

Canning House is a centre for information and contact on Spain, Portugal and Latin America in the UK. It promotes the teaching of Spanish andPortuguese, organises cultural events, runs a lending library (50,000 books), and offers an information service on classes, courses and opportunities in Britain and abroad.

AGE RANGE:
Any
NUMBERS PASSING THROUGH:
Several thousand
HOW TO CONTACT:
Telephone, letter or in person to Education Department for information and leaflets, advice and contacts. Contact Library for books

REGIONS SERVICED:
UK
SPECIAL NEEDS PROVISION:
Enquiries welcome
COSTS/WAITING LISTS:
Annual subscription for students: £10.
Information leaflets: £3. Course fees around
£50. No waiting lists

HITCH-HIKERS' MANUAL – BRITAIN
(publication)
Vacation Work Publications
9 Park End Street
Oxford OX1 1HJ
Tel: 0865 241978 Fax: 0865 790885

This guide provides information on hitching
techniques, route planning, the law, which lifts
to turn down and hitch-cycling. The Town
Guide covers 200 British towns and pinpoints
the best places to stand when trying to hitch out
and explains how to reach these positions on
foot or by public transport. It also includes 38
pages of motorway maps showing where you
would be unwise to hitch, would be breaking
the law and where you are most likely to have
the shortest wait.
ISBN 0 907638 26 0.   Available through
libraries, bookshops (price £3.95), or direct
from the above address (price £5.45 inc. p&p).

HOLIDAY CARE SERVICE
2 Old Bank Chambers
Station Road
Horley
Surrey RH6 9HW
Tel: 0293 774535 Fax: 0293 784647
Minicom: 0293 776943

A national charity that advises on holidays for people who are elderly, disabled, single parents, on low income or anyone who has difficulty in finding a suitable holiday. Also provides competitive travel insurance designed for people with a pre-existing medical condition, their friends and family, runs Tourism for All Holidays, a low-cost holiday scheme, and operates a reservation service for accessible accommodation throughout the UK which offers discounted rates to those who book through the service. The Holiday Care Awards recognise excellent service in the tourism industry for people with disabilities.

AGE RANGE:
Any (18+ for volunteer helpers)
HOW TO CONTACT:
Telephone, SAE, fax or minicom for information sheets listing holiday ideas or information about volunteering
REGIONS SERVICED:
UK
SPECIAL NEEDS PROVISION:
Service for people with special needs

COSTS/WAITING LISTS:
All information is free

HOME FROM HOME (publication)
Central Bureau for Educational Visits and
Exchanges
Seymour Mews
London W1H 9PE
Tel: 071 725 9402 (credit card orders)

Have you ever wanted to find out what it is like
to live in another country? Do you want to
improve your language skills and make lasting
friendships internationally? *Home From Home*
has all the answers. It is an authoritative guide
to over 120 bona fide organisations arranging
home stays, exchanges, home exchanges, farm
stays and term stays in more than 50 countries.
You could stay with a French family in Paris,
sample dhal with a Nepalese family, exchange
hospitality with an Italian partner, study for a
term in a Bavarian school, discover Ashanti
traditions in Ghana, teach English to a family in
Japan or swap your home for one in the USA.
ISBN 0 900087 85 4. Price £6.99. Available
from bookshops or direct from the above address
(price £8.49 inc. p&p).

HORTICULTURAL VOLUNTEERS IN SCOTLAND (HVS)

c/o Horticultural Therapy Scotland
4 Drum Street
Edinburgh
EH17 8QG
Tel: 031 658 1096

If you have experience and/or basic qualifications in horticulture, have worked in some capacity with people with special needs, and are looking for a way to use your skills, Horticultural Volunteers in Scotland will help. They help projects use horticulture as therapy for people with disabilities, by providing a volunteer with horticultural skills. You may help in preparing a new site for a horticultural therapy unit, or train clients and care staff in basic horticultural tasks. Horticultural Volunteers in Scotland will place you in a project that reflects your own particular skills and interests. Minimum period of service is 6 months, the maximum 1 year. Board, lodging and pocket money provided throughout your stay.

AGE RANGE:
18+
HOW TO CONTACT:
Letter or telephone to above address
REGIONS SERVICED:
Scotland (see entry for Land Use Vulunteers for rest of UK)

HOTEL AND CATERING TRAINING COMPANY (HCTC)
Careers Department
International House
High Street
Ealing
London W5 5DB
Tel: 081 579 2400

The HCTC supplies a wide range of advice and information on all aspects of careers in the hotel and catering industry – what courses to take, training opportunities, ways into the industry etc. It also provides training programmes for young people leading to National and Scottish Vocational Qualifications. Free literature and information packages available on request.

ICYE-UK
c/o National Youth Office
Board of Education
Church House
Great Smith Street
London SW1P 3NZ
Tel: 071 222 9011 (ext. 407)

ICYE-UK is part of the worldwide ICYE movement, founded in 1949. Its primary commitments are to fight racism and promote environmental issues. The UK programme offers the chance to go abroad for a year-long voluntary experience. Selected participants go to one of

30 countries to take part in projects. These include drug rehabilitation, rural and health development projects, peace education, ecological projects, youth centre, Third World shops, hospitals and refugee centres.

Participants live with a host family or at their workplace. The scheme costs £3,000, which covers flight, insurance and living expenses for 1 year.

INDEPENDENT RADIO DRAMA PRODUCTIONS LTD (IRDP)
PO Box 518
Manningtree
Essex CO11 1XD
Tel: 0206 395795 Fax: 0206 395795

IRDP is dedicated to encouraging young people to write for radio. They run free radio writing and acting workshops, which can be organised on request. They are also responsible for the Woolwich Young Radio Playwrights' Competition, which offers professional writing opportunities in radio and theatre. Annual national competitions lead to production and broadcast of half-hour theatre readings. The radio plays are premiered on London's Independent Speech radio station and then taken on a tour of independent and BBC local radio services.

AGE RANGE:
Up to 25

NUMBERS PASSING THROUGH:
500
HOW TO CONTACT:
Telephone 0206 395795 for leaflets and
further information
REGIONS SERVICED:
UK
SPECIAL NEEDS PROVISION:
Workshops for special needs groups available
COSTS/WAITING LISTS:
No costs or waiting lists. Contact IRDP at
least a month before a workshop. Workshops
are advertised by leaflet in schools and
colleges

INDEPENDENT SCHOOLS CAREERS
ORGANISATION (ISCO)
12A Princess Way
Camberley
Surrey GU15 3SP
Tel: 0276 21188 Fax: 0276 691833

ISCO produces a range of aptitude and ability
tests and questionnaires to help in the selection
of careers, further and higher education. These
can be arranged either through the Camberley
address or preferably through the ISCO London
Office at 27 Marylebone Road, London, NW1
5JS (Tel: 071 487 3660). ISCO also produces
the following publications which can be
obtained from the Publications Department at
the Camberley address: *The Sixthformer's Guide
to visiting Universities and Colleges*; information

sheets on 107 careers; guideline sheets on Options at 16+, 18+, gap years, etc.; *Opportunities in the Gap Year; CareerScope* magazine (published three times a year with articles of interest on careers and higher education); *The Guide to Erasmus Courses at UK Universities and Colleges.*

In addition to its publications ISCO supports the work of careers and other staff, pupils and parents in independent schools.

INDIAN VOLUNTEERS FOR COMMUNITY SERVICE (IVCS)
12 Eastleigh Avenue
Harrow
Middlesex HA2 0UF
Tel: 081 864 4740

Applicants are placed initially in a selected rural development project in north India for two weeks as observers and paying guests. After this period of adjustment and orientation they are given a choice of other projects to move on to. Some of these projects will accept applicants in some sort of volunteering capacity for longer periods and many will provide board and lodging free if the applicant is able to make him/herself useful. Length of stay is flexible. No placements are possible between April and September.

AGE RANGE:
18+

NUMBERS PASSING THROUGH:
70
HOW TO CONTACT:
SAE
REGIONS SERVICED:
UK
SPECIAL NEEDS PROVISION:
No provision
COSTS/WAITING LISTS:
Annual membership fee of £10 to IVCS. If
selected, a payment of £48, which includes 2
weeks' board and lodging at the initial
project, an orientation day and printed
material. Individuals are responsible for their
own air fares, travel in India and pocket
money. Past applicants have raised money
through local appeals and sponsored events

INDUSTRIAL COMMON OWNERSHIP MOVEMENT (ICOM)
Vassalli House
20 Central Road
Leeds LS1 6DE
Tel: 0532 461738 Fax: 0532 440002

ICOM can provide help and advice to anyone
involved in setting up or running a workers' co-
operative. A co-operative is a system where all
the people working in a business or enterprise
own and control the business. ICOM produce
various factsheets and publications and can
advise on legal issues affecting co-ops and
sources of finance as well as putting you in

touch with other co-ops. ICOM can also provide details of local Co-operative Development Agencies.

AGE RANGE:
Any
HOW TO CONTACT:
Letter, phone or fax for leaflets and
information
REGIONS SERVICED:
UK
SPECIAL NEEDS PROVISION:
No special provision but anyone can use the
services of ICOM
COSTS/WAITING LISTS:
Cost of membership depends on the size of co-op. Courses cost from £75. Various books and publications for sale

---

INSIGHT INTO MANAGEMENT COURSES
(Careers Research and Advisory Centre)
Sheraton House
Castle Park
Cambridge
CB3 0AX
Tel: 0223 460277 Fax: 0223 311708

Insight Courses give post-16 students, undergraduates and postgraduates an insight into management. Students from a range of disciplines can meet individuals working in a wide variety of different organisations and gain experience of teamwork, analysing problems and making decisions under pressure. You will be encouraged to examine a wide range of career possibilities, discover what it is really like working in particular management areas and gain a general understanding of business priorities and the world of work.

AGE RANGE:
Post-16 students and undergraduates and postgraduates

NUMBERS PASSING THROUGH:
4,015 in 1992

HOW TO CONTACT:
CRAC mainly provide careers information through their publications, not through individual contact. For details of the range of careers books/publications contact Hobsons Publishing, Bateman Street, Cambridge. Tel: 0223 354551. For information about 'Insight into Management' courses contact address above

REGIONS SERVICED:
UK

COSTS/WAITING LISTS:
Courses cost £35-£75

INSTANT MUSCLE LTD (IM)
Springside House
84 North End Road
London W14 9ES
Tel: 071 603 2604 Fax: 071 603 7346

Instant Muscle provides free, intensive, one-to-one business counselling and enterprise training, particularly for unemployed and disadvantaged people. IM will guide you through all the skills you need, such as taxation, marketing, accounting, book-keeping and market research until your business is fit to be up and running. It also offers a free 24-month aftercare service to all new businesses started at its Centres or on board its innovative Mobile Training Units.

REGIONAL ADDRESSES:
East Anglia: 7 Tey Road, Earls Colne,
Colchester CO6 2LG Tel: 0787 222027
Humberside: Ground Floor, Carmelite House,
Posterngate, Hull HU1 2JN
Tel: 0482 588202
London: same as Head Office
North-west: Lakeside Opportunities Centre,
Bowness Road, Middleton, Manchester
M24 4NU Tel: 061 654 6874
South Wales: 13 Market Street, Pontypridd,
Mid-Glamorgan CF37 2ST Tel: 0443 486200
Yorkshire: 24b Hallgate, Doncaster
DN1 3NG Tel: 0302 364956
AGE RANGE:
18-59
HOW TO CONTACT:
Telephone for an appointment or write to the nearest Regional Office
REGIONS SERVICED:
See above
SPECIAL NEEDS PROVISION:
Enquiries welcome

COSTS/WAITING LISTS:
All services are free. Waiting lists vary
between regions – in some, opportunities are
almost immediately available

INSTITUTE FOR CITIZENSHIP STUDIES
Queen Mary and Westfield College
University of London
Mile End Road
London E1 4NS
Tel: 071 975 5539 Fax: 071 607 7067

The purpose of this Institute, which was founded
by the then Speaker of the House of Commons
Bernard Weatherill, is to encourage citizenship,
in particular amongst young people. It runs
competitions to offer opportunities to practise
citizenship skills like letter writing and debating,
as well as preparing materials to enable young
people and their teachers to consider how
democracy developed and how it works today.

INSTITUTE FOR COMPLEMENTARY MEDICINE
21 Portland Place
London W1N 3AF

Alternative medicine covers a wide range of
practices such as homoeopathy, where the whole
person is taken into account in treatment rather
than just individual symptoms, herbal medicine,

acupuncture, reflexology and osteopathy to name just a few. Some training courses in alternative medicine require previous conventional medical training while others do not (homoeopathic doctors are medically qualified – although you can train and practise as a homoeopath without training as a doctor first). For more information on training available in alternative medicine send an SAE to the above address.

INSTITUTE OF CHARTERED ACCOUNTANTS IN ENGLAND AND WALES
Chartered Accountants' Hall
PO Box 433
Moorgate Place
London EC2P 2BJ
Tel: 071 920 8100

The Institute of Chartered Accountants in England and Wales is the largest professional accountancy body in Europe with over 102,000 members. Its role is to educate and train members, to undertake technical work, to preserve the professional independence of chartered accountants and to maintain high standards of professional conduct. Members of the Institute work in a wide range of fields including public practice (i.e. for accountancy firms), in industry and commerce and the public sector. For further information on how to become a chartered accountant please contact the Institute's Student Recruitment Section at the above address or phone 071 920 8677.

INSTITUTE OF PUBLIC RELATIONS
The Old Trading House
15 Northburgh Street
London EC1V 0PR
Tel: 071 253 5151

Public Relations Officers work towards promoting the image of organisations in either the private or public sector. Private industry, central and local government, public services, trade unions and most other large organisations use PR to some extent to present themselves in the best way possible to the press, public, local communities, Parliament, local councils, employees etc. using a variety of means e.g. press releases, reports, magazines, speeches etc. PR Officers either work for an agency or are employed by an individual organisation. The Institute of Public Relations can provide an information pack which outlines what public relations is all about and gives information on career development.

INSTITUTE OF TRAVEL AND TOURISM (ITT)

113 Victoria Street
St Albans
Hertfordshire AL1 3TJ
Tel: 0727 854395

The ITT can provide a basic information pack, mainly aimed at school leavers and those thinking of changing their careers towards travel and tourism. It contains useful advice and information, lists of ITT-approved colleges and the courses they offer, recommended reading and useful further contacts. Current price is £3. Contact above to check details of price and availability.

INTERNATIONAL ASSOCIATION FOR THE EXCHANGE OF STUDENTS FOR TECHNICAL EXPERIENCE (IAESTE)

Central Bureau for Educational Visits and
Exchanges
Seymour Mews
London W1H 9PE
Tel: 071 486 5101 Fax: 071 935 5741

IAESTE is an independent, non-political worldwide organisation which arranges course-related paid work placements for degree-level students in fields such as engineering, sciences, agriculture and the applied arts. Most last for up to 12 weeks during the summer, although longer placements may be available. Contact the Central Bureau at the above address for more information.

INTERNATIONAL CHRISTIAN YOUTH EXCHANGE (ICYE)
c/o Church of England Youth Services
Board of Education
Church House
Great Smith Street
London SW1P 3NZ
Tel: 071 222 9011 (ext. 407)

ICYE is a Federation of National Committees, co-ordinated by a central office in Berlin. It offers youth the possibility to spend 1 or a half-year abroad participating in school or voluntary work programmes as a means of intercultural learning and global education, teaching the individual how to live as a member of an increasingly multi-cultural society.

AGE RANGE:
16-27
HOW TO CONTACT:
Telephone or letter to the above address for detailed information
REGIONS SERVICED:
30 countries in all continents
COSTS:
Travel cost, insurance and administrative expenses

INTERNATIONAL DIRECTORY OF VOLUNTARY WORK (publication)
Vacation Work Publications
9 Park End Street
Oxford OX1 1HJ
Tel: 0865 241978 Fax: 0865 790885

Directory which includes details of over 500 organisations wanting help from all types of people for all types of work. Covers both short- and long-term residential work in Britain and around the world, and non-residential work in the UK for those with the time to help a local organisation or charity. Opportunities exist for both skilled and unskilled people – dentists can work for 2 years on a development project in Malawi, or students can work on an archaeological dig in France for a few weeks, or can help an inner-city shelter for homeless people.
ISBN 1 85458 085 X.   Available through libraries, bookshops (price £8.95), or direct from the above address (price £9.95 inc. p&p).

INTERNATIONAL HEALTH AND BEAUTY COUNCIL (IHBC)
46 Aldwick Road
Bognor Regis
West Sussex PO21 2PN

The International Health and Beauty Council can provide a general careers information pack

covering the full range of jobs in the beauty
industry, plus job-profiles and suggested career
paths.

AGE RANGE:
Any
HOW TO CONTACT:
SAE to above address
REGIONS SERVICED:
UK

INTERNATIONAL SOCIAL AND
EDUCATION EXCHANGES (ISEE)
150 Bonnyton Drive
Eaglesham
Glasgow G76 0LU
Tel: 041 429 8722 Fax: 041 429 2117

ISEE can provide information, contacts, support,
training, resources and general advice on any
aspect of international youth mobility.

REGIONAL ADDRESSES:
Contact through above address
AGE RANGE:
In practice over 90% of those using ISEE are
aged 12-27, but anyone can use the service
HOW TO CONTACT:
By letter or telephone to above address for
further information
REGIONS SERVICED:
UK and abroad

SPECIAL NEEDS PROVISION:
ISEE has taken a special interest in the
opening up of access to international
opportunities to socially and physically
disadvantaged groups
COSTS/WAITING LISTS:
No costs or waiting lists, but some replies at
certain times of the year may take some time

INTERNATIONAL STUDENT PLAYSCRIPT
COMPETITION (ISPC)
World Student Drama Trust
20 Lansdowne Road
Muswell Hill
London N10 2AU
Tel: 081 883 4586 Fax: 081 883 7142

This annual competition is open to current or
recent students. Applicants must have been full
or part-time students on or after 1 January of the
year before the year of entry and scripts must be
entered by 30 November. There are no
restrictions on length, subject, setting etc. but
scripts must be in English, or translated into
English, and be unperformed. All scripts will be
considered for first performance by the National
Student Theatre Company (see separate entry)
or the young professional Springboard Theatre
Company and each entry will receive a written
criticism. The winner receives the World Student
Drama Trust Award of £400 and, if practicable,
a rehearsed reading at the following National
Student Drama Festival (see separate entry).

AGE RANGE:
Any
HOW TO CONTACT:
Details and entry forms available from above
address (but do not send scripts there)
REGIONS SERVICED:
UK and abroad
COSTS/WAITING LISTS:
Entry is free

INTERNATIONAL THEATRE EXCHANGE
(ITE)
Marjorie Havard
19 Abbey Park Road
Grimsby
Humberside DN32 0HJ
Tel: 0472 343424

International Theatre Exchange is the UK centre
of the International Amateur Theatre Association,
an organisation whose main aim is to promote
cultural exchange in the area of the performing
arts and arts education. It organises and conducts
international theatre workshops, festivals and
theatrical exchange visits, many of which are
based around youth and student theatre. All the
work of the ITE is carried out by experienced
people volunteering their services and funding
is provided by 'friends' – individuals and groups
involved in theatre in any of its forms, whether
student, amateur, professional, school, fringe or
community theatre. Write to the above address
for details of forthcoming events.

AGE RANGE:
Any
HOW TO CONTACT:
Contact the secretariat at the above address
for further information
REGIONS SERVICED:
UK
COSTS/WAITING LISTS:
Individual annual subscription is £6; group
subscription is £10. International work
involves costs such as air fares and groups
need to fund-raise to cover costs. It is often
worthwhile approaching businesses for
sponsorship and Local Authorities sometimes
assist with educational projects. Exchanges
and visits can take 12 months or more to fully
organise

INTERNATIONAL VOLUNTARY SERVICE (IVS)

IVS aims to provide ways for individuals from
various countries to work together on socially
useful projects, in the hope of promoting peace
and understanding between people of different
nations. Each year they operate around 60 work
camps in Britain and hundreds abroad. Work
camps bring together a mix of volunteers, aged
18 and over, from different countries and
backgrounds. The volunteers live and work co-
operatively. Work camps typically last between
2 and 4 weeks, with a wide range of projects

being offered from camp to camp. They could
involve work with children or disabled people,
conservation, renovation, or solidarity with
disadvantaged minorities. Wherever possible
the work camps offer a small 'study element' to
allow volunteers to find out about the underlying
issues that make the work important.

REGIONAL ADDRESSES:
North of England: IVS (North), 188 Roundhay
Road, Leeds LS8 5PL
South of England: IVS (South), Old Hall East,
Bergholt, Near Colchester CO7 6TQ
Scotland: IVS (Scotland) St John's Church,
Princes Street, Edinburgh EH2 4BJ
Northern Ireland: see separate entry below
AGE RANGE:
18+
HOW TO CONTACT:
Letter plus SAE to appropriate regional office
for information pack
REGIONS SERVICED:
England and Wales. See also entries for IVS
Scotland and IVS Northern Ireland
SPECIAL NEEDS PROVISION:
IVS promote open access and equal
opportunities in all their activities. Some
projects, however, may not be suitable for
people with disabilities – further information
available on request
COSTS/WAITING LISTS:
Volunteers pay for their own travel to work
camps. Assistance may be available – more

details from IVS. Work camp fees range from
£45-£85

INTERNATIONAL VOLUNTARY SERVICE
(NORTHERN IRELAND)
122 Great Victoria Street
Belfast BT2 7BG
Tel: 0232 238147

IVS, through the Teenage Workcamp Scheme
(TWS), provides opportunities for 16-19 year-
old volunteers to work together with their
European peers, through a programme of
weekends and 2-week work camps. The
emphasis of the TWS is on young people who
would not normally have the opportunity to
travel. After 1 year, opportunities exist to become
more involved in organising your own activities,
using the IVS international network.
International Workcamps consist of an
international group of volunteers. They last for
2-3 weeks and take place throughout Europe
and America. Volunteers pay their own way to
the camp and are offered food and
accommodation in exchange for their labour.

AGE RANGE:
16-19 for Teenage Workcamp Scheme (TWS);
18+ for International Workcamps and
regional voluntary work; 21+ for Asia/Africa
exchange
NUMBERS PASSING THROUGH:
c 150 per year

HOW TO CONTACT:
Telephone or in person for advice and
information. Also information available on
other organisations
REGIONS SERVICED:
Northern Ireland
SPECIAL NEEDS PROVISION:
Some opportunities available. Varies
according to work camp programme
COSTS/WAITING LISTS:
TWS is £2.50 per residential night in Northern
Ireland. TWS work camps in Europe cost £90
including all travel. International Workcamps
registration and IVS membership costs are
dependent on income (volunteer is
responsible for own travel). Camps in Eastern
Europe cost an extra £30+. Apply for TWS
from January to March

INTERNSHIPS USA 1994 (publication)
Vacation Work Publications
9 Park End Street
Oxford OX1 1HJ
Tel: 0865 241978 Fax: 0865 790885

Internship is the American word for short-term
work experience that enables students and
graduates to get invaluable on-the-job training
for a possible future career by acquiring the
skills, ability and experience that can only be
gained by a genuine period of work with an
established organisation. 38,000 career-
orientated positions in the USA are listed in

fields ranging from business to theatre, communications to science. Many are open to British students. The book explains when, where and how to apply for both positions and work permits.

ISBN 1 56079 286 8. Available through libraries, bookshops (price £16.95), or direct from the above address (price £19.45 inc. p&p).

JOBCENTRES

Jobcentres have the largest computer-based vacancy system in the country, displaying local job vacancies and vacancies from other parts of the country and overseas. If you find a suitable vacancy one of the staff will be happy to discuss it with you and then phone the employer to arrange an interview. Jobcentres can also offer advice to help with your job search through things like Jobclubs and Job Search Seminars, as well as information on opportunities to become self-employed. Consult your local telephone directory for your nearest Jobcentre.

JOBS IN EUROPE (publication)
52 Queen's Gardens
London W2 3AA
Tel: 071 724 5346 Fax: 071 221 3408

Jobs in Europe is a magazine which comes out monthly, giving advice and information on how to go about working in Europe. It is written by people who have worked in Europe themselves and who have also written books on the subject. *Jobs in Europe* gives job news, job ads and information in an average of 36 pages per month. The magazine is available on subscription from the above address, or you can just buy one sample issue. The company also runs a helpline, Euro Buro, (see separate entry).

JOHN HALL PRE-UNIVERSITY INTERIM COURSE
12 Gainsborough Road
Ipswich
Suffolk IP4 2UR
Tel: 0473 251223 Fax: 0473 288009

The pre-university interim course has been running for 30 years. It lasts about 7 weeks running from late January to mid March. It is about European Civilisation. The course begins with an introduction in London, and thereafter in Venice. There are optional extensions to the course held in Florence and Rome. The course is for students who have just left school – the average age is 18. It is open to Arts and Science students alike. No previous knowledge of European art or music history is required. It offers a foretaste of a university style of learning and living. The course is a programme of lectures, classes, walk-abouts and special study visits, language teaching, photography, and life-drawing and painting classes, and free time and individual visits.

AGE RANGE:
c 18
HOW TO CONTACT:
Write to above
REGIONS SERVICED:
UK and USA
COSTS/WAITING LISTS:
1994 : c £3,150. Scholarships offered by the
National Association of Decorative and Fine
Arts Societies (NADFAS), but only to
applicants who have been members of Young
NADFAS for at least 2 consecutive years and
who are under 19 at the time of application

JUBILEE SAILING TRUST (JST)
Test Road, Eastern Docks
Southampton
Hampshire SO1 1GG
Tel: 0703 631395/631388 Fax: 0703 638625

Jubilee Sailing Trust offers young people aged
16 and over the opportunity to experience the
challenge and adventure of crewing a 490-ton
tall ship at sea for up to 10 days regardless of
their physical ability. Voyages comprise an
equal number of physically handicapped and
able-bodied people aged 16 to 70.

AGE RANGE:
16+
HOW TO CONTACT:
Telephone or letter (with SAE) to the Public
Relations Department

REGIONS SERVICED:
UK, Channel Islands, Republic of Ireland,
overseas
SPECIAL NEEDS PROVISION:
Provision for physically disabled
COSTS/WAITING LISTS:
UK voyages range from £220 (3 days) to £650
(10 days); Canaries voyages from £400 (8
days) to £630 (19 days). Associate
membership is £15 per year. There are
various bursaries and Trusts from which some
funding is available – details from JST.
Applications should be made 2 months in
advance

JUNIOR ASTRONOMICAL SOCIETY (JAS)
36 Fairway
Keyworth
Nottingham NG12 5DU

The JAS is open to beginners and more
experienced amateur astronomers of all ages.
There are four meetings each year in London
and occasional meetings and weekend courses
away from London. Publications include the
Popular Astronomy magazine four times a year
as well as news circulars, usually about six
times a year. The society also provides a GCSE
advisory service and an instrument advisory
service, and society officials are pleased to
correspond with young people to provide help
and guidance. Members may contribute to
specialist observing sections.

AGE RANGE:
Any
NUMBERS PASSING THROUGH:
Nearly 3,000 members
HOW TO CONTACT:
Write with SAE to above address for
information leaflet and an application form
REGIONS SERVICED:
UK and overseas
SPECIAL NEEDS PROVISION:
Require notice of attendance as some
activities may not be accessible
COSTS/WAITING LISTS:
Annual UK subscription is £10 per year
which includes all publications. Weekend
courses are charged at cost for
accommodation, food etc.

KIBBUTZ REPRESENTATIVES
1A Accommodation Road
London NW11 8ED
Tel: 081 458 9235 Fax: 081 455 7930

An opportunity to live and work on a Kibbutz in
Israel. A Kibbutz is a co-operative community
and in exchange for working you will be provided
with accommodation, meals and all the leisure
facilities and activities of the Kibbutz.
Occasional trips around the country will be
arranged and a small allowance provided to
cover essentials. You need to be in good
physical and mental health, have at least eight
weeks to spare and be interested in participating

in an alternative and communal lifestyle.

AGE RANGE:
18-32
NUMBERS PASSING THROUGH:
3,000
HOW TO CONTACT:
SAE to address above for information and
application forms
REGIONS SERVICED:
UK
SPECIAL NEEDS PROVISION:
No provision
COSTS/WAITING LISTS:
Registration fee approx £45; return fare to
Israel (varies according to time of year);
insurance £32-£80. Costs are the same
whether you go for 8 weeks or 6 months
(present maximum). Applications normally
take 3-6 weeks to process but applications for
July and August should be sent by April

KIBBUTZ VOLUNTEER (publication)
Vacation Work Publications
9 Park End Street
Oxford OX1 1HJ
Tel: 0865 241978 Fax: 0865 790885

A guide to life on a Kibbutz. The book gives
details of 200 Kibbutzim, and describes what to
expect when working in one. Also gives details
of other vacation and short-term work available
in Israel – the Moshav Movement, conservation,

archaeological digs, fruit-picking, voluntary work with Palestinian refugees, au pair work and hotel jobs in Eilat. Sections devoted to Kibbutz Ulpan, money, customs, food and drink, where to stay, and generally how to see the country as an insider rather than a tourist.

ISBN 1 85458 021 3. Available through libraries, bookshops (price £5.95), or direct from the above address (price £7.45 inc. p&p).

LABOUR PARTY
150 Walworth Road
London SE17 1JT
Tel: 071 701 1234

LAND USE VOLUNTEERS (LUV)
c/o Horticultural Therapy
Goulds Ground
Vallis Way,
Frome
Somerset BA11 3DW
Tel: 0373 464782 Fax: 0373 464782

If you have experience and/or basic qualifications in horticulture, have worked in some capacity with people with special needs, and are looking for a way to use your skills, LUV will help. They help projects use horticulture as therapy for people with disabilities by providing a volunteer with horticultural skills. You may help in preparing a new site for a horticultural therapy unit, or train clients and care staff in basic horticultural tasks. LUV will place you in a project that reflects your own particular skills and interests. Minimum period of service is 3 months, the maximum 1 year. Board, lodging and pocket money are provided throughout your stay.

AGE RANGE:
18+
HOW TO CONTACT:
Letter or telephone to above address for application form and fuller details
REGIONS SERVICED:
England, Wales, Northern Ireland (see entry for Horticultural Volunteers in Scotland for Scottish equivalent)
SPECIAL NEEDS PROVISION:
LUV act as a clearing house, matching volunteers with projects. Any volunteer with special needs would be carefully placed in a project which had committed their support

LAURA ASHLEY FOUNDATION
33 King Street
London WC2
Tel: 071 497 2503

The Laura Ashley Foundation will consider applications for course fees in cases of hardship for any course held at a further education college, e.g. City and Guilds, foundation courses, nursery nursing, 'A' level, GCSE or BTEC.

AGE RANGE:
18+
NUMBERS PASSING THROUGH:
150
HOW TO CONTACT:
Telephone or letter for information and an
application form
REGIONS SERVICED:
UK
SPECIAL NEEDS PROVISION:
Anyone can apply
COSTS/WAITING LISTS:
Apply before the course begins

LAW SOCIETY
Careers and Recruitment Office
227-228 The Strand
London WC2R 1BA
Tel: 071 242 1222

The Law Society produce a range of careers
leaflets and brochures and can provide advice
and information about training and developing
a career as a solicitor. The Recruitment team
can also provide advice on CVs, interview
technique and job availability.

REGIONAL OFFICES:
Scotland: Legal Education Department, 26
Drumsheugh Gardens, Edinburgh EH3 7YR
Tel: 031 226 7411
Northern Ireland: 98 Victoria Street, Belfast
BT1 3JZ Tel: 0232 231614

(These are separate jurisdictions with their own Law Society. Please contact them direct.)

LIBERAL DEMOCRATS
4 Cowley Street
London SW1P 3NB
Tel: 071 222 7999

LIGHTS, CAMERA, ACTION!
Careers in Film, Television and Video
(publication)
British Film Institute
21 Stephen Street
London W1P 1PL
Tel: 071 255 1444

An invaluable guide to media employment opportunities. Gives sound advice on types of job available, qualifications required, recent changes in the industry and first steps along a career path. Useful job profiles and interesting case studies are included.
ISBN 0 85170 343 7. Updated annually. Available from public libraries, bookshops (£9.95) or direct from the above address (price £10.95 inc. p&p).

LITTLE THEATRE GUILD OF GREAT BRITAIN (LTG)
Secretariat
Ann Mattey
Flat 6, 34 Broadwater Down
Tunbridge Wells
TN2 5NX

LTG members are independent, non-commercial companies producing several plays a year. There are 70 member theatres, most of which have a youth or junior section and provide some form of training for young people, workshops and student productions. If you have an interest in any aspect of theatre, the LTG can direct you to your nearest suitable member company or alternatively look up the theatres in your area at your local library.

REGIONAL ADDRESSES:
Three regional offices: Northern (including Scotland), Midland and Southern – details from above
AGE RANGE:
Any
HOW TO CONTACT:
Send SAE to above address or call 0892 534710 for further information including details of the nearest suitable LTG member
REGIONS SERVICED:
UK
SPECIAL NEEDS PROVISION:
Each member theatre of the LTG varies in

facilities and provision
COSTS/WAITING LISTS:
Annual subscriptions/membership fees vary
as do course and workshop fees. There is
often a limit to the number of training places
available and those wishing to participate
join a waiting list. 6 months is a usual
waiting time

LIVEWIRE
Hawthorn House
Forth Banks
Newcastle-upon-Tyne NE1 3SG
Tel: 091 261 5584 Fax: 091 261 1910

Livewire can provide information, advice and
support to young people who are thinking of
starting up in business, and to those already
established in business. Sponsored by Shell
(UK) Ltd, there are three key elements to the
Livewire service.

The Enquiry and Link Up Service: young people
anywhere in the UK can be linked to appropriate
local advice and support on starting up in
business.

The Business Start Up Awards: £175,000 worth
of cash awards and help in kind is available
through this awards competition in a series of
county, regional, national and UK events. It is
based on submission of a business plan for a
new business and awards are made by
independent judging panels.

Business Growth Challenge: a management development programme for young owner-managers of established businesses.

REGIONAL ADDRESSES:
Livewire England: The Fishergate Centre, 4 Fishergate, York YO1 4AB Tel: 0904 620105 Fax: 0904 651260
Livewire Scotland: Romano House, 43 Station Road, Corstorphine, Edinburgh EH12 7AF Tel: 031 334 9876 Fax: 031 316 4521
Livewire Northern Ireland: Young Business Centre, 103-107 York Street,
Belfast BT15 1AB Tel: 0232 328000 Fax: 0232 439666
Livewire Cymru: Greenfield Valley Enterprise Centre, Greenfield Road, Greenfield, Holywell, Clwyd CH8 7QB Tel: 0352 710199 Fax: 0352 715210

AGE RANGE:
16-25 for Enquiry Service and Start Up Awards. Up to 35 for Business Growth Challenge

NUMBERS PASSING THROUGH:
£175,000 worth of awards shared between approx. 300 young businesses nationally. 10,000 young people linked to information/ advice. 500 people helped through the Business Growth Challenge

HOW TO CONTACT:
Telephone UK or national Livewire offices above. Information is usually available in Careers Offices, Jobcentres and Local Enterprise Agencies. Or write to one of the

following Freepost adresses:
Livewire UK, Freepost, Newcastle-upon-
Tyne NE1 1BR
Livewire Cymru, Freepost,
Holywell CH8 7YZ
Livewire Scotland, Freepost, Edinburgh
EH12 0PE
Livewire Northern Ireland, Freepost,
Belfast BT15 1BR
REGIONS SERVICED:
UK
SPECIAL NEEDS PROVISION:
Support is available to any young person
regardless of ability
COSTS/WAITING LISTS:
No costs. All enquiries are dealt with
promptly

LIVEWIRE
BUSINESS START UP AWARDS
for contact details see main Livewire entry

This awards scheme is open to entrants aged 16-
25 who submit a business plan to their local
Livewire co-ordinator which is then assessed by
independent judging panels. Over 80 awards
presentations take place each year at county,
regional and national levels leading to the
prestigious Livewire UK Finals. Each year up to
£175,000 is given in awards. The scheme
provides an opportunity for young businesses,
advisers, organisers and sponsors to mix and
learn from one another.

LOCAL ENTERPRISE COMPANIES
(SCOTLAND)
Contact through Jobcentre or telephone
directory

Youth Training, Employment Training and
Enterprise Allowance Schemes in Scotland are
all managed by Local Enterprise Companies.
Their programmes are structured for the area in
which they operate, and they can provide advice
and information on all aspects of youth training
in Scotland.

LOCAL ENTERPRISE DEVELOPMENT UNIT
(LEDU)
LEDU House
Upper Galwally
Belfast BT8 4TB
Tel: 0232 491031 Fax: 0232 691432

As well as offering financial assistance, LEDU
can provide advice, guidance and information
to anyone in Northern Ireland on setting up in
business.

REGIONAL ADDRESSES:
Six regional offices throughout Northern
Ireland – full details from the above address
AGE RANGE:
17+
NUMBERS PASSING THROUGH:
400-500

HOW TO CONTACT:
Contact through any local LEDU regional
office or direct at above address
REGIONS SERVICED:
Northern Ireland
SPECIAL NEEDS PROVISION:
Disabled programmes available
COSTS/WAITING LISTS:
None

THE LOCAL GOVERNMENT MANAGEMENT BOARD

Arndale House
Arndale Centre
Luton LU1 2TS
Tel: 0582 451166

There are three main types of employment in
local government: professionals such as
accountants and architects who train in their
own field first and take up employment in local
government; specialists who train in a specific
area of local government such as Environmental
Health Officers; and administrators and clerical
workers who carry out the day-to-day running
of local government affairs. The Local
Government Management Board can provide
further information about training and career
structure for specialists, administrators and
clerical workers.

LONDON COLLEGE OF FASHION
20 John Prince's Street
London W1M 0BJ
Tel: 071 629 9401

The London College of Fashion, as well as offering a wide variety of training and courses in all aspects of fashion including clothing, tailoring, fashion hairstyling, embroidery etc., also produces a range of leaflets and can offer advice and information covering many aspects of the beauty industry, including background information about starting up and developing a career in modelling.

MARINE CONSERVATION SOCIETY
9 Gloucester Road
Ross-on-Wye
Herefordshire
HR9 5BU
Tel: 0989 66017 Fax: 0989 67815

Information on all aspects of marine conservation; factsheets for students/pupils; advice on careers in marine sciences; surveys, including marine curios, marine debris and wildlife projects ,which encourage young people to take an active role e.g. Beach Watch, Marine Curio Survey; clothing with a conservation message. MCS Sales Ltd stock many publications and gifts suitable for young people.

REGIONAL ADDRESSES:
List of local groups available from main office
AGE RANGE:
Any
NUMBERS PASSING THROUGH:
6,000 enquiries from young people
HOW TO CONTACT:
SAE to Enquiry Secretary for membership
leaflet, factsheets and information
REGIONS SERVICED:
UK
COSTS/WAITING LISTS:
Annual membership fee: £12
Student/child: £8

MEDIA COURSES UK (publication)
British Film Institute
21 Stephen Street
London W1P 1PL
Tel: 071 255 1444

An up-to-the-minute guide to media courses
currently available at colleges and universities.
It lists both practical and academic courses on
film, television, video and photography. Syllabus
analysis, entry qualifications and contacts for
further information on each course are also
included.
ISBN 0 85170 441 7. Updated annually.
Available from public libraries, bookshops
(£7.95) or direct from the above address (price
£8.50 inc. p&p).

THE MERLIN TRUST
The Dower House
Boughton House
Kettering
Northamptonshire NN14 1BJ
Tel: 0536 82279

The Merlin Trust was set up in memory of keen
naturalists Sir David Scott and his son Merlin,
who was killed during the Second World War
aged 20. It offers practical assistance to young
horticulturalists who are driven by their love of
plants. Assistance takes the form of grants of up
to £500 for study projects either in Britain or
abroad. Projects can involve photography,
painting, written observations, seed collecting,
or help with conservation projects, especially
involving garden plants. Travelling and other
expenses are paid. Please note that grants are
not normally given for postgraduate study or to
fund highly technical, laboratory-based research.

AGE RANGE:
18-30, though age matters less than a genuine
keenness for plants, gardens or gardening.
Applicants should be able to show that their
proposed applications will help them in their
careers
NUMBERS PASSING THROUGH:
An average of 75 a year
HOW TO CONTACT:
Write for simple application form, enclosing a
large A4 SAE, to the above address

REGIONS SERVICED:
UK
COSTS/WAITING LISTS:
No costs. Applications dealt with on a first
come, first served basis

MINORITIES ARTS ADVISORY SERVICE LTD
(MAAS)
4th Floor
28 Shacklewell Lane
London E8 2EZ
Tel: 071 254 7295
(Advice and Information line)

MAAS is an arts development agency strongly
involved in the advancing and promotion of the
black arts sector by providing advice and
information, research, initiating conferences and
seminars and providing information on training
opportunities for administrators, artists and
cultural workers. The Advice and Information
services are available to artists and arts
organisations, students and researchers,
educational and training agencies and members
of the general public. They also publish an
inter-cultural arts magazine, *Artrage*, containing
interviews, articles, listings and reviews on fine
arts, the performing arts, literature and the media
arts.

AGE RANGE:
Any

HOW TO CONTACT:
Write or telephone for advice and
information
REGIONS SERVICED:
UK

MOBILITY INTERNATIONAL
228 Borough High Street
London SE1 1JX
Tel: 071 403 5688 Fax: 071 378 1292

Mobility International organises projects in the
UK and abroad for disabled young people of
different nationalities and with different abilities.
The aim is to give all young people – regardless
of their needs – the chance to learn new skills
and gain confidence through international travel.
Some projects are only open to people with a
particular disability, others can be enjoyed by
everybody. If you are disabled MI may have a
project for you – brush up on a foreign language,
improve your employment prospects, meet new
friends. Assistance available towards the cost of
bringing a helper/companion with you. Full
details of opportunities available are in the
annual programme.

AGE RANGE:
16-30 (but this is flexible)
HOW TO CONTACT:
Telephone, letter, fax or in person for an
annual programme of events and activities

REGIONS SERVICED:
UK
SPECIAL NEEDS PROVISION:
See above
COSTS/WAITING LISTS:
Costs of activities and events vary and some
funding is available from various sources
such as LEAs, trusts etc.

MUSIC IN SCOTLAND TRUST (MIST)
PO Box 183
Glasgow G3 8DG
Tel: 041 204 1961

The Music in Scotland Trust is a unique charity
which assists young people between 18 and 25
by securing funding and providing music-related
information and advice to those wishing to set
up in business in the Scottish music industry.
The Trust has close links with the Prince's
Scottish Youth Business Trust and can assist
with everything from helping with the
development of a business plan to providing
places at music industry seminars and helps in
a wide variety of ways according to need.

AGE RANGE:
18-25
NUMBERS PASSING THROUGH:
500
HOW TO CONTACT:
Telephone or letter (with SAE) or by

contacting the Prince's Scottish Youth
Business Trust in your area
REGIONS SERVICED:
Scotland
SPECIAL NEEDS PROVISION:
Enquiries welcome
COSTS/WAITING LISTS:
No costs or waiting lists

MUSICIANS UNION (MU)
60-62 Clapham Road
London SW9 0JJ
Tel: 071 582 5566 Fax: 071 582 9805

The Musicians Union exists to support those
who earn their living, or part of it, from any kind
of music. Any kind of musician is welcome,
from early music specialists through to rappers.
Benefits include access to legal advice about
musical employment, contracts advice, career
advice, insurance for equipment, and access to
a wealth of information covering all aspects of
the music industry.

REGIONAL ADDRESSES:
East/North-east: 193 Dogsthorpe Road,
Peterborough PE1 3AT Tel: 0733 557555
Fax: 0733 898224
London: as Head Office above
Midlands: Unit A, Benson House, Lombard
Street, Birmingham B12 0QR
Tel: 021 622 3870 Fax: 021 622 5361

North/North-east: 327 Roundhay Road, Leeds
LS8 4HT Tel: 0532 481335 Fax: 0532 481292
North-west: 40 Canal Street, Manchester M1
3WD Tel: 061 236 1764   Fax: 061 236 0159
Scotland: 135 Wellington Street, Glasgow G2
2XD Tel: 041 248 3723 Fax: 041 204 3510
South-east: as Head Office above
South-west: 131 St George's Road, Bristol BS1
5UW Tel: 0272 265438   Fax: 0272 253729

AGE RANGE:
Any

HOW TO CONTACT:
Letter, telephone or fax for membership
details and application forms

REGIONS SERVICED:
UK

SPECIAL NEEDS PROVISION:
Enquiries welcome

COSTS/WAITING LISTS:
Membership costs vary depending on how
much you are earning from your music

NABC-CLUBS FOR YOUNG PEOPLE
369 Kennington Lane
London SE11 5QY
Tel: 071 793 0787 Fax: 071 820 9815

Clubs affiliated to NABC-CYP exist to encourage
the development of young people in a co-
operative and enjoyable environment. There is
no typical club – most are just places where
young people go for enjoyment and to participate

in an activity of their choice. In more and more clubs members are forging vital links with their local communities, perhaps by fund-raising for a local cause, or through helping the elderly and disabled. Whilst sport is important in all the clubs, there are also opportunities for other pursuits to enable young people to achieve personal development which might otherwise be denied to them. Club members are encouraged to participate in activities such as the Duke of Edinburgh's Award, Operation Raleigh and Community Sports Leader Awards. There are also opportunities for creativity in the visual arts, drama and music, often using the latest techniques.

HOW TO CONTACT:
Letter or phone for general/local information
REGIONS SERVICED:
Throughout the UK 2,500 clubs are affiliated to NABC-CYP. Local club details are available from Central Office.
SPECIAL NEEDS PROVISION:
Enquiries welcome

NATIONAL ASSOCIATION FOR THE CARE AND RESETTLEMENT OF OFFENDERS
169 Clapham Road
Stockwell
London SW9 0PU
Tel: 071 582 6500

NACRO can provide information concerning criminal offences, the police, the courts and criminal records. In nine areas of England NACRO run Youth Activities Units where young people participate in organising their own activities when previously there were very few. Projects recruit volunteers (including 15-21 year-olds) to help develop new provision. NACRO also has a number of Youth Training and Employment Training Schemes.

REGIONAL ADDRESSES:
Youth Activities Unit address:
NACRO YAU, Princess House, 105-107 Princess Street, Manchester M1 6DD Tel: 061 236 0588
AGE RANGE:
Any
NUMBERS PASSING THROUGH:
3,000
HOW TO CONTACT:
Letter to above address for information on current projects or suitable alternatives
REGIONS SERVICED:
Criminal justice information service available nationwide. Location of youth projects varies
SPECIAL NEEDS PROVISION:
Young people with physical disabilities will be accommodated wherever possible. Those with learning difficulties are especially welcome if these are causing school, social or integration problems
COSTS/WAITING LISTS:
Occasionally contributions are required towards the costs of activities

NATIONAL ASSOCIATION OF VOLUNTEER BUREAUX (NAVB)
St Peter's College
College Road
Saltley
Birmingham B8 3TE
Tel: 021 327 0265 Fax: 021 327 3696

NAVB can give you details of your nearest Volunteeer Bureau. Volunteer Bureaux offer advice and information on volunteering opportunities in your local area. A Bureau will also be able to put you in touch with organisations in your local area who want to recruit volunteers.

AGE RANGE:
Any
HOW TO CONTACT:
Letter, telephone or fax to above address
REGIONS SERVICED:
England, Wales and Northern Ireland
SPECIAL NEEDS PROVISION:
Volunteer Bureaux cater for people with special needs

NATIONAL ASSOCIATION OF YOUTH ORCHESTRAS (NAYO)

Ainslie House
11 St Colme Street
Edinburgh EH3 6AG
Tel: 031 225 4606 Fax: 031 225 3568

The NAYO exists to represent youth orchestras (including chamber, symphonic, wind and jazz orchestras) throughout the country and to foster their development. The association organises an Anglo-German youth music week each summer for musicians of both countries aged 15-25, can arrange tuition/coaching for young musicians and has a free ticket scheme for Edinburgh and Glasgow Festivals of British Youth Orchestras. The NAYO publishes a news bulletin, *Full Orchestra,* containing news of youth orchestras, courses, future events, foreign travel etc., can provide ideas for concert programmes, advice on overseas travel, exchange of platforms etc. and is happy to deal with enquiries about youth music from anyone.

AGE RANGE:
No specific age range
HOW TO CONTACT:
By letter for advice and information
REGIONS SERVICED:
UK
SPECIAL NEEDS PROVISION:
Services open to all young people with an interest in music

NATIONAL ASSOCIATION OF YOUTH THEATRES (NAYT)

Unit 1304 The Custard Factory
Gibb Street
Digbeth
Birmingham B9 4AA
Tel: 021 608 2111 Fax: 021 608 2333

The NAYT holds the most comprehensive list of youth theatres in the UK (over 700 which involve at least 40,000 young people). They can put you in contact with your local group, provide more information about youth theatre and give informal advice regarding theatre as a hobby and as a career. If you already have experience and are interested in starting your own youth theatre, NAYT has a range of services that can help you.

AGE RANGE:
No specific age range
NUMBERS PASSING THROUGH:
Indirectly, approximately 20,000
HOW TO CONTACT:
Easiest to contact by letter (with SAE) for individual advice (if applicable)
REGIONS SERVICED:
UK
SPECIAL NEEDS PROVISION:
Details available of youth theatres which cater for or work solely with young people with special needs, as well as specific advice relating to special needs

COSTS/WAITING LISTS:
Membership costs about £15 annually for
groups and individuals. Course fees vary
from £5 for a day course to £90 for a
weekend. Financial support is sometimes
available for young people from various
sources wishing to attend events or
conferences through NAYT

NATIONAL BOARD FOR NURSING, MIDWIFERY AND HEALTH VISITING

Contact the relevant national board for
information on courses and careers in nursing
including hospital nursing, midwifery,
community nursing, occupational health nursing
and working as a health visitor. You can also
obtain information on training from the Regional
Nursing Officer at your nearest NHS Regional
Health Authority.

NATIONAL BOARDS:
England: Resource and Careers Services, Chantry
House, 798 Chesterfield Road
Sheffield S8 0SF   Tel: 0742 551064/5
Northern Ireland: RAC House, 79 Chichester
Street, Belfast BT1 4JR Tel: 0232 238152
Scotland: 22 Queen Street, Edinburgh EH2 1JX
Tel: 031 226 7371
Wales: 13th Floor, Pearl Assurance House,
Greyfriars Road, Cardiff CF1 3AG   Tel: 0222
395535

NATIONAL COACHING FOUNDATION
(NCF)
114 Cardigan Lane
Headingley
Leeds LS6 8BJ
Tel: 0532 744802

The NCF can give information about developing a career as a sports coach – how to get in, coaching courses, and lists of useful further contacts. The NCF provides courses and publications on sports coaching.

REGIONAL ADDRESSES:
A list of national coaching courses across the UK is available from the above address
AGE RANGE:
Any
HOW TO CONTACT:
Large SAE required for careers factsheets.
Letter or telephone for information and advice
REGIONS SERVICED:
UK
SPECIAL NEEDS PROVISION:
Enquiries welcome

NATIONAL COUNCIL FOR DRAMA
TRAINING (NCDT)
5 Tavistock Place
London WC1H 9SM
Tel: 071 387 3650

The NCDT can provide a list of the professional courses in acting and stage management which it has accredited on receipt of a stamped and addressed envelope.

NATIONAL COUNCIL FOR THE TRAINING OF JOURNALISTS (NCTJ)
Latton Bush Centre
Southern Way
Harlow
Essex CM18 7BL
Tel: 0279 430009

Trainee journalists study and train for professional qualifications approved by the NCTJ, who can provide information about courses in journalism – where they are held, entry requirements, duration etc. Please mark all written correspondence 'Pre-entry'.

NATIONAL EXTENSION COLLEGE (NEC)
18 Brooklands Avenue
Cambridge CB2 2HN
Tel: 0223 316644 Fax: 0223 313586

The National Extension College offers a wide range of courses which people of all ages can start any time and study at their own pace and in their own home. Over 150 Home Study courses leading to GCSEs, 'A' levels, RSA, professional qualifications and degrees are available. Students are given on-going support by experienced personal tutors – usually by letter or telephone – leading to examinations which can be taken when and if the student chooses. Full courses list available from NEC.

AGE RANGE:
Any
HOW TO CONTACT:
Telephone, letter or fax for free Guide to Courses
REGIONS SERVICED:
UK
SPECIAL NEEDS PROVISION:
Enquiries welcome
COSTS/WAITING LISTS:
Price list of courses available from NEC

NATIONAL FEDERATION OF CITY FARMS (NFCF)
AMF House
93 Whitby Road
Brislington
Bristol BS4 3QF
Tel: 0272 719109

NFCF brings the countryside to the city by setting up and running small farm holdings in built-up areas where many of us live. For more information about the work of NFCF, addresses of farms in your local area and advice on how to become involved in the city farm movement – either voluntarily or as a worker – contact the address above.

AGE RANGE:
Any
HOW TO CONTACT:
Letter to above address. SAE required for
written information
REGIONS SERVICED:
UK

NATIONAL FEDERATION OF GATEWAY CLUBS
117 Golden Lane
London EC1Y 0RT
Tel: 071 454 0454 Fax: 071 608 3254

Gateway clubs offer leisure opportunities to
people of all ages with a learning disability. The
activities provided aim to advance the personal
development of club members by promoting
choice and independence. Members are
encouraged to become involved in the wider
community through the club. The Gateway
Award incorporates these aims and activities
into a progressive award scheme. Able-bodied
volunteers always needed to help with the work
of the clubs.

REGIONAL ADDRESSES:
South: as Head Office above
East: 4 Scotgate, Stamford, Lincs PE9 2YB
Tel: 0780 51199
West: 84 Aldridge Road, Perry Bar,
Birmingham B42 2TD Tel: 021 356 7306

North: 43 East Parade, Harrogate, North
Yorkshire HG1 5LQ Tel: 0423 568162/3
Northern Ireland: Segal House, 4 Annadale
Avenue, Belfast BT7 3JH Tel: 0232 691351
Wales: 169A City Road, Cardiff CF2 2JB Tel:
0222 494933

AGE RANGE:
Any
NUMBERS PASSING THROUGH:
40,000 members
HOW TO CONTACT:
Letter or telephone to Head Office or regional
offices who will put you in touch with nearest
Gateway group
REGIONS SERVICED:
England, Northern Ireland, Wales
SPECIAL NEEDS PROVISION:
Exclusively for people with learning
disabilities, although any young people can
join clubs as volunteers
COSTS/WAITING LISTS:
Gateway clubs set their own membership fees
which are usually very low or even free

NATIONAL FEDERATION OF MUSIC SOCIETIES (NFMS)
Francis House
Francis Street
London SW1P 1DE
Tel: 071 828 7320 Fax: 071 828 5504

NFMS is the national body covering all types of
music societies. They can put you in touch with

a local society or offer help and advice to anyone who wants to set up a new music club or society. Most of their member societies are orchestras and choirs but they are keen to encourage other types of music such as jazz, steel bands, folk music, Indian music etc.

REGIONAL ADDRESSES:
12 regions – contact through Head Office
AGE RANGE:
Any
HOW TO CONTACT:
Telephone Head Office who will put you in touch with a local regional contact
REGIONS SERVICED:
England, Wales and Scotland
SPECIAL NEEDS PROVISION:
Depends on individual societies
COSTS/WAITING LISTS:
Costs vary between societies

NATIONAL FEDERATION OF YOUNG FARMERS CLUBS (NFYFC)
National Agricultural Centre
Stoneleigh Park
Kenilworth
Warwickshire CV8 2LG
Tel: 0203 696544 Fax: 0203 696559

The services provided by YFCs include educational services e.g. courses, seminars, publications and training aids; many social functions; competitions held at regional and national level; the opportunity to travel via the international exchange programme; a wide range of sporting activities; encouragement for young people to take an interest in and express an opinion on farming and countryside issues.

REGIONAL ADDRESSES:
Wales: YFC Centre, Llanelwedd, Builth Wells, Powys LD2 3SY Tel: 0982 553502
AGE RANGE:
10-26
NUMBERS PASSING THROUGH:
37,500 members
HOW TO CONTACT:
Telephone or letter to Head Office or any County Office (listed in telephone book)
REGIONS SERVICED:
All of Wales and the majority of England
SPECIAL NEEDS PROVISION:
No special provision but every effort made to accommodate special requirements when the need arises
COSTS/WAITING LISTS:
Annual subscriptions vary between £5 and £10

NATIONAL MUSEUM OF PHOTOGRAPHY, FILM AND TELEVISION (NMPFT)
Pictureville
Bradford
West Yorkshire BD1 1NQ
Tel: 0274 727488 (Museum), 0274 725347 (Education Unit) Fax: 0274 723155

The museum has six storeys of interactive exhibitions and displays taking you into the fascinating worlds of television, film and photography. It also houses Britain's only IMAX cinema – with daily showings of a changing programme of films on the 52' x 64' screen – and is the home to the first museum resident theatre company, Action Replay, whose regular performances around the Museum bring displays and exhibitions to life. The Education Unit organises a programme of talks, workshops, demonstrations etc. as well as special events and courses for young people including the Co-op Young People's Film and Video Festival, summer workshops and much more. The Museum, jointly with Bradford University, runs a BSc course in Electronic Imaging.

AGE RANGE:
Any
NUMBERS PASSING THROUGH:
750,000 each year
HOW TO CONTACT:
By letter or phone
REGIONS SERVICED:
UK
SPECIAL NEEDS PROVISION:
Museum is accessible to people with special needs with ramps and lifts to the entrance and all levels. IMAX cinema can accommodate two wheelchairs – advance booking for these spaces is strongly recommended

COSTS/WAITING LISTS:
Charges made for some events/workshops.
School groups should make contact approx. 1
term in advance. Individuals should book for
IMAX 1 week in advance

NATIONAL RECORDER SCHOOL OF SCOTLAND (NYROS)
Scottish Amateur Music Association
PO Box 1085
Bearsden
Glasgow G61 4AP
Tel: 0360 60021

Young musicians are invited to apply for the
1994 course which will be held at Craigie
College, Ayr in September. No audition required
but players should be Grade 4 to benefit fully
from the course. Auditions for the Advanced
Group will be held during the first session.

AGE RANGE:
Any
NUMBERS PASSING THROUGH:
70
HOW TO CONTACT:
By telephone or letter for further information
REGIONS SERVICED:
UK but mainly Scotland
SPECIAL NEEDS PROVISION:
Special tuition at an advanced level is
available

COSTS/WAITING LISTS:
There is a course fee of £80 which includes
tuition, accommodation and the services of a
professional Director. Some Local Authority
grants may be available. Waiting lists can be
up to 6 months preceding the next year's
course

NATIONAL RESOURCE CENTRE FOR
DANCE (NRCD)
University of Surrey
Guildford
Surrey GU2 5XH
Tel: 0483 509316

NRCD was established to provide information
on all aspects of dance and will direct enquiries
to other sources where appropriate. Membership
of NRCD offers access to a reference library/
archive (also open to visitors), courses and
seminars, a range of directories/publications/
catalogues/periodicals, and to news of NRCD's
latest activities/courses/plans etc.

MEMBERSHIP:
Corporate: £40; Group: £30; Individual: £10

NATIONAL SOCIETY FOR EDUCATION IN ART AND DESIGN (NSEAD)
The Gatehouse
Corsham Court
Corsham
Wiltshire SN13 0BZ
Tel: 0249 714825

The NSEAD produce a *A Guide to Courses and Careers in Art, Craft and Design* (£12.15 inc. p&p), a publication providing general information about all routes to gaining employment in the field of art, craft and design. A free booklist of publications related to art and design is also available on request.

NATIONAL STUDENT DRAMA FESTIVAL (NSDF)
20 Lansdowne Road
Muswell Hill
London N10 2AU
Tel: 081 883 4586 Fax: 081 883 7142

The NSDF gives an annual national platform for 1 week during the Easter vacation for the work of talented students, with productions often transferring to the Edinburgh Festival. You don't need to enter a production or be a student to attend and see the 14 or so selected productions, join in the discussions, write for the daily Festival newspaper, join the Tech Team, help with the organisation or participate in the excellent range of daily, professionally led workshops. Contact the NSDF at the above address for details of how to enter a production or participate in the Festival.

AGE RANGE:
Any, but usually about 17+
HOW TO CONTACT:
Contact above for further information
REGIONS SERVICED:
UK

NATIONAL STUDENT THEATRE COMPANY (NSTC)
20 Lansdowne Road
Muswell Hill
London N10 2AU
Tel: 081 883 4586 Fax: 081 883 7142

The NSTC is open to all current British students or recent graduates and aims to channel the best student talents, especially those discovered through the annual National Student Drama Festival (NSDF – see separate entry), into an outstanding company, of which the hallmarks are excellence, professional discipline, total commitment and high entertainment value. The company mainly operates in the summer vacation and forms afresh after each NSDF (around Easter). Technicians, admin and publicity personnel should ideally first apply to help at the Easter NSDF. Actors and musicians should apply from the third week in April onwards with auditions held from May. Several

productions are taken to the Edinburgh Fringe
Festival each year, where the company has
been particularly successful.

AGE RANGE:
17+
HOW TO CONTACT:
Contact above address
REGIONS SERVICED:
UK
COSTS/WAITING LISTS:
For the last 2 years the company has been
unsponsored, which means that members
have to be able to support themselves. Any
profits are shared, but there is fierce
competition for audiences at the Edinburgh
Festival and no one should rely on receiving
anything back. So you will need to find
accommodation costs (flat-sharing can cost
around £55 a week for 4 weeks in
Edinburgh), travel and food costs, as well as
any London rehearsal expenses. The NSTC
can find you accommodation in Edinburgh,
but not, usually, in London.

NATIONAL TRUST (ACORN PROJECTS)
PO Box 12
Westbury
Wiltshire BA13 4NA
Tel: 0373 826826 Fax: 0373 827162

If you have 1 or 2 weeks to spare, or even just a
weekend, why not volunteer for an Acorn

Working Holiday, helping on an outdoor conservation project on a site in the care of the National Trust? Projects cover a wide range of tasks and you could be helping to maintain woodland paths, drystone walling, restoring farm buildings, or even surveying cliff vegetation. Food and accommodation are provided. There are over 420 projects taking place all year round. A comprehensive brochure is available free from the Volunteer Office at the above address.

REGIONAL ADDRESSES:
Available from Head Office
AGE RANGE:
16+
NUMBERS PASSING THROUGH:
3,500 per annum
HOW TO CONTACT:
Telephone or write to the National Trust Volunteer Office at the above address
REGIONS SERVICED:
England, Wales and Northern Ireland
COSTS/WAITING LISTS:
1 week usually costs about £35; weekend projects about £10. Fees go towards the cost of food and accommodation. Volunteers pay their own travelling expenses

NATIONAL TRUST FOR SCOTLAND
CONSERVATION VOLUNTEERS (NTS)
The Conservation Volunteer Co-ordinator
5 Charlotte Square
Edinburgh EH2 4DU
Tel: 031 226 5922 Fax: 031 243 9302

Conservation volunteers carry out practical conservation work at countryside properties in the care of the Trust throughout Scotland. There are two ways to become involved – Thistle Camps and the local Conservation Volunteers groups. Thistle Camps, lasting 1 or 2 weeks, take place between March and October each year and are located throughout Scotland on Trust properties. The five local groups – Glasgow, Lothian, Grampian, Tayside and Highland – work weekends, throughout the year, and undertake valuable conservation-related work that otherwise might never be possible. By taking part in projects you can learn such traditional skills as drystone walling, footpath construction or woodland management and make a positive contribution to the care and protection of Scotland's countryside and wildlife. Opportunities are available to attend courses in countryside skills and to learn at first hand how the Ranger/Naturalist service works.

REGIONAL ADDRESSES:
Five Regional Offices. Contact Head Office in the first instance

AGE RANGE:
16+
HOW TO CONTACT:
Write to the Conservation Volunteer Co-ordinator at the above address for full details
COSTS/WAITING LISTS:
The Thistle Camp programme is published in January and rapidly becomes fully booked; applicants are advised to book early. The five local group programmes are published twice yearly, in March and September

---

NATIONAL UNION OF STUDENTS (NUS)
Nelson Mandela House
461 Holloway Road
London N7 6LJ
Tel: 071 272 8900 Fax: 071 263 5713

NUS provides information and services to all young people continuing education after school, whether in further or higher education. Advice and information can be provided on welfare matters such as student hardship, grants and housing; educational matters (although not on actual courses) and legal help plus much more.

REGIONAL ADDRESSES:
Available from Head Office
AGE RANGE:
Any
HOW TO CONTACT:
Telephone Head Office for advice and

services. Regional Offices for union
developments etc.
REGIONS SERVICED:
UK
SPECIAL NEEDS PROVISION:
Information service available
COSTS/WAITING LISTS:
No costs for information

**NATIONAL VOCATIONAL
QUALIFICATIONS (NVQs)**
National Council for Vocational
Qualifications
222 Euston Road
London NW1 2BZ
Tel: 071 387 9898

NVQs are work-related qualifications based on
national standards set by industry and
commerce, designed to reward individuals who
can demonstrate competence in their
performance at work. Each NVQ is made up of
a number of units. Each unit is certificated
separately, which enables you to choose which
units to study and at the pace that suits you best.
It is up to you how and where you study,
whether at work, at college or at home. More
information on NVQs is available from schools
careers services and Careers Offices (look in the
phone book under 'C').

AGE RANGE:
Any

HOW TO CONTACT:
Letter or telephone to above address
REGIONS SERVICED:
England, Wales and Northern Ireland. See
entry SCOTVEC for Scottish provision

NATIONAL YOUTH AGENCY (NYA)
17-23 Albion Street
Leicester LE1 6GD
Tel: 0533 471200 Fax: 0533 471043

The National Youth Agency is the central agency
providing information, advice and curriculum
development materials for young people and all
those who work with them. Its activities include
answering enquiries using the agency's extensive
library facilities, compiling regularly updated
reading and resource lists and information packs,
publishing a range of new materials on issues
which affect young people, and generally
providing an overview of what is going on for
young people throughout the UK.

HOW TO CONTACT:
Letter, telephone or fax to above address
REGIONS SERVICED:
UK
COSTS/WAITING LISTS:
None for information

NATIONAL YOUTH BRASS BAND OF SCOTLAND (NYBBS)

Scottish Amateur Music Association
PO Box 1085
Bearsden
Glasgow G61 4AP
Tel: 0360 60021

Young brass musicians are invited to audition for a place in the NYBBS. The 1994 course will be held at St Andrews University, Fife from 5-11 July. Candidates must have attained a standard equivalent to Grade 6 and be prepared to sight-read, be proficient in scales and arpeggios and to perform two contrasting pieces.

AGE RANGE:
Up to 21
NUMBERS PASSING THROUGH:
73
HOW TO CONTACT:
By telephone or letter for further information
REGIONS SERVICED:
UK but mainly Scotland
SPECIAL NEEDS PROVISION:
Special tuition at an advanced level available
COSTS/WAITING LISTS:
There is a course fee of £195 which includes tuition, accommodation and the services of a professional conductor. Some local authority grants may be available. The Carnegie UK Trust has funded a special bursary scheme for those in need. Applications are treated on

merit. Waiting lists can be up to 6 months preceding the next year's course

---

NATIONAL YOUTH JAZZ ORCHESTRA OF GREAT BRITAIN (NYJO)
11 Victor Road
Harrow
Middlesex HA2 6PT
Tel: 081 863 2717 Fax: 081 863 8685

NYJO holds open rehearsals for anybody interested in a career in jazz. They can provide the opportunity for young people to rehearse with a professional big band and to go on to perform professionally. Applicants need a high level of musical aptitude, but this can be decided upon at rehearsals.

AGE RANGE:
Up to 25
NUMBERS PASSING THROUGH:
c 150
HOW TO CONTACT:
Letter, fax, telephone
REGIONS SERVICED:
UK
SPECIAL NEEDS PROVISION:
Enquiries welcome
COSTS/WAITING LISTS:
None

NATIONAL YOUTH MUSIC THEATRE
(NYMT)
2 Bow Street
Covent Garden
London WC2E 7BA
Tel: 071 836 9791 Fax: 071 240 7949

The NYMT's artistic policy is primarily to create and perform new music theatre works for performance by young people to the highest artistic standards. As well as cast and instrumental performers, an NYMT production will also involve young people in the technical, backstage and wardrobe departments, as well as front of house, box office, publicity and administration, offering them a valuable learning experience. For those not selected through annual auditions, the NYMT holds residential weekend workshops in the spring and autumn which you do not need to audition for.

AGE RANGE:
Workshop courses 11-19; cast performers 11-19; instrumentalists mainly 11-19; technical staff, front of house, box office, press, PR, admin assistants 16-25
HOW TO CONTACT:
By telephone or letter (with SAE) for information and application forms for workshops and/or national annual auditions
REGIONS SERVICED:
UK

SPECIAL NEEDS PROVISION:
No provision as yet
COSTS/WAITING LISTS:
A residential workshop weekend costs about
£75. Residential, rehearsal and performance
weeks cost about £150 per week. There are
various possible sources of funding e.g.
schools, Local Education Authorities, Prince's
Trust, individual fund-raising activities, local
sponsorship etc. Contact in September for
auditions, any time for workshops and in
January-April for working backstage, box
office etc.

NATIONAL YOUTH ORCHESTRA OF GREAT BRITAIN (NYO)
Causeway House
Lodge Causeway
Fishponds
Bristol BS16 3HD
Tel: 0272 650036 Fax: 0272 585311

Musicians under the age of 18 who play
orchestral instruments and have achieved Grade
8 with distinction in Associated Board
Examinations or are of an equivalent standard
can apply to join the NYO. Auditions are held
each year for about 50 places and those selected
meet on three residential courses a year with
over 150 other young musicians to rehearse and
perform, with coaching from top professional
musicians and prestigious conductors. Each

course lasts about 10 days and ends with concerts at venues such as the Proms in London, Symphony Hall, Birmingham, Glasgow, Leeds, Newcastle etc.

AGE RANGE:
19 and under
NUMBERS PASSING THROUGH:
155
HOW TO CONTACT:
Telephone or letter for further information and an application form
REGIONS SERVICED:
UK
SPECIAL NEEDS PROVISION:
Applications welcome
COSTS/WAITING LISTS:
Course fees are £200 per course plus travel. Funding is available from various sources e.g. Local Education Authorities, trusts, local business, NYO Bursary Fund etc. The NYO provides full board and travel to concerts. About 400 people audition for approx. 50 places each year. Applications must be received by 30 June for auditions in September/October and entry into the Orchestra at Christmas

NATIONAL YOUTH STRING ORCHESTRA OF SCOTLAND (NYSOS)

Scottish Amateur Music Association
PO Box 1085
Bearsden
Glasgow G61 4AP
Tel: 0360 60021

Young musicians are invited to audition for a place in the NYSOS. The 1994 course will be held at St Andrews University, Fife from 7-13 August. Candidates must have attained a standard equivalent to Grade 7 and be prepared to sight-read, be proficient in scales and arpeggios and to perform two contrasting pieces.

AGE RANGE:
Up to 21
NUMBERS PASSING THROUGH:
60
HOW TO CONTACT:
By telephone or letter for further information
REGIONS SERVICED:
UK but mainly Scotland
SPECIAL NEEDS PROVISION:
Special tuition at an advanced level available
COSTS/WAITING LISTS:
There is a course fee of £195 which includes tuition, accommodation and the services of a professional conductor. Some local authority grants may be available. Waiting lists can be up to 6 months preceding the next year's course

NATIONAL YOUTH THEATRE OF GREAT BRITAIN (NYT)
443-445 Holloway Road
London N7 6LW
Tel: 071 281 3863 Fax: 071 281 8246

The NYT gives young people the chance to join a team which mounts productions in professional theatres. Productions may take place in London or tour the country or occasionally visit a theatre abroad. The NYT's members join in all departments of theatre work – not just acting – such as design, lighting and sound, costume and stage management. Enthusiasm and an interest in theatre are more important than talent.

AGE RANGE:
14-21
NUMBERS PASSING THROUGH:
c 500
HOW TO CONTACT:
By letter to above asking for an audition or interview depending on which area of theatre you are interested in. Auditions are held throughout the UK
REGIONS SERVICED:
UK
SPECIAL NEEDS PROVISION:
To date no special provision has been necessary as all members have fitted in perfectly well regardless of ability
COSTS/WAITING LISTS:
Audition/Interview Fee: £6. Acting courses

for first-year members: Junior Course:£115 (2 weeks); Senior Course: £165 (3 weeks). After first year there is no fee, but members have to meet the cost of accommodation, travel and subsistence. Funding may be available from Local Education Authorities, Prince's Trust etc. and the NYT has its own Bursary Fund to help in difficult cases. Apply in October of each year. All applicants are seen and many re-apply the following year

NATIONAL YOUTH WIND ENSEMBLE/ NATIONAL YOUTH SYMPHONIC BAND OF SCOTLAND
Scottish Amateur Music Association
PO Box 1085
Bearsden
Glasgow G61 4AP
Tel: 0360 60021

Young musicians are invited to audition for a place in the bands. A 1994 course for the bands will be held from 1-8 August at St Andrews University, Fife. Candidates must have attained a standard equivalent to Grade 6 and be prepared to sight-read, be proficient in scales and arpeggios and to perform two contrasting pieces.

AGE RANGE:
Up to 21
NUMBERS PASSING THROUGH:
90

HOW TO CONTACT:
By telephone or letter for further information
REGIONS SERVICED:
UK but mainly Scotland
SPECIAL NEEDS PROVISION:
Special tuition at an advanced level available
COSTS/WAITING LISTS:
There is a course fee of £195 which includes
tuition, accommodation and the services of a
professional conductor. Some Local
Authority grants may be available. Waiting
lists can be up to 6 months preceding the
next year's course

NORMAN HART MEMORIAL FUND
European Movement
158 Buckingham Palace Road
London SW1W 9TR

The Norman Hart Memorial Fund offers grants
for young people undertaking work or study
projects in European Countries. A limited
number of grants to cover travel and related
costs are offered each year to supplement finance
from other sources, or as initial funding for
applicants seeking further support elsewhere.
Awards are made to young people of UK
nationality and residence who plan short periods
of study or work on projects that further the aims
of European unification. Particular stress is
placed on the individual initiative shown by the
applicants. The projects can be in the political,
economic, social, cultural, professional,

vocational, industrial or commercial fields and applicants, if awarded a grant, are asked to report to the trustees on the conclusion of their projects.

AGE RANGE:
18-25
NUMBERS PASSING THROUGH:
Nine grants totalling £3,000 made in 1991
HOW TO CONTACT:
By letter only to the Secretary of the Trust for a leaflet, explanatory notes and an application form
REGIONS SERVICED:
UK
COSTS/WAITING LISTS:
Applications may be made at any time of the year though submission in the early months is recommended. Applications for grants for projects to be undertaken during the summer months should be submitted by 31 May at the latest

---

OCCUPATIONS (publication)
Careers and Occupational Information Centre
(COIC)
PO Box 348
Bristol
BS99 7FE
Tel: 0272 777199

Occupations a unique careers directory. An invaluable reference book, it lists over 600 different types of jobs and careers from unskilled work to professional occupations. Each entry describes the type of work involved, the working environment, pay and conditions, job opportunities and prospects, personal characteristics required, entry requirements and training available as well as where to go to find out more information. Price £23.00. Available in bookshops, Careers Offices, libraries or direct from the above address (price £25.30 inc. p&p).

OCEAN YOUTH CLUB (OYC)
The Bus Station
South Street
Gosport
Hampshire PO12 1EP
Tel: 0705 528421; Bookings 0705 501211
Fax: 0705 522069

Ocean Youth Club is a national voluntary youth organisation which aims to provide young people no matter what their circumstances with the opportunity to experience the challenge and adventure of life at sea. We operate ten ocean-going vessels based around the British Isles for young people aged 12 upwards. No previous sailing experience is required and we provide all the safety equipment, instruction, food and insurance. All you need to be is reasonably fit and able to swim. It's a prime opportunity to meet new friends – you will be involved in everything on board from sailing and navigation to cooking and cleaning, under the watchful eye of a certified skipper and a team of qualified watch leaders. Those who wish to continue sailing with OYC can join our training scheme and progress to skipper if they wish. You are also encouraged to get involved in the boats' winter refits and attend reunions and parties at the end of the sailing season.

REGIONAL ADDRESSES:
Central office: The Bus Station, South Street, Gosport, Hampshire PO12 1EP Tel: 0705 528421
Northern Ireland: Rodgers Quay, Carrickfergus Marina, Carrickfergus, Co. Antrim BT38 8BE Tel: 09603 66776
Scotland: Kip Marina, Inverkip PA16 0AS Tel: 0475 521294
North-west: CCE Business Centre, Windmill Lane, Denton, Tameside M34 3QS Tel: 061 335 9032
London: PO Box 730, 20 Farringdon Street, London EC4A 4PP Tel: 071 325 2960

AGE RANGE:
12-24

NUMBERS PASSING THROUGH:
4,000 sailed in 1992

HOW TO CONTACT:
By telephone to your nearest office above or by letter to Central Office, Gosport

REGIONS SERVICED:
UK and rest of Europe

SPECIAL NEEDS PROVISION:
OYC regularly run cruises for young people

with special needs. All vessels are fitted with
audio compasses to assist visually impaired
voyagers

COSTS/WAITING LISTS:
Voyages cost about £30-£40 a day depending
on the time of season. OYC does have a
grant scheme but young people are
encouraged to raise some funds themselves.
Peak season always books up early –
telephone for availability

OCKENDEN VENTURE
Constitution Hill
Woking
Surrey GU22 7UU
Tel: 0483 772012/3 Fax: 0483 750774

Volunteers are recruited to look after refugees at
various homes and reception centres in the UK,
giving them the opportunity, through working
as part of a team and using initiative, to learn
about others and themselves in all types of
situations. Volunteers are normally recruited
for 1 year, but shorter-term vacancies do
occasionally occur. The main recruitment period
is in August/September. Volunteers receive
board and lodging and between £22 and £25 a
week pocket money.

REGIONAL ADDRESSES:
Contact through HQ
AGE RANGE:
18+

NUMBERS PASSING THROUGH:
8 volunteers at any one time
HOW TO CONTACT:
Letter with SAE for further information
REGIONS SERVICED:
UK
SPECIAL NEEDS PROVISION:
No provision
COSTS/WAITING LISTS:
Advisable to enquire a few months in advance

ODYSSEY TRAVEL CLUB
Odyssey International
21 Cambridge Road
Waterbeach
Cambridge CB5 9NJ
Tel: 0223 861079 Fax: 0223 861079

The number of young people travelling or taking a year out from education is on the increase. Many others would like to travel but don't have anyone to go with or are put off by expensive single supplements. The Odyssey Travel Club can help by bringing together like-minded travellers with similar interests and plans. If you are seeking a companion or just travel advice contact the Odyssey Travel Club.

AGE RANGE:
17+
NUMBERS PASSING THROUGH:
2,000

HOW TO CONTACT:
Telephone or letter for further information
REGIONS SERVICED:
UK
SPECIAL NEEDS PROVISION:
No special provision
COSTS/WAITING LISTS:
Annual membership fee is £20, which
includes contact service, advice line,
quarterly newsletter, discounted activity
breaks/holidays and discounted travel
insurance

THE OPEN COLLEGE (OC)
Customer Services
St Paul's
781 Wilmslow Road
Didsbury
Manchester M20 8RW
Tel: 061 434 0007

The Open College offers a range of work skills
courses through 'open learning'. This system
allows you to study at your own pace using
specially designed course books, audio and
visual tapes. Open College training materials
offer a valuable learning experience in their
own right. However, to gain full benefit from
studying our materials we recommend that you
obtain tutor support from a local college or
training centre. This is advisable for all learners,
but it is usually essential if you wish to work
towards a qualification.

REGIONAL ADDRESSES:
All enquiries through above address
AGE RANGE:
Any
REGIONS SERVICED:
UK
SPECIAL NEEDS PROVISION:
Anyone can use the Open College
COSTS/WAITING LISTS:
From £25 to over £120

THE OPEN UNIVERSITY (OU)
Walton Hall
Milton Keynes MK7 6AA
Tel: 0908 274066

The Open University offers a different way of
studying a degree-level course. Learning is
through correspondence materials, audio and
radio and television broadcasts and course books
as well as residential summer courses. The
structure of the courses allows students to study
at their own pace.

AGE RANGE:
Over 18
HOW TO CONTACT:
Write to the Central Enquiry Service (CES),
PO Box 200, Walton Hall, Milton Keynes
MK7 6YZ Tel: 0908 653231
REGIONS SERVICED:
UK and Europe

SPECIAL NEEDS PROVISION:
The OU has a specialist adviser for students
with disabilities
COSTS/WAITING LISTS:
Details of course fees are available from CES.
Help may be available from the Local
Education Authority

OPERATION RALEIGH see RALEIGH
INTERNATIONAL

OPPORTUNITIES FOR PEOPLE WITH
DISABILITIES
1 Bank Buildings
Princes Street
London EC2R 8EU
Tel & Fax: 071 726 4961 Minicom: 071 726
4963

Opportunities for People with Disabilities finds
fulfilling employment for disabled people. Job-
seekers who have successfully found jobs have
a number of types of disability – deafness,
blindness, epilepsy, amputation, cerebral palsy,
spina bifida, paraplegia, multiple sclerosis,
learning difficulties and many more. To date,
over 3,000 people with disabilities have found
employment through its network of Regional
Operating Centres. Opportunities is a sponsor
of the Sheltered Placement Scheme, and operates
three Jobclubs for disabled people, two of which
are specialist Jobclubs for deaf people.

AGE RANGE:
16-65
HOW TO CONTACT:
Telephone, fax or letter plus SAE to local
Regional Operating Centre (details from
above address)
REGIONS SERVICED:
UK
COSTS/WAITING LISTS:
Free service and immediate access

OPSIS
National Association for the Education,
Training and Support of Blind and Partially
Sighted People
Albany House
5 New Street
Salisbury
Wiltshire SP1 2PH
Tel: 0722 410234 Fax: 0722 410044

Opsis is an association of six charities all
providing support services for blind and partially
sighted people. Education at all levels and
vocational training are particular features.
Visually impaired people or their parents who
would like more information are invited to
contact the Secretary General at the above
address. They will then be put in direct touch
with one of the Opsis member organisations.

AGE RANGE:
Up to 21 (or older, by discussion)

HOW TO CONTACT:
Letter, telephone or fax to above address
REGIONS SERVICED:
UK
COSTS/WAITING LISTS:
Dependent on services provided

ORGANISATION FOR BLACK ARTS ADVANCEMENT AND LEARNING ACTIVITIES (OBAALA)
Obaala House
225 Seven Sisters Road
London N4 2DA
Tel: 071 263 1918

OBAALA aims to create a greater awareness of Black art, runs a bookshop and gallery, a summer arts school, and an annual project for 11-16 year-old African-Caribbean young people.

OUTSET – Action on Disability
18 Creekside
London SE8 3DZ
Tel: 081 692 7141 Fax: 081 469 2532

Outset is the national charity which develops technology-related employment opportunities for people with disabilities. Through a network of ten centres they provide information technology and business skills training. This is backed by job-match and post-recruitment support. Outset's Consultancy Service works with Local Authorities, Health Authorities, trusts, TECs and the private sector to improve local opportunities and service provision. Outset also offers Disability Awareness Training and has an Initiatives Database providing information on all aspects of employment and disability. Outset's Business Services Division runs a mailing house and office services bureaux directly employing people with disabilities. The division offers a wide range of services to a variety of clients.

OUTWARD BOUND TRUST
Chestnut Field
Regent Place
Rugby
Warwickshire CV21 2PJ
Tel: 0788 560423 Fax: 0788 541069

The Outward Bound Trust runs a wide range of adventure courses and expeditions, available to all. The courses can be 'centre-based' at one of Outward Bound's residential settings, or you can find yourself trekking through the wilderness with little more than a tent between you and the elements. The courses and programmes usually run for between a week and a month and they provide a range of opportunities for you to enjoy the experience and challenge of adventure. Activities include rock-climbing, abseiling, the Outward Bound ropes course, orienteering, sailing, Canadian canoeing and kayaking, caving and expeditions. The expedition courses are probably the most challenging and demanding of the courses on offer. They take place in wilderness areas, with every night spent under canvas, often far from civilisation. Outward Bound recommend that people attend courses as individuals although they will accept group enquiries. Whatever, you are encouraged to participate as part of a team and to stretch yourself to the limits on these courses. The Trust also run other types of schemes, including City Challenge courses where participants are given the opportunity for personal development through a series of challenging placements working with disadvantaged people in the community, or Urban Schemes which were developed to enable young people from the inner cities to benefit from Outward Bound courses. A network of centres is developing throughout Europe, so there are opportunities abroad too. Contact Head Office for a brochure covering the full range of opportunities on offer.

REGIONAL ADDRESSES:
There are a number of regional centres.
Details of your nearest centre from Head Office
AGE RANGE:
Any. Minimum 14
NUMBERS PASSING THROUGH:
c 500
HOW TO CONTACT:
By letter or telephone to Head Office for advice, information and brochure

REGIONS SERVICED:
UK
SPECIAL NEEDS PROVISION:
Enquiries welcome
COSTS/WAITING LISTS:
The fees for all courses are fully inclusive of
all accommodation, specialist equipment,
tuition etc. They range from approx. £180-
£550. Young people between 14 and 24 may
qualify for financial help up to 50% of the
cost of a course. Details from the Trust.
Courses during the summer months do tend
to get filled quickly, so apply early

OVERSEAS JOBS EXPRESS
PO Box 22
Brighton BN1 6HX
Tel: 0273 440220 Fax: 0273 440229

Overseas Jobs Express publishes a fortnightly
newspaper for international job-seekers. Each
issue contains editorial features and job
vacancies in up to 30 job categories: those of
particular interest to young people include
agriculture, education (particularly TEFL), hotel
and catering, nanny and au pair, sales and
marketing, seasonal and secretarial. Overseas
Jobs Express also publishes books and guides:
*Casual Work Worldwide, Working Holidays in
Australia, Teaching English Abroad, Working
inTravel and Tourism, Voluntary Work
Worldwide* and *Au Pair and Nanny Jobs
Worldwide.*

COSTS/WAITING LISTS:
Newspaper is sold on subscription – 3 months
(6 issues) costs £18. The books and guides listed
above are all priced at £5.99 (inc. p&p)

OVERSEAS PLACING UNIT (EMPLOYMENT SERVICE) (OPU)

c/o Rockingham House
13 West Street
Sheffield S1 4ER

The OPU can give advice and guidance through
Jobcentres to anyone who wants to take up
employment overseas .

AGE RANGE:
18+ for vacancy applications; 16+ for
information packs
NUMBERS PASSING THROUGH:
500-800 enquiries monthly
HOW TO CONTACT:
By visiting any Jobcentre for information on
specific countries
REGIONS SERVICED:
UK
SPECIAL NEEDS PROVISION:
Each enquiry dealt with individually
COSTS/WAITING LISTS:
The service is free. Contact your local
Jobcentre at least 1 month before you intend
travelling

OVERSEAS VOLUNTEER SCHEME OF THE BRITISH AND FOREIGN SCHOOL SOCIETY
The Richard Mayo Hall
Eden Street
Kingston-upon-Thames KT1 1HZ
Tel: 081 546 2379

The BFSS Overseas Volunteers Scheme, working in liaison with existing school and community links, provides financial help to school leavers wishing to spend from 9 months a year teaching in a developing country. It also supports educational visits to Britain by people from developing countries.
For more information, please write to the Secretary.

PARTNERS IN EUROPE
The Prince's Trust
8 Bedford Row
London WC1R 4BA
Tel: 071 405 5799 Fax: 071 831 7280

Partners in Europe aims to support young people in developing lasting links with European counterparts. Small development grants (maximum £500) called Go and See and more substantial follow-up grants called Go Ahead are available for young people with ideas for working with a European counterpart. Partners in Europe is part of the Prince's Trust and is sponsored by Severn Trent plc.

AGE RANGE:
Under 26 and out of full-time education.
Under 31 for people with disabilities
NUMBERS PASSING THROUGH:
Approximately 200 grants awarded each year
HOW TO CONTACT:
By phone or letter
REGIONS SERVICED:
UK

PEAK PARK CONSERVATION VOLUNTEERS (PPCV)

The Volunteers Organiser
Peak Park Joint Planning Board
Aldern House
Baslow Road
Bakewell
Derbyshire DE45 1AE
Tel: 0629 814321 (ext. 339)
Fax: 0629 812659

The National Park Ranger Service enables volunteers of all ages and backgrounds to become actively involved in many types of practical conservation projects throughout the Peak District National Park. The projects include footpath construction and erosion control, fencing, walling, tree-planting, scrub clearance, simple nature reserve management and much more. The project tasks are led by a Ranger/ Supervisor and tools, materials and a lunchtime brew are provided. Tasks are arranged all year

round for each weekend although limited
opportunities exist during the midweek period.

AGE RANGE:
14-66
NUMBERS PASSING THROUGH:
Over 3,000 per year
HOW TO CONTACT:
Telephone, letter, fax or in person for
information and leaflets
REGIONS SERVICED:
Peak National Park
SPECIAL NEEDS PROVISION:
Enquiries welcome
COSTS/WAITING LISTS:
Membership is 50p per year for individuals

PENFRIENDS WORLDWIDE
PO Box 87
Douglas
Isle of Man
Tel: 0624 612035

International correspondence service accepting
members of all ages from any country in the
world. Special sections for stamp collectors,
language students etc.

AGE RANGE:
Any
HOW TO CONTACT:
By letter for brochure containing full

information plus application form
REGIONS SERVICED:
UK
COSTS/WAITING LISTS:
16 and under: £5 fee; 17+: £10 fee

PETRA (EUROPEAN COMMUNITY PETRA PROGRAMME)

c/o The Central Bureau for Educational Visits
and Exchanges
Seymour Mews House
Seymour Mews
London SW1H 9PE
Tel: 071 486 5101

PETRA is a European Community programme
for the vocational training of young people and
their preparation for adult and working life. It
has recently been extended, and the revised
programme now incorporates the EC Young
Worker Exchange Programme. One of the ways
PETRA can be of direct benefit to young people
is by providing financial support for individuals
aged 16-27 to benefit from a vocational training/
work experience placement in another EC
Member State.

Short-term placements are aimed at young
people in initial vocational training and are
normally of 3 weeks' duration. Long-term
placements are aimed at those who are either in
employment, available on the labour market or
taking part in an advanced training programme
after starting work. The average duration of

these placements is 3 months.

Financial assistance is available as a contribution towards accommodation, food, insurance, pocket money, language tuition, local travel, travel costs to and from host country (normally 75% of economy fare). In the case of short-term projects, grants will only be made payable to project organisers and not to individuals.

AGE RANGE:
16-27

HOW TO CONTACT:
Contact the Central Bureau at the above address for details of how to apply to take part in the programme

REGIONS SERVICED:
UK

SPECIAL NEEDS PROVISION:
Enquiries welcome

COSTS/WAITING LISTS:
No costs to individuals – placements are funded by the EEC and training organisations

---

PHAB
12-14 London Road
Croydon CR0 2TA
Tel: 081 667 9443 Fax: 081 681 1399

PHAB is an organisation working towards the integration of physically disabled people into the community via youth clubs, holidays and training facilities. Join a PHAB club and participate alongside young people with and

without a physical disability in a wide range of
activities, e.g. sailing, rock-climbing, snooker,
table tennis etc., as well as enjoying holidays
together and weekends away. Enquiries from
volunteers welcome.

REGIONAL ADDRESSES:
Details available from Head Office
AGE RANGE:
Any
NUMBERS PASSING THROUGH:
18,000
HOW TO CONTACT:
Letter, telephone or fax, ideally through
regional offices (see telephone directory), but
can be contacted through Head Office for
information on clubs, holidays, activities etc.
REGIONS SERVICED:
UK
SPECIAL NEEDS PROVISION:
All members can participate in any activity
COSTS/WAITING LISTS:
Small club subscription. Some activities/
holidays are subsidised by various trusts

PLAID CYMRU
51 Cathedral Road
Cardiff CF1 9HD
Tel: 0222 231944

THE POETRY SOCIETY
22 Betterton Street
London WC2H 9BU
Tel: 071 240 4810 Fax: 071 240 4818

The Society is a membership organisation which aims to promote all aspects of poetry and encourage interest in poetry including among young people. They can provide advice and information on poetry competitions, workshops, contact names and addresses of relevant organisations as well as details on how to go about getting poetry published. The Society's Education Department administrates the WH Smith Poets in Schools Scheme and publishes the termly *Schools Poetry Review*.

AGE RANGE:
Any
NUMBERS PASSING THROUGH:
400-500
HOW TO CONTACT:
By telephone or letter (with SAE) for advice and further information
REGIONS SERVICED:
UK
SPECIAL NEEDS PROVISION:
Anyone with an interest in poetry can use the services of the society
COSTS/WAITING LISTS:
None

POLICE RECRUITMENT DEPARTMENT
F5-Division
Room 516
Home Office
50 Queen Anne's Gate
London SW1H 9AT
Tel: 071 273 3797

The 40+ police forces in England and Wales recruit independently so if you are interested in joining a particular force write to the Chief Officer of that force for further information. You can contact the Police Recruitment Department. above (Police Division for Scotland, RUC Recruiting Branch for Northern Ireland) for leaflets and information about careers in the police force in general covering the nature of the work, range of opportunities and entry requirements.

REGIONAL OFFICES:
Scotland: Police Division, Scottish Office, Home and Health Department, St Andrews House, Edinburgh EH1 3DE Tel: 031 556 8400
Northern Ireland: RUC Recruiting Branch, RUC Headquarters, Brooklyn, Knock Road, Belfast BT5 6LE Tel: 0232 451881

THE PRINCE'S SCOTTISH YOUTH
BUSINESS TRUST (PSYBT)
6th Floor
Mercantile Chambers
53 Bothwell Street
Glasgow G2 6TS
Tel: 041 248 4999 Fax: 041 248 4836

The aim of the Prince's Scottish Youth Business Trust is to provide seedcorn finance and professional support to young people in Scotland, aged 18-25, whoever they are and wherever they come from, so that they can set up and continue to run their own businesses. The Trust has particular concern for the disadvantaged. Applicants must have a viable business idea, be unable to raise all or part of the finance necessary to set up their own business and be able to work at their business full-time. The Trust offers free professional advice; access to pre-start training; loans of up to £5,000 over a period of up to 5 years at 4% interest; grants of up to £1,000; assistance from professional advisers once the applicant has started trading for a minimum period of 2 years.

REGIONAL ADDRESSES:
18+ Regional Managers – details available from Head Office
AGE RANGE:
18-25
NUMBERS PASSING THROUGH:
460 businesses were set up in the 1990/91

financial year, 437 in 1991/92, 411 in 1992/
93

HOW TO CONTACT:
Contact nearest regional manager through
one of the 44 Enterprise Trusts throughout
Scotland

REGIONS SERVICED:
Scotland

SPECIAL NEEDS PROVISION:
Applications welcome

COSTS/WAITING LISTS:
There are no waiting lists but it normally
takes 12 weeks or more to prepare an
application/business plan and complete the
necessary training before the application is
ready to be processed

THE PRINCE'S TRUST AND THE ROYAL
JUBILEE TRUSTS
8 Bedford Row
London WC1R 4BA
Tel: 071 430 0524 Fax: 071 831 7280

Aim is to assist young people who are in some
way disadvantaged. Grants up to £800 for an
individual or £2,500 for a group are provided to
enable development of individual potential or
to be of service to others in the community. The
Trusts' primary focus for projects is on those
which address needs that are otherwise ignored
and that are original in provision. Shortfall in
statutory funding will not be considered nor will
general fund-raising.

REGIONAL ADDRESSES:
59 local committees covering the UK. Each
have their own contact number available
from the phone book or from the national
number above

AGE RANGE:
14 to 25 inclusive

NUMBERS PASSING THROUGH:
Several thousand grants made each year

HOW TO CONTACT:
By telephone or letter which will be followed
up by a member of the local committee

REGIONS COVERED:
UK

COSTS/WAITING LISTS:
There are no costs to applicants and grants
are not repayable. Committees should be
able to act quickly, the majority providing
funding within 1 month of application

THE PRINCE'S TRUST VOLUNTEERS
8 Jockey's Fields
London WC1R 4BW
Tel: 071 430 0378 Fax: 071 404 5339

A national programme which provides young
people with the opportunity for personal
development training and experience while
working with and in their local community.
Each 15-strong team of volunteers includes a
full mix of young people from different
backgrounds, all walks of life and those who are

employed, unemployed or in education. Each team participates in a 60-day programme which includes team-building, a residential experience and 40 days of either individual placement or team project work in the community. These community opportunities will include environmental and caring experiences. Volunteers who successfully complete the Programme receive a City and Guilds Profile of Achievement, a Prince's Trust Volunteers Certificate and the opportunity during the Programme to attain personal skills qualifications such as the Community Sports Leader Award and a First Aid Certificate.

AGE RANGE:
16-25
NUMBERS PASSING THROUGH:
2,000 per year
HOW TO CONTACT:
Letter or telephone to the above address
REGIONS SERVICED:
UK

THE PRINCE'S YOUTH BUSINESS TRUST (PYBT)
5 Cleveland Place
London SW1Y 6JJ
Tel: 071 321 6500 Fax: 071 839 6494

The Trust is a registered charity which aims to help unemployed young people who would not otherwise have the opportunity to develop their self-confidence, achieve economic independence or contribute to the community through the medium of self-employment. Loans up to £5,000 on easy repayment terms and grants up to £1,500 are awarded to young people with a good business idea but without adequate means to finance it. In addition to finance the Trust provides each supported business with a volunteer Business Adviser and directs the young people to suitable enterprise training. Applicants must have tried but failed to raise all their necessary finance elsewhere.

REGIONAL ADDRESSES:
38 regional addresses throughout England, Wales and Northern Ireland. Consult local telephone directory or call the Head Office at the above address (for Scotland see Prince's Scottish Youth Business Trust

AGE RANGE:
18-29 (up to 30 for disabled people)

NUMBERS PASSING THROUGH:
Approx. 25,000 enquiries each year leading to about 3,000 people receiving grants or loans

HOW TO CONTACT:
By letter or telephone

REGIONS SERVICED:
All parts of England, Wales and Northern Ireland

SPECIAL NEEDS PROVISION:
Applications from disabled people and people from ethnic minorities welcome

COSTS/WAITING LISTS:
There are no costs to the applicant in
applying and no waiting list. All proposals
are evaluated on their individual merits

PROJECT 67
10 Hatton Garden
London EC1N 8AH
Tel: 071 831 7626 Fax: 071 404 5588

Project 67 arranges for over 2,000 people a year
to go to Israel on three types of working holiday
on a 'package holiday' basis. There are Kibbutz
and Moshav holidays, which last for a minimum
of 2 months, and archaeological digs. Departures
take place throughout the year, with placement
guaranteed. Project 67 is the official UK
representative of the Kibbutz movement and
arranges Kibbutz holidays (age limits 18-32) on
which volunteers receive free accommodation,
meals, laundry, pocket money, recreational
facilities and occasional trips in exchange for
working a 6-day week. On a Moshav holiday
(age limits 21-35) work is mainly agricultural.
Free accommodation is provided (usually self-
contained). In exchange for their work volunteers
receive a monthly salary which may be increased
if overtime is worked. Project's archaeological
digs are organised in conjunction with the
Ministry of Antiquities and Universities; a variety
of programmes are offered on several sites
throughout Israel, in which anyone over the age
of 18 can participate. Accommodation varies

from site to site. Project 67 has its own office in Tel Aviv which can take care of the needs of volunteers while they are in Israel.

AGE RANGE:
18-35
NUMBERS PASSING THROUGH:
c 4,000
HOW TO CONTACT:
For more details those interested can visit Project's London office to watch a video, otherwise telephone or send SAE for a brochure
REGIONS SERVICED:
UK
SPECIAL NEEDS PROVISION:
No special provision but enquiries welcome
COSTS/WAITING LISTS:
Cost is approx £270. This is for the minimum period for any holiday of 8 weeks. A 1-year ticket might only be £20 more. Usually no waiting lists except in busy periods

---

PROJECT TRUST
The Hebridean Centre
Ballyhough
Isle of Coll
Scotland PA78 6TB
Tel: 08793 444 Fax: 08793 357

Project Trust is an educational trust that places volunteers overseas each year in posts where they have the opportunity to do useful work for

a year between school and higher education.
Since 1968 it has sent over 2,000 volunteers to
39 different countries. Project aims to give
young people a better understanding of the
world outside Europe through living and working
overseas. The three main categories of project
are teacher-aides, social services and outdoor
activities. Projects are chosen which do not
take work from a local person, and which offer
work that is both satisfying to the volunteer and
useful to the host nation.

AGE RANGE:
17-19
NUMBERS PASSING THROUGH:
180-200 each year
HOW TO CONTACT:
By letter to the Director at above address for
an information leaflet and application form
REGIONS SERVICED:
UK
SPECIAL NEEDS PROVISION:
No provision
COSTS/WAITING LISTS:
The average cost is about £3,250. Project
Trust provides about £500; volunteers need to
raise £2,950. The Trust has a finance officer
who can advise how to go about fund-raising,
through sponsored events, charities, industry,
local business etc. Projects start in August/
September and you can apply 18 months
before. Applications close usually in the
previous November

QUAKER INTERNATIONAL SOCIAL PROJECTS (QISP)
Friends' House
Euston Road
London NW1 2BJ
Tel: 071 387 3601 Fax: 071 388 1977

QISP projects bring together people of different nationalities, backgrounds and cultures who would like to be involved in a 1-3-week voluntary project. The projects are innovative and are initiated by a local community who need volunteers to help them carry out some task that aims to make life more positive for others. There are many different types of projects e.g. play schemes, projects in psychiatric hospitals, manual and women only projects, study projects etc. QISP projects offer you the chance to meet, live and work with people you might not otherwise meet, learn from each other, develop new skills and find out for yourself just what a group of 12 or so complete strangers from all over the world can do when they work together.

AGE RANGE:
18+ (16-18 for International Youth Projects)
NUMBERS PASSING THROUGH:
200 young people in UK, 100 sent abroad
HOW TO CONTACT:
In person, by telephone, SAE or fax for information about current projects
REGIONS SERVICED:
UK

SPECIAL NEEDS PROVISION:
QISP is open to volunteers of all abilities and
any special needs are considered when
planning projects
COSTS/WAITING LISTS:
There is a registration fee from £3 to £25
depending on income. Accommodation and
foo are free and some travel subsidies are
available. Apply in January for Easter projects
and in April/May for summer projects

RAC MOTOR SPORTS ASSOCIATION (RAC MSA)
Motor Sports House
Riverside Park
Colnbrook
Slough SL3 0HG
Tel: 0753 681736

The RAC MSA produce a comprehensive booklet
about starting up in the various types of motor
sports, and about the different types of jobs that
are available. It can give information about
schools, circuits and a range of other specialised
contact information covering motor sports
throughout the UK.

RALEIGH INTERNATIONAL
Raleigh House
27 Parsons Green Lane
London SW6 4HS
Tel: 071 371 8585 Fax: 071 371 5116

Raleigh International is a charity which aims to develop young people by giving them the opportunity to carry out demanding environmental and community projects in the UK and remote parts of the world. Raleigh is recruiting over 1,000 young people between the ages of 17 and 25 and over 350 members of staff aged 25+ for expeditions in 1993/94 to Chile, Guyana, Namibia, Zimbabwe, Mauritius, Russia and Malaysia. No skills are necessary except the ability to swim and speak basic English.

REGIONAL ADDRESSES:
Contact through Head Office
AGE RANGE:
17+
NUMBERS PASSING THROUGH:
1,000+
HOW TO CONTACT:
Send an A4 SAE to Head Office
REGIONS SERVICED:
Worldwide
SPECIAL NEEDS PROVISION:
Participants must be physically capable of looking after themselves. Raleigh cannot accommodate young people with severe learning difficulties but physical disabilities do not present a problem
COSTS/WAITING LISTS:
Participants are asked to raise between £500 and £2,950 through sponsorship and fund-raising events. Many companies send employees as part of a training programme

and there are a number of grants available
from Training Enterprise Councils, Local
Authorities and charitable trusts

REMPLOY LTD
415 Edgware Road
Cricklewood
London NW2 6LR
Tel: 081 452 8020 Fax: 081 452 6898

Remploy Ltd, a state-funded manufacturing and
services company with 9,500 severely disabled
employees, provides special needs training,
sheltered employment and progression to jobs
in open industry and commerce.

REGIONAL ADDRESSES:
Check with local Jobcentres for Remploy
factories in your area
AGE RANGE:
16+
NUMBERS PASSING THROUGH:
Approximately 150 disabled young people
take part in Remploy YT and ET courses each
year. While there is no guarantee of a
permanent job, approximately 100 are
employed at the end of their training
HOW TO CONTACT:
Applicants registered as severely disabled
(Category 2, Green Card) must be referred to
Remploy by the Disability Employment
Adviser at a Jobcentre

REGIONS SERVICED:
There are 96 Remploy factories throughout
the country

SPECIAL NEEDS PROVISION:
A wide range of courses available including
those aimed at providing vocational
qualifications to national standards

COSTS/WAITING LISTS:
There are more young people applying than
places available

ROAD TRANSPORT INDUSTRY TRAINING
BOARD (RTITB)

The RTITB can offer advice and supply information
brochures covering courses and careers throughout
the road transport industry. They are a good first
point of contact whether you want to be a
mechanic, auto electrician, car fitter, driver, car
salesperson, transport manager etc.

REGIONAL ADDRESSES:
England and Wales: Capitol House, Empire
Way, Wembley, Middlesex HA9 0NG
Tel: 081 902 8880
Northern Ireland: Nutts Corner Training
Centre, 15 Dundrod Road, Crumlin, Co.
Antrim BT29 4SS Tel: 0232 825653
Scotland: Training Services, Hardie Road,
Livingstone, West Lothian EH54 8AR Tel:
0506 416355

ROTARY YOUTH EXCHANGE PROGRAMME
Rotary International
Kinwarton Road
Alcester
Warwickshire B49 6BP
Tel: 0789 765411 Fax: 0789 765570

The object of the Rotary Youth Exchange Programme is to promote international understanding and goodwill by bringing young people into contact with each other so that they can understand other ways of life, learn the thinking and culture of other countries and open lasting friendships. Youth exchanges give an opportunity for travel, education and self-dependence. Young people have to be selected by an interviewing panel of the local Rotary Club and they have to be sponsored by the Rotary Club.

REGIONAL ADDRESSES:
Over 1,700 clubs around Britain and Ireland
AGE RANGE:
16-22
NUMBERS PASSING THROUGH:
10,000 worldwide
HOW TO CONTACT:
Send SAE to Head Office, who will put you in contact with a local club
REGIONS SERVICED:
UK
SPECIAL NEEDS PROVISION:
Enquiries welcome

COSTS/WAITING LISTS:
Individuals are responsible for transport,
insurance/registration and spending money

ROUGH GUIDE TO CAREERS
BSS
PO Box 29 (SEDO)
Manchester M12 6AD
Tel: 061 272 7722

BSS publishes guides to various careers to
accompany the *Rough Guides to Careers* series
shown on BBC2. There are a number of titles
available covering a wide range of career
opportunities. Each guide gives details of the
different jobs and careers available in a particular
field (e.g. sport and leisure, finance, tourism,
working in Europe), what each job actually involves
told by people who do it and the training
opportunities available. For details of the guides
available, contact BSS at the above address.

COSTS/WAITING LISTS:
Guides cost between £1.50 and £3.95

ROYAL ACADEMY OF DANCING (RAD)
36 Battersea Square
London SW11 3RA
Tel: 071 223 0091 Fax: 071 924 3129

RAD caters for dancing for anyone whether as
a pastime or professional career. Students can

attend lessons at HQ or at any of the registered teachers' schools located worldwide – lists available from above. The Academy caters for dancers at every stage of their professional career from dancing examinations, to awards that help entry into companies, to training as teachers. There are summer schools for all ages and a Junior Friends club and magazine.

REGIONAL ADDRESSES:
Details available from Head Office
AGE RANGE:
Any
HOW TO CONTACT:
Telephone, letter or in person
REGIONS SERVICED:
UK and 58 countries overseas
SPECIAL NEEDS PROVISION:
There is provision for teaching students with special needs
COSTS/WAITING LISTS:
Membership of the academy is £42; Friends of the Academy £21.   Ballet classes and course fees vary

ROYAL ACADEMY OF DRAMATIC ART
(RADA)
62-64 Gower Street
London WC1E 6ED
Tel: 071 636 7076 Fax: 071 323 3865

RADA offer courses in acting, stage management and specialist diploma courses. They also offer a 4-week summer vacation Drama Workshop in Shakespearean acting, and a 2-week course in Set Design. Competition for places is tough, although the entry criteria for each course are different. Fuller details in the college prospectus.

AGE RANGE:
18+
HOW TO CONTACT:
Letter plus large SAE for further information
REGIONS SERVICED:
UK
COSTS/WAITING LISTS:
Application forms should be submitted by the November prior to the year for which entry is sought

ROYAL AIR FORCE CAREERS

Contact your nearest RAF Careers Information Office (see telephone directory) for details of careers and training in the RAF or alternatively if you are still at school contact the RAF Schools Liaison Officer through your careers department.

ROYAL INSTITUTE OF BRITISH ARCHITECTS (RIBA)
Education Department
66 Portland Place
London W1N 4AD
Tel: 071 580 5533

Architecture involves a mixture of artistic skill and technology. As well as designing a building to look attractive an architect also needs the necessary technical knowledge to ensure that it is practical to build the structure he or she has designed so training is quite a lengthy process. The majority of architects work in private practice but many also work for Local Authorities and government departments. Contact the RIBA for information on training and career development. Opportunities also exist for architectural technicians working as part of a team assisting architects on a particular project. Contact the British Institute of Architectural Technicians for its training requirements at 397 City Road, London EC1V 1NE Tel: 071 278 2206/8

ROYAL LIFE SAVING SOCIETY UK (RLSS UK)
Mountbatten House
Studley
Warwickshire B80 7NN
Tel: 0527 853943 Fax: 0527 854453

If you want to learn to look after yourself – or

take care of others – in the water, RLSS have courses for you, ranging from very basic to professional-level qualifications for lifeguards, which can lead to a job in the leisure industry or active membership of a volunteer lifeguard club. Whatever your swimming ability a life-saving course will make you safer in the water. People with special needs welcome.

REGIONAL ADDRESSES:
Details from Head Office
AGE RANGE:
Any
NUMBERS PASSING THROUGH:
200,000
HOW TO CONTACT:
Phone, letter, fax, or in person to Head Office for advice, information, leaflets etc. about the work of RLSS UK, and for local contact information
REGIONS SERVICED:
UK
SPECIAL NEEDS PROVISION:
No special provision but participation welcome
COSTS/WAITING LISTS:
Membership: £9.50. Programmes cost from nothing to £1.50. Exam fees range from 75p-£15. No waiting lists, but some programmes only run at particular times of the year

ROYAL NATIONAL COLLEGE FOR THE BLIND (RNCB)
College Road
Hereford HR1 1EB
Tel: 0432 265725 Fax: 0432 353478

The RNCB is the major further education establishment in the UK offering preparation for open employment and higher education for visually handicapped students. The college offers specialist training, development of independence and mobility skills, experience with the latest technology, employment counselling and much more. Entry is via an assessment and the emphasis is on potential rather than qualifications.

AGE RANGE:
16+
NUMBERS PASSING THROUGH:
200+
HOW TO CONTACT:
Contact direct by telephone, fax or letter or through the Specialist Careers Officer in the Careers Centre or the Disability Employment Adviser in the Jobcentre
REGIONS SERVICED:
UK and overseas
SPECIAL NEEDS PROVISION:
Exclusively for visually handicapped students
COSTS/WAITING LISTS:
Course fees may be paid by Local Education Authorities or Employment Service

ROYAL NATIONAL THEATRE EDUCATION
Upper Ground
South Bank
London SE1 9PX
Tel: 071 261 9808 Fax: 071 620 1197

The Education Department of the Royal National Theatre is responsible for a range of activities and resources including main stage productions for young people; mobile touring productions which visit schools, colleges and theatres throughout the UK; printed study packs and resource materials; weekend courses for students and teachers and cut-price ticket schemes (see also WH Smith Interact). Joining Royal National Theatre education means you will receive regular information about forthcoming events.

AGE RANGE:
Any
HOW TO CONTACT:
By letter or fax to the Education Department at the above address
REGIONS SERVICED:
UK
SPECIAL NEEDS PROVISION:
Variety of workshops planned according to special needs
COSTS/WAITING LISTS:
Small voluntary contribution for regular newsletter. There is usually a charge for workshops

ROYAL NAVY AND ROYAL MARINES CAREERS

For information on careers in the Royal Navy and Royal Marines contact your local Royal Navy Careers Information Office – address of your nearest one is available from the telephone directory. If still at school you can contact the Navy Schools Liaison Officer through the Careers Department. Alternatively you could write to Officer Enquiry Section, DNR, Ministry of Defence, Old Admiralty Building, London SW1A 2BE

ROYAL SOCIETY FOR THE PREVENTION OF CRUELTY TO ANIMALS (RSPCA)
Causeway
Horsham
West Sussex RH12 1HG
Tel: 0403 264181 Fax: 0403 241048

The RSPCA is the world's largest animal welfare charity. It receives no money from the government and has no direct link with any political party. It works to prevent cruelty and to encourage kindness to animals. You can become involved by joining the Society as a member, helping to raise funds, helping out at events, raising awareness etc. The RSPCA is a very good source of information about all aspects of animal welfare.

REGIONAL ADDRESSES:
Contact Head Office for regional addresses
AGE RANGE:
Any
HOW TO CONTACT:
Letter, telephone or fax for general
information and membership forms
REGIONS SERVICED:
UK
SPECIAL NEEDS PROVISION:
Enquiries welcome
COSTS/ WAITING LISTS:
Animal Action Club Membership (up to 17
years) £4.50 per year

RSA EXAMINATIONS BOARD (RSA)
Progress House
Westwood Way
Coventry CV4 8HS
Tel: 0203 470033 Fax: 0203 468080

With over 1 million candidates every year, RSA
Examinations Board is one of the UK's leading
providers of vocational and non-vocational
qualifications. Courses are available in more
than 8,000 centres, including schools, further
education colleges, higher education colleges
and the workplace. There are more than 200
schemes and courses in subjects ranging from
business or office skills through language courses
to warehousing and wholesaling. RSA is the
awarding body for many NVQs and the new

GNVQs. Its standards are recognised by employers and education institutions at home and abroad.

REGIONAL ADDRESSES:
Midlands/Anglia: Bradford Court, Bradford Street, Birmingham B12 0NX
North: 1 Albion Place, Leeds LS1 6JL
South-east: 8 John Adam Street, London WC2N 6EZ
South-west: contact Coventry Head Office
AGE RANGE:
14+
NUMBERS PASSING THROUGH:
More than 1,000,000 candidates in 1992
HOW TO CONTACT:
Write to or call RSA or contact colleges and training organisations direct
REGIONS SERVICED:
UK and Ireland
SPECIAL NEEDS PROVISION:
RSA publishes a booklet outlining its pro-active approach to special needs. Call RSA for a copy
COSTS/WAITING LISTS:
Costs vary according to the course concerned. Call RSA or the centre concerned for details

THE RSNC WILDLIFE TRUSTS PARTNERSHIP
The Green
Witham Park
Waterside South
Lincoln LN5 7JR
Tel: 0522 544400 Fax: 0522 511616

The Wildlife Trusts are concerned with all aspects of wildlife protection.   There are many opportunities for getting involved in local conservation projects and initiatives which aim to create a better future for wildlife. Contact RSNC for information about activities in your area and how you can get involved. RSNC also produce information about careers in the environment.

REGIONAL ADDRESSES:
Branches throughout the UK
AGE RANGE:
Any
HOW TO CONTACT:
Letter, telephone or fax to above address for general information and details of your nearest branch
REGIONS SERVICED:
UK

RURAL DEVELOPMENT COMMISSION
(New Entrants Training Scheme)
141 Castle Street
Salisbury
Wiltshire SP1 3TP
Tel: 0722 336255 Fax: 0722 332769

The Commission promotes and assists jobs and communities in rural areas of England. They provide training opportunities for young employees of small rural businesses in a wide variety of occupations e.g. upholstery, forgework, plastics, woodworking machinery, saddlery, thatching, furniture-making etc.

REGIONAL ADDRESSES:
Details available from Head Office
AGE RANGE:
Any
NUMBERS PASSING THROUGH:
300 (on training scheme)
HOW TO CONTACT:
Telephone or letter to Head Office
REGIONS SERVICED:
Rural areas of England only (i.e. where the population does not exceed 10,000 people)
SPECIAL NEEDS PROVISION:
Provision is dependent on the nature of the course
COSTS/WAITING LISTS:
There is no cost to the trainee under the New Entrants Training Scheme

RYA SEAMANSHIP FOUNDATION
RYA House
Romsey Road
Eastleigh
Hampshire SO5 4YA
Tel: 0703 629962 Fax: 0703 629924

The Young Skippers scheme, run by the Seamanship Foundation, is designed to give young people (14-23) the opportunity to skipper a yacht and experience the responsibility of command. It provides small cruising yachts and invites young people to sail them at a price which just covers running costs. The Challenger scheme, also run by the Seamanship Foundation, gives young people and adults with a physical disability the opportunity to sail trimarans at a number of centres around the country. Blind sailing courses are run each year for visually impaired people aged 17+, and are structured for beginners through to experienced sailors.

AGE RANGE:
14+
HOW TO CONTACT:
Letter or telephone for general information
REGIONS SERVICED:
UK
SPECIAL NEEDS PROVISION:
See above
COSTS/WAITING LISTS:
Young Skipper Scheme cruise fees are £100-£140 for 7-10 day cruise. Blind Sailing Week

fees are about £120. Challenger fees vary
with each boat

SAIL TRAINING ASSOCIATION
(STA Schooners)
2a The Hard
Portsmouth PO1 3PT
Tel: 0705 832055/6 Fax: 0705 815769

The aim of the STA is to help young people learn
about themselves, their capabilities and
awareness of others in an exciting and
demanding voyage on the UK's largest sail-
training schooners – the 150ft 'Sir Winston
Churchill' and 'Malcolm Miller'. You do not
need any previous experience of the sea or
sailing, just an awareness that you are
undertaking a challenge, both physically and
psychologically, that will stand you in good
stead for the rest of your life. During your
voyage you and 38 other trainees of varying
backgrounds will take a large sailing ship across
nearly 1,000 miles of unpredictable sea. You
will be part of the ship's company and as such
will take an active part in the care and
maintenance of the ship as well as watch duties,
including look-out, steering, sail-trimming,
galley work and ship cleaning. All voyages
count towards the Duke of Edinburgh's Award
scheme – Gold Award Residential qualification
or the scheme's interest section.

REGIONAL ADDRESSES:
Comprehensive list of regional committees
available from Head Office

AGE RANGE:
16-24

NUMBERS PASSING THROUGH:
c 1,000

HOW TO CONTACT:
Telephone, letter or fax to Head Office for
advice and information

REGIONS SERVICED:
UK

SPECIAL NEEDS PROVISION:
Each case is dealt with individually

COSTS/WAITING LISTS:
Low season – 2 weeks £500; high season –
£770, inclusive of all food and equipment,
raised from own activities. STA volunteer
committees around the country hold fund-
raising events and Head Office can advise on
funds and trusts. It is advisable to book as
early as possible

SAVE THE CHILDREN FUND (SCF)
17 Grove Lane
Camberwell
London SE5 8RD
Tel: 071 703 5400

SCF is the UK's largest international voluntary
agency concerned with child health and welfare.
It operates major projects in more than 30
countries overseas, as well as many programmes

in the UK. For survival it depends on financial support from the general public, and on volunteers in over 800 fund-raising branches throughout the UK.

AGE RANGE:
Any
HOW TO CONTACT:
Letter or telephone to above address
REGIONS SERVICED:
UK

A SCHOOL YEAR ABROAD (ASSE)
PO Box 20
Harwich
Essex CO12 4DQ
Tel: 0255 506347 Fax: 0255 240952

The student exchange scheme exists to give the opportunity to young people to spend a school year abroad (current participating countries: USA, Canada, France, Germany, Iceland, Australia, New Zealand, Japan) and/or receive into their family a student of a similar age to themselves from abroad. As a participant you would live with a volunteer family and attend the local school. You would become a member of the family and community, experiencing the life of a young citizen of that country.

REGIONAL ADDRESSES:
Scotland, Northern Ireland, South-east, East

and North-east: PO Box 20, Harwich, Essex
CO12 4DQ Tel: 0255 506347
Fax: 0225 240952
Wales, West and South-west contact:
K.M.Wright, ASSE, 4 Cunningham Close,
Sketty, Swansea, SA2 8LG
Tel & Fax: 0792 205317

AGE RANGE:
16-18 for the North American High School
Year Programme

NUMBERS PASSING THROUGH:
60 travelling abroad in 1993/94

HOW TO CONTACT:
Telephone or letter for general information
and contact with previous participants

REGIONS SERVICED:
UK

SPECIAL NEEDS PROVISION:
Can't cater for special needs

COSTS/WAITING LISTS:
Costs vary depending on destination and
length of stay. A year at a USA high school
for example will cost £3,170 plus pocket
money. Most participants are funded by
parents but some have successfully
approached local businesses and charities for
sponsorship. Apply as early as possible
during the school year previous to departure
and not later than 1 March

SCOTS FIDDLE SCHOOL
Scottish Amateur Music Association
PO Box 1085
Bearsden
Glasgow G61 4AP
Tel: 0360 60021

Young musicians are invited to attend the 1994 course which will be held at St Andrews University, Fife from 1-4 August. No audition is required.

AGE RANGE:
Any
NUMBERS PASSING THROUGH:
20
HOW TO CONTACT:
By telephone or letter for further information
REGIONS SERVICED:
UK but mainly Scotland
SPECIAL NEEDS PROVISION:
Special tuition at all levels available
COSTS/WAITING LISTS:
There is a course fee of £145 which includes tuition, accommodation and the services of professional musicians. Some local authority grants may be available. Waiting lists can be up to 6 months preceding the next year's course

SCOTTISH ARTS COUNCIL
12 Manor Place
Edinburgh EH3 7DD
Tel: 031 226 6051

See entry for Arts Council

SCOTTISH ASSOCIATION OF YOUNG FARMERS (SAYF)
Young Farmers Centre
Ingliston
Edinburgh EH28 8NE
Tel: 031 333 2445 Fax: 031 333 2488

Young Farmers care about the countryside, and delve into all kinds of rural issues for 'grass roots' information. There are some 120 clubs throughout Scotland which organise activities such as discos and parties, drama and international travel, sporting competitions (anything from curling to tug-of-war, football and ten-pin bowling), speech-making contests and craft-making. They organise special courses which help young people to develop leadership skills and confidence in public speaking. They are part of an international network of young people whose interests lie in meeting people and caring for the countryside. Members make friends worldwide – exchange visits are arranged between clubs in the UK and as far away as Australia, Finland, Sweden, Switzerland, Canada and America.

AGE RANGE:
14-26
HOW TO CONTACT:
Letter or telephone to Head Office for
information about your nearest Young
Farmers Club
REGIONS SERVICED:
Scotland

SCOTTISH BUSINESS IN THE COMMUNITY
(SBC)
Romano House
43 Station Road
Corstorphine
Edinburgh EH12 7AF
Tel: 031 334 9876 Fax: 031 316 4521

SBC can give general information on all aspects
of setting up and maintaining your own business,
plus details of agencies in your local area from
where you can obtain more specific information
and advice.

AGE RANGE:
Any
HOW TO CONTACT:
Letter, telephone or fax for general
information
REGIONS SERVICED:
Scotland
SPECIAL NEEDS PROVISION:
Enquiries welcome

SCOTTISH CONSERVATION PROJECTS TRUST (SCP)
Balallan House
24 Allan Park
Stirling FK8 2QG
Tel: 0786 479697 Fax: 0786 465359

Action Breaks are 7-14 day practical, residential conservation projects for people aged 16+ held throughout Scotland. Midweek groups in Inverness, Falkirk, Edinburgh and Glasgow organise non-residential projects for mainly unemployed volunteers aged over 16. Operation Brightwater projects are water-based projects carried out by groups in various parts of Scotland, mainly for over 16s but there are some opportunities for younger people. There are also weekend training courses in environment skills and 6- and 12-month Vocational Training Courses leading to a recognised City and Guilds Certificate. There are also long-term volunteering and leadership opportunities.

REGIONAL ADDRESSES:
Contact through Head Office
AGE RANGE:
16+
NUMBERS PASSING THROUGH:
11,000 total volunteers (about 8,000 young people)
HOW TO CONTACT:
Telephone or letter to Head Office

REGIONS SERVICED:
Whole of Scotland and outer islands, Orkney and Shetland
SPECIAL NEEDS PROVISION:
Some provision on certain schemes
COSTS/WAITING LISTS:
Student membership is £8. Action Breaks cost £3 per day. There are no costs for Midweek Projects or Operation Brightwater. Training courses cost £24 per weekend

---

SCOTTISH CO-OPERATIVES DEVELOPMENT COMMITTEE (SCDC)
Building 1, 1st Floor
Templeton Business Centre
Templeton Street
Bridgeton
Glasgow G40 1DA
Tel: 041 554 3797

The SCDC is an organisation which can give free advice to anyone proposing to start a business and who might be interested in a co-operative structure. Free advice from SCDC will explain what a co-operative is and how it could work for your business. They can assist in preparing a business plan, and ultimately can help you to register your company. After start-up SCDC will stay on hand with advice and assistance through the early months.

AGE RANGE:
Any

HOW TO CONTACT:
Telephone or letter to Head Office for details
of regional offices
REGIONS SERVICED:
Scotland

SCOTTISH COUNCIL FOR EDUCATIONAL TECHNOLOGY (SCET)
74 Victoria Crescent Road
Glasgow G12 9JN
Tel: 041 334 9314 Fax: 041 334 6519

SCET provides information and advice on all
aspects of open/flexible learning and topics
relating to education, training and educational
technology. They run training workshops and
have an extensive range of education and training
films and videos. They develop software for
education and offer consultancy on database
design, hypermedia and software solutions.
SCET's Information Resource Centre has a large
collection of open learning packages available
for reference.

AGE RANGE:
Any
HOW TO CONTACT:
Telephone, letter, fax or in person to the
Information Resource Centre for information
or referral to another agency if appropriate
REGIONS SERVICED:
UK and worldwide

SPECIAL NEEDS PROVISION:
SCET has developed SEND (Special Education Needs Database) an information database for those with special educational needs which offers information on: Software: 500 programs found useful for special needs; Hardware: 200 add-on devices, communication aids and other products; Developments: Details of projects on micros in special educational needs; Events: Relevant seminars, conferences; Contacts: Names and addresses of organisations who can offer help and advice

COSTS/WAITING LISTS:
There is no charge for information. Costs for services vary

SCOTTISH NATIONAL ASSOCIATION OF YOUTH THEATRE (SNAYT)
Old Athenaeum Theatre
179 Buchanan Street
Glasgow G1 2JZ
Tel: 041 353 1866 Fax: 041 333 1021

The SNAYT is a resource and development service for youth theatre in Scotland and can provide information and advice to anyone with an interest in young people's theatre, either directly or by referring to other organisations.

AGE RANGE:
12-25

HOW TO CONTACT:
Letter, phone or fax for further information
REGIONS SERVICED:
Scotland, has contacts across UK
SPECIAL NEEDS PROVISION:
Can put people in touch with relevant
organisations
COSTS/WAITING LISTS:
None for information
Membership subscriptions £10-£50

SCOTTISH NATIONAL PARTY (SNP)
6 North Charlotte Street
Edinburgh
Lothian EH2 4FH
Tel: 031 226 3661

SCOTTISH SILVER JUBILEE & CHILDREN'S BURSARY FUND
1 Woodside Road
Tullibody, Alloa
Clackmannanshire FK10 2QQ
Tel: 0259 723935

If you are under 25 and have an idea that would benefit the community in some way this bursary fund may be able to give you a grant to help with your project. You can apply on your own or with others (you don't have to be a member of a club or organisation). If you want to apply, write down your plans, find out how much it will cost and get in touch with the Fund.

AGE RANGE:
Under 25
NUMBERS PASSING THROUGH:
20 grants awarded
HOW TO CONTACT:
Telephone or letter for information and an
application form
REGIONS SERVICED:
Scotland
SPECIAL NEEDS PROVISION:
Anyone under 25 can apply for grants
COSTS/WAITING LISTS:
Applications are usually dealt with as
received

SCOTTISH SPORTS COUNCIL
Caledonia House
South Gyle
Edinburgh EH12 9DQ
Tel: 031 317 7200 Fax: 031 317 7202

The Scottish Sports Council provides information
on sport in Scotland and initiates opportunities
for people to participate in sport at any level of
ability.

AGE RANGE:
Any
HOW TO CONTACT:
Telephone or letter for information,
publications and contact addresses of sports
organisations

REGIONS SERVICED:
Scotland
SPECIAL NEEDS PROVISION:
Information on disabled sports
COSTS/WAITING LISTS:
There is a charge for some publications
although many are free

SCOTTISH VOCATIONAL EDUCATION COUNCIL (SCOTVEC)
Hanover House
24 Douglas Street
Glasgow G2 7NQ
Tel: 041 248 7900 Fax: 041 242 2244

SCOTVEC qualifications are open to all.
SCOTVEC is Scotland's national body
responsible for vocational qualifications. They
work in partnership with industry and commerce,
government and education and training
providers. This ensures that the qualifications
remain up to date and relevant to the changing
needs of employment. SCOTVEC's
qualifications include National Certificate
Modules, general SVQs, HNCs and HNDs. All
these qualifications are recognised by employers
throughout the UK and internationally.

AGE RANGE:
Any
HOW TO CONTACT:
Write to the above address

REGIONS SERVICED:
Scotland. For England, Wales and Northern
Ireland see entry for Business and Technology
Education Council (BTEC)

SCOTTISH YOUNG PERSONS VIDEO COMPETITION
Learning Systems Division
Scottish Council for Educational Technology
74 Victoria Crescent Road
Glasgow G12 9JN

This video competition is an annual event with
prizes for an overall winner and for the best
programmes in the primary, secondary and further
education sectors. It is open to those aged 21 and
under who are at an established school or college
in Scotland and who are not involved
professionally in broadcast media. Each year
there is a theme for entries and also a category for
scripts/storyboards so you can enter even if you
don't have access to production equipment. Write
to the above address for further information.

SCOTTISH YOUTH DANCE FESTIVAL (SYDF)
The Assembly Rooms
54 George Street
Edinburgh EH2 2LR
Tel: 031 220 6320

The SYDF runs the annual Youth Dance Festival

in Scotland which includes all types of dance plus the chance to perform alongside professional companies. They also administrate the Mitchell Trust Dance Bursary as well as promoting young people's participation in dance through information networking.

AGE RANGE:
14-25
NUMBERS PASSING THROUGH:
300 directly involved
HOW TO CONTACT:
Telephone or letter with SAE for information on the Dance Festival and other activities as well as opportunities for dance in Scotland
REGIONS SERVICED:
Mainly Scotland, but also UK and Europe
SPECIAL NEEDS PROVISION:
Enquiries welcome
COSTS/WAITING LISTS:
Cost of attendance at the 1993 Festival was £155 + VAT residential and £95 + VAT non-residential. Information and advice is free

---

SCOTTISH YOUTH THEATRE (SYT)
Old Athenaeum Theatre
179 Buchanan Street
Glasgow G1 2JZ
Tel: 041 332 5727 Fax: 041 333 1021

SYT wants to hear from anyone, anywhere in Scotland, aged 12-21, who is interested in the performing arts. They offer the chance to

experience all aspects of performance art while
working with theatre professionals. A very wide
range of activities is available including touring
workshops, youth theatre festivals, a playwright
festival, professional training and much more.

AGE RANGE:
12-21
NUMBERS PASSING THROUGH:
10,000+
HOW TO CONTACT:
Letter, telephone, fax or in person for details
of activities
REGIONS SERVICED:
UK but mainly Scotland
SPECIAL NEEDS PROVISION:
Extensive provision e.g. a variety of mixed
ability projects and workshops
COSTS/WAITING LISTS:
Costs for festivals, courses, tuition etc. vary
and SYT can offer advice on fund-raising

THE SCOUT ASSOCIATION
Baden-Powell House
Queen's Gate
London SW7 5JS
Tel: 071 584 7030 Fax: 071 581 9953

Scouts are young men and women who take
part in a very wide range of outdoor activities
including climbing, abseiling, canoeing, sailing,
hiking, mountaineering etc., as well as
community work, international projects

throughout the world, training in a variety of different areas and a personal development programme.

REGIONAL ADDRESSES:
Available from HQ
AGE RANGE:
Venture Scouts 15-20 years, other sections 6-15 years
NUMBERS PASSING THROUGH:
556,000 members
HOW TO CONTACT:
Contact local group (Local Authority has list of Scout groups in area) or Headquarters above
REGIONS SERVICED:
UK with international projects throughout the world
SPECIAL NEEDS PROVISION:
Scout Link Clubs deal specifically with special needs scouting
COSTS/WAITING LISTS:
Subscriptions vary from group to group

SEA CADET CORPS (SCC)
202 Lambeth Road
London SE1 7JF
Tel: 071 928 8978

The Sea Cadet Corps is a voluntary youth organisation comprised of 400 units scattered throughout the country, providing facilities for the Cadets to take part in activities in which self-discipline, leadership and a sense of responsibility to the community are encouraged. The accent is on the sea; sailing and boat work have a high priority and most units have access to water and boats. Other activities include band training, communications, engineering, model-making, swimming, visits to ships, expeditions and much more. All cadets can take part in adventure training, map- reading and the Duke of Edinburgh's Award Scheme.

REGIONAL ADDRESSES:
Six regional addresses – details available from Head Office
AGE RANGE:
12-18
NUMBERS PASSING THROUGH:
17,000 members
HOW TO CONTACT:
Telephone, letter or fax to Head/Regional Office or contact local Sea Cadet Unit
REGIONS SERVICED:
UK
SPECIAL NEEDS PROVISION:
Some restriction on physical disability
COSTS/WAITING LISTS:
Voluntary monthly contribution. Part assistance with travel costs for selected field trips

SEA RANGER ASSOCIATION (SRA)
HQTS 'Lord Amory'
Dollar Bay
631 Manchester Road
London E14 9NU
Tel: 071 987 1757

The SRA gives girls and young women the chance to canoe, row, sail (board, dinghy and off-shore), camp, learn first aid etc.; help the community, e.g. at hospitals, childrens homes; fund-raise for other charities, make new friends, meet regularly and have fun.

REGIONAL ADDRESSES:
Available through General Secretary
AGE RANGE:
10-21
NUMBERS PASSING THROUGH:
750
HOW TO CONTACT:
Telephone or SAE to General Secretary, Vera Simpson, 91 Sherwood Avenue, Streatham Vale, London SW16 5EL Tel: 081 764 3694 for advice and information plus details of local contact
REGIONS SERVICED:
England
SPECIAL NEEDS PROVISION:
Enquiries welcome
COSTS/WAITING LISTS:
Annual subscription: £3; membership fees: 25p-50p per week; payments for specific

events, e.g. £10-£20 for regatta and activity
weekend camp

SHELL BETTER BRITAIN CAMPAIGN
Red House
Hill Lane
Great Barr
Birmingham B43 6LZ
Tel: 021 358 0744 Fax: 021 358 5250

The Shell Better Britain Campaign provides
advice and support for any voluntary group
which is carrying out a practical project to
improve their local environment. There is a free
information pack which includes a 68-page
booklet, *Guide to a Better Britain,* and details of
their grant scheme. The grant scheme is only
applicable to voluntary groups.

AGE RANGE:
Any
NUMBERS PASSING THROUGH:
95 young people's groups received grants
during 1993
HOW TO CONTACT:
Letter to Head Office for an information pack
and details of grant scheme
REGIONS SERVICED:
UK
SPECIAL NEEDS PROVISION:
No special provision
COSTS/WAITING LISTS:
None

SHELL TECHNOLOGY ENTERPRISE PROGRAMME (STEP)
Shell (UK) Ltd
Shell Mex House
Strand
London WC2R 0DX
Tel: 071 257 3185

STEP offers selected university and polytechnic students placements with a host company for 8 weeks during the summer vacation to complete a project which is specified by and benefits the firm. The scheme gives students an insight into how business works and the opportunity to learn about teamwork, problem-solving, communication and decision-making. Students make presentations about their projects at local awards ceremonies and the winners compete at the STEP National Awards ceremony.

AGE RANGE:
No specific age-range – open to students in their penultimate year of a degree or higher diploma course
NUMBERS PASSING THROUGH:
400 in 1991, 800 in 1992
HOW TO CONTACT:
The best way to contact is through one of the various agencies which deal with the STEP programme – Careers Offices, TECs, universities, colleges etc. A full list is available from the above address or ask at your Careers Office for an application form

REGIONS SERVICED:
UK
SPECIAL NEEDS PROVISION:
No special provision
COSTS/WAITING LISTS:
No costs. Students receive a weekly training
allowance of £100 for the 8 weeks

SHEPLEY-SHEPLEY TRUST
12 Manor Place
Edinburgh EH3 7DD
Tel: 031 226 6051 Fax: 031 225 9833

The Trust can offer grants from their Youth Arts
Fund ranging from £50 to £2,000 for arts projects
which show enterprise, innovation and potential
for development. Applicants must be resident
in Scotland and applying in connection with
projects to be undertaken in Scotland. Projects
can involve anything from film, video and rock
music to dance, drama, literature and the visual
arts and crafts.

AGE RANGE:
16-25
NUMBERS PASSING THROUGH:
Approx. 100 applications from 500 enquiries
HOW TO CONTACT:
Letter for further information and an
application form
REGIONS SERVICED:
Scotland

SPECIAL NEEDS PROVISION:
All applications are dealt with on an equal
opportunities basis
COSTS/WAITING LISTS:
Closing dates are three times per year (exact
dates available on request) and applicants
hear results within 1 month of closing date

SKILL: NATIONAL BUREAU FOR STUDENTS
WITH DISABILITIES
336 Brixton Road
London SW9 7AA
Tel: 071 274 0565 (voice/minicom)
Fax: 071 274 7840

Skill is a national voluntary organisation which is
working to develop opportunities for people with
disabilities and learning difficulties in all types of
post-16 education, training and employment.
Amongst other activities Skill offers an information
service to students, their families and staff who
work with them and produces a range of
publications and information sheets. The
Information Service can help with general and
specific enquiries e.g. about applying to further
and higher education, financial entitlements, and
getting the right support services in education.
Skill is currently developing its Information Service
to cover graduate employment issues.

REGIONAL ADDRESSES:
Contact through Central Office

AGE RANGE:
16+

HOW TO CONTACT:
Information Service is available by phone (voice/minicom), enquiries between 2pm and 5pm, Monday to Friday. Letters can be sent to the above address

REGIONS SERVICED:
UK

COSTS/WAITING LISTS:
Advice and information by phone and letter is free. Information sheets are usually free to students. Price of publications available on request

---

SOCIAL DEMOCRATIC AND LABOUR PARTY (SDLP)
38 University Street
Belfast BT7 1FZ
Tel: 0232 323428

SOCIAL INVENTIONS COMPETITION
The Institute for Social Inventions
20 Heber Road
London NW2 6AA
Tel: 081 208 2853 Fax: 081 452 6434

The Institute of Social Inventions runs an annual competition, with prizes for both adults and young people, for novel ideas and projects that will improve the quality of life within our society. A social invention is defined as a new and imaginative solution to a social problem – not a product, nor a technological invention, nor a patentable device – but a means by which society can be improved upon. Good examples of past social inventions include the Open University and *Which?* magazine – new combinations of existing ideas, new ways for people to relate to each other, new organisational structures or whatever. ISI offer £1,000 a year for the best social invention, and they are editors of *The Book of Visions – An Encyclopaedia of Social Innovations* (price £18.49 inc p&p).

AGE RANGE:
Any
HOW TO CONTACT:
Letter, telephone or fax to above address
REGIONS SERVICED:
UK
SPECIAL NEEDS PROVISION:
Enquiries welcome

SOCIETY OF VOLUNTARY ASSOCIATES (SOVA)
1-4 Brixton Hill Place
London SW2 1HJ
Tel: 081 671 7833

SOVA is a national charity which has schemes throughout the country that recruit and train volunteers to befriend people who have offended. The aims of this are to give support and advice, to encourage independence, and to break the cycle of re-offending. SOVA specialises in training local volunteers to work with the probation service. The volunteers in return give their time, commitment and enthusiasm to assist in supporting offenders and their families in the community, thereby helping to reduce crime. The tasks that volunteers undertake are likely to be influenced by their location, and individual interests and skills. Some examples are befriending of people on probation; supporting the partners and families of people in prison; teaching literacy or numeracy skills; providing support to individuals or families in court, etc.

SPONSORSHIP FOR STUDENTS
(publication)
Careers and Occupational Information Centre
(COIC)
PO Box 348
Bristol BS99 7FE
Tel: 0272 777199

Many companies help young people financially with their studies. *Sponsorship for Students* combines features and advice on the ins and outs of sponsorship with details of of employers offering sponsorship to young people while they take professional or technical degrees. It lists rare opportunities for young people to gain extra financial support and work experience at a time when finances are stretched and

experience at a premium. Available from COIC
(price £5 inc. p&p).

SPORTS COUNCIL
16 Upper Woburn Place
London WC1H 0QP
Tel: 071 388 1277 Fax: 071 383 5740

The Sports Council Information Service provides
contact addresses and information on all aspects
of sport. Details of career opportunities and
courses are available.

REGIONAL ADDRESSES:
Ten regional offices – addresses available
from Head Office
AGE RANGE:
Any
HOW TO CONTACT:
Letter with SAE to Information Centre
REGIONS SERVICED:
UK (see separate entries for Scotland, Wales
and Northern Ireland)
SPECIAL NEEDS PROVISION:
Information on disabled sports
COSTS/WAITING LISTS:
None

SPORTS COUNCIL FOR NORTHERN IRELAND
House of Sport
Upper Malone Road
Belfast BT9 5LA
Tel: 0232 381222 Fax: 0232 682757

The aims of the Sports Council are to further sport and physical recreation in Northern Ireland. If you need any general advice or information about a particular sport and how to get involved, the Sports Council will be able either to help or to point you in the right direction.

AGE RANGE:
Any
HOW TO CONTACT:
By letter to the Information Officer
REGIONS SERVICED:
Northern Ireland
SPECIAL NEEDS PROVISION:
Information on disabled sports
COSTS/WAITING LISTS:
No costs for information

SPORTS COUNCIL FOR WALES
Information Centre
Sophia Gardens
Cardiff CF1 9SW
Tel: 0222 397571

The Sports Council for Wales can provide

information on all sports provision throughout Wales – special needs provision, minority interest sports, major sporting events etc. They can give information about provision in your local area, and can give advice about developing a career in sport and related occupations.

AGE RANGE:
Any
HOW TO CONTACT:
By telephone or letter for further information on any aspect of sport
REGIONS SERVICED:
Wales

SPRINGBOARD
1 Denmark Street
London WC2H 8LP
Tel: 071 497 8654

Springboard is the careers advice centre for hotels, catering, leisure and tourism. It can provide advice and up-to-date information on the wide variety of opportunities within this industry, training and qualifications that may be required, where to find the training, what your typical career path could be – all tailored to your own individual needs and aspirations. At the Springboard offices there are computer storyboards which you can go through in your own time, looking at job descriptions of more than 200 different types of career. These can be printed out for you to take away. This is backed up with our careers advisers' first-hand knowledge of the industry and literature from a variety of progressive companies within hotels, catering, leisure and tourism. Assistance with CV preparation and job-search skills.

AGE RANGE:
All ages
NUMBERS PASSING THROUGH:
Approximately 10,000 per year
HOW TO CONTACT:
Either call in or contact the above address by letter or telephone
REGIONS COVERED:
Greater London area, but written and telephone enquiries are handled on a national basis

---

STAGIAIRES
The UK Offices of the European Commission
Information Office
Jean Monnet House
8 Storey's Gate
London SW1P 3AT

The European Commission, the European Parliament and the Economic and Social Committee all run schemes of in-service training for about 300 trainees each year, known as 'stagiaires'. The largest one is run by the European Commission. The training period begins with a general introduction to Community matters, followed by attachments to departments with advisers to supervise your work. That gives you the opportunity to see how the Commission works from the inside. At the end of each 'stage', the work of each stagiaire is assessed and given a certificate. Trainees need to be under 30 and with either university degrees or equivalent. It is an advantage to have shown an interest in European affairs in your work or studies. For full information contact the above address.

ST JOHN AMBULANCE
National Headquarters
1 Grosvenor Crescent
London SW1X 7EF
Tel: 071 235 5231 Fax: 071 235 0796

As a member of St John Ambulance you can learn everything from first aid to abseiling, from camping to working in the community and much more. St John Cadets aims for a balance of fun and responsibility. You can participate in the Duke of Edinburgh's Award Scheme and The Challenge – an award scheme covering various activities, open to all over 15 year-olds, not just St John members. There is also a St John connected society called Links, which operates in universities, polytechnics and higher and further education colleges.

REGIONAL ADDRESSES:
Organised on a county basis; all counties have an HQ listed in the telephone directory. Wales and Northern Ireland have their own

national HQs and in Scotland St John
Ambulance operates through a sister
organisation:

Scotland: St Andrew's, Milton Street, Glasgow
Tel: 041 332 4031

Wales: Priory for Wales, Lisvane Road,
Llanishen, Cardiff CF4 5XT Tel:
0222 750222

Northern Ireland: Erne Purdysburn Hospital,
Saintfield Road, Belfast BT8 8RA Tel:
0232 799393

AGE RANGE:
Badgers 6-10; Cadets 10-18; Adult members
18+

NUMBERS PASSING THROUGH:
22,000 Badgers, 25,000 Cadets

HOW TO CONTACT:
By letter or telephone to the Youth Services
Department at National HQ or contact
County HQ via telephone directory

REGIONS SERVICED:
UK

SPECIAL NEEDS PROVISION:
Membership is open to all young people who
can learn first aid

COSTS/WAITING LISTS:
Small weekly divisional subscription plus
some uniform costs

THE STOCK EXCHANGE
Careers and Employment Office
The Stock Exchange
Old Broad Street
London EC2N 1HP
Tel: 071 588 2355

The main opportunities on the stock exchange or in the financial markets are as a market-maker, stockbroker, investment analyst or in administration. Market makers deal in stocks and shares on the stock exchange in order to make a profit. Stockbrokers work on behalf of clients wishing to make investments by either advising on the value of stocks and shares or directly by buying from or selling to market-makers. Investment analysts investigate and advise on the investment prospects of companies or particular industries usually either for stockbroking firms or for large investors such as pension funds. Administrative and clerical staff carry out back-up duties such as processing transactions etc. Market makers, stockbrokers and investment analysts study for the professional examinations of the Stock Exchange Council. For further information on careers and training in the stock exchange or financial markets contact either the Stock Exchchange at the above address or individual companies (see telephone directory under 'Investment Consultants' or 'Stockbrokers and Market-makers').

STRATHCLYDE INTERNATIONAL RESOURCES CENTRE

St Patrick's Primary School
10 Perth Street
Glasgow G3 8UQ
Tel: 041 227 3889 Fax: 041 227 2085

The International Resources Centre can provide information, advice, publications, training, contacts and any other type of help requested on any aspect of international work, e.g. exchanges, working abroad, job placements, European legislation, European Community schemes and much more.

AGE RANGE:
Any

NUMBERS PASSING THROUGH:
Over 3,000 per year

HOW TO CONTACT:
Telephone, letter, fax or in person for leaflets, information, local visits, details of courses etc.

REGIONS SERVICED:
Specifically Strathclyde, but will deal with enquiries from anywhere in the UK

SPECIAL NEEDS PROVISION:
The Centre has particular interest and expertise in special needs areas

COSTS/WAITING LISTS:
Service is free. Enquiries are dealt with as they are received

STUDENT CHRISTIAN MOVEMENT (SCM)
186 St Paul's Road
Balsall Heath
Birmingham B12 8LZ
Tel: 021 440 3000 Fax: 021 446 4060

SCM supports the initiatives and programmes of over 70 groups which meet regularly in universities and colleges. Each local group has its own programme of events, run by students and for students, usually involving invited speakers, discussions and visits. There are regional and national conferences and training events. SCM is an ecumenical movement which encourages open enquiry into the nature of Christian faith and action. It is a member of the World Student Christian Federation and arranges regular exchanges and visits between students of different national movements.

REGIONAL ADDRESSES:
Northern England: St Peter's House, Precinct Centre, Oxford Road, Manchester M13 9GH Tel: 061 273 5752
Scotland: University Chaplaincy Centre, 1 Bristo Square, Edinburgh EH8 9AL Tel: 031 667 4321
Wales and southern England: 186 St Paul's Road, Balsall Heath, Birmingham B12 8LZ Tel: 021 446 5554
AGE RANGE:
Any

REGIONS SERVICED:
England, Scotland and Wales

STUDENT GRANTS AND LOANS: A BRIEF GUIDE (publication)

DFE Publications Centre
PO Box 2193
London E15 2EU
Tel: 081 533 2000 Fax: 081 533 7700

GRANTS

If you have not had grant before and you are offered a place on a designated course at college or university, you may be eligible for a mandatory award (fees plus means-tested maintenance grant) from the LEA where you live. In general, designated courses are full-time or sandwich courses of higher education, or certain courses of initial teacher training.

In Scotland you get grants from the Scottish Office Education Department. Tuition fees are usually paid in full for UK students and the amount you get for living expenses may depend on your parents' income. However, if you are married, your grant will be assessed on your spouse's income. In addition to the basic maintenance grant, there are allowances which provide extra support to disabled students, mature students, those with dependants and those required to maintain a second home.

LOANS

To qualify for a student loan you must meet the same residence rules as for grants. You must also be a full-time student on a higher education course and aged under 50 when your course starts. You must also have a bank or building society account that can handle direct credits and debits. You can only apply once in each academic year of your course and for only one course at a time.

This information and much more is in *Student Grants and Loans: A brief guide,* which is available from school, college and LEA careers libraries or free of charge from the above address. If you decide to go for further education (instead of higher education), you should contact your LEA to find out what they can offer you. This is because FE grants are discretionary and different LEAs have different policies.

STUDENT INDUSTRIAL SOCIETY (SIS)
Quadrant Court
49 Calthorpe Road
Edgbaston
Birmingham B15 1TH
Tel: 021 454 6769 Fax: 021 456 2715

Run by students for students, SIS exists to enable students in higher education to gain a greater understanding of employers in industry, business and commerce, with the special purpose of emphasising the importance of industry, heightening awareness of the issues and opportunities in the world of work and developing students' personal transferable skills, all of which should ease the transition into working life. SIS has 60 campus-based societies at institutions of higher education across the British Isles. With some 16,000 members it is the UK's largest non-political student society. Each society is run by a committee which organises a variety of events including visits to companies, presentations by companies, business games, skills training and a wide variety of social activities.

AGE RANGE:
Any
HOW TO CONTACT:
Contact SIS at your institution if there is one, or alternatively contact the full-time National Team at the above address

---

STUDENT LOAN COMPANY LTD
100 Bothwell Street
Glasgow G2 7GD
Tel: 041 306 2000 Fax: 041 306 2005

The Student Loans Scheme is a government funded loans scheme which is administered by Student Loan Company Ltd. It provides for loans to be made towards students' living costs. There are different amounts of loan available, depending on whether you are living at home or away from home, and on whether you are studying in London or outside London. For full details of the scheme contact Student Loan Company.

STUDENTS ABROAD LTD
Whitehorse Chambers
36 Whitehorse Street
Baldock
Hertfordshire SG7 6QQ
Tel: 0462 490939 Fax: 0462 490111

The agency places au pairs and mothers' helps in Austria, Belgium, France, Germany, Greece, Holland, Italy, Spain, Switzerland, UK and USA. Minimum stay in Europe is 6 months (there are a limited number of summer posts for 2–3 months in France, Spain and Italy). 12 months stay for USA. Also places qualified nannies in Canada, France, Greece and Italy for a minimum of 12 months. The international agency network has been established for over 17 years.

AGE RANGE:
18-27 for au pairs (18-25 USA). No upper age limit for mothers' helps and nannies
NUMBERS PASSING THROUGH:
More than 600 annually
HOW TO CONTACT:
Please send a large SAE for information leaflet and an application form. Telephone enquiries welcome

REGIONS SERVICED:
UK
SPECIAL NEEDS PROVISION:
Rarely able to find placements for people with
special needs due to the nature of the work

STUDY HOLIDAYS (publication)
Central Bureau for Educational Visits and
Exchanges
Seymour Mews House
Seymour Mews
London W1H 9PE
Tel: 071 486 5101 Fax: 071 935 5741
Tel: 071 725 9402 (credit card orders)

If you need to brush up language skills in
preparation for exams, want to learn another
language for enjoyment or to further knowledge
of the country and culture, then *Study Holidays*
has details of a European language course that
can provide just what you are looking for.
Actually being in another country, learning
formally or informally, is an ideal way to become
confident and fluent in a second language.
Study Holidays has just about all the information
you need on holiday courses in 26 European
languages, where you can receive expert tuition
and stay in an area where you can put your
language skills into practice. There is also
practical information on accommodation, travel,
sources for bursaries, grants and scholarships
and language teaching resources.

ISBN 0 90087 90 0. Price £7.95. Available through bookshops or direct from the above address (price £9.45 inc. p&p).

SUE RYDER FOUNDATION
Cavendish
Suffolk CO10 8AY
Tel: 0787 280252

The Sue Ryder Foundation is an international charity formed in 1953. They run 80 homes in 24 different countries for the sick and disabled and offer opportunities for voluntary service in Britain which allow young people to work alongside staff and to meet other volunteers, some of different nationality. Volunteers do whatever work is necessary which may include helping with patients, domestic, office or other duties and in return receive free simple accommodation and meals plus pocket money.

AGE RANGE:
16+
NUMBERS PASSING THROUGH:
c 50 volunteers per year
HOW TO CONTACT:
By letter or telephone to Mr Wilkinson at the above address for information on the foundation and an application form
REGIONS SERVICED:
UK

SPECIAL NEEDS PROVISION:
No provision
COSTS/WAITING LISTS:
Volunteers have to meet their own travel costs

SUMMER JOBS USA 1994 (publication)
Vacation Work Publications
9 Park End Street
Oxford OX1 1HJ
Tel: 0865 241978 Fax: 0865 790885

Thousands of jobs listed at employers' request for students in the United States and Canada. Ranches, summer camps, national parks, theatres, resorts, restaurants etc. Information is given on board and lodging. Wages up to £750 per month. Includes special section giving advice on legal requirements and visa procedure for non-US citizens, plus comments from employers on the specific advantages of particular jobs. Many US summer employers welcome applicants from Britain and Europe. ISBN 1 56079 280 9. Available through libraries, bookshops (price £9.95) or direct from the above address (price £11.45 inc. p&p).

SUMMER MUSIC
22 Gresley Road
London N19 3JZ
Tel: 071 272 5664

Summer Music arrange courses and classes for musicians and singers throughout the year at various locations. There is a programme of weekend courses for singers (solo and choral), guitarists, cellists, violinists, flautists, pianists, trumpeters plus Tai Chi and story-writing. There is an 8-day summer school at Wellington College in Berkshire offering classes in, amongst others, string quartets, symphony orchestra, choirs, story-writing, composing, wind ensembles, sight- singing, opera, music theatre, conducting and contemporary music.

REGIONAL ADDRESSES:
All enquiries to London office
AGE RANGE:
14+
NUMBERS PASSING THROUGH:
Over 400
HOW TO CONTACT:
By telephone or letter for details of courses available
REGIONS SERVICED:
UK
SPECIAL NEEDS PROVISION:
Most venues are fully accessible

COSTS/WAITING LISTS:
The 8-day summer school currently costs
£200 plus VAT for residents and £150 plus
VAT for non-residents. Weekend courses
cost from £78

SURVIVAL INTERNATIONAL
310 Edgware Road
London W2 1DY
Tel: 071 723 5535 Fax: 071 723 4059

Survival International is a worldwide
movement to support tribal peoples. It
stands for their right to decide their own
future and helps them protect their lands,
environment and way of life. Its work is
wholly funded by subscriptions from
members and donations from supporters.
You can help by becoming a member and
taking an active part in one of its letter-
writing campaigns.

TANGENTS
Central Hall
West Tollcross
Edinburgh EH3 9BP
Tel: 031 229 1950 Fax: 031 229 0339

The broad aim of Tangents is to bring together
the young people of Scotland in a variety of
ways to ensure their active participation, and a
voice, in all issues relating to young people –

homelessness, the environment, the law etc. The emphasis is on young people working for themselves to become actively involved and make their opinions and views known on a local, regional and national level. Tangents work with many youth projects in Scotland and can offer young people access to a variety of resources including training, support (from national staff or local workers), representation and access to a national network of young people. Membership is open to any young person in Scotland aged 16-25.

AGE RANGE:
16-25
HOW TO CONTACT:
Telephone, letter or in person
REGIONS SERVICED:
Scotland
SPECIAL NEEDS PROVISION:
Any young person can participate in
Tangents' activities
COSTS/WAITING LISTS:
None

TEACHING ABROAD
10 Drew Street
Brixham
Devon TQ5 9JU
Tel & Fax: 0803 855565

Teaching Abroad sends young people to teach conversational English in Moldavia, Romania and Ukraine. Their salary is their food and housing for the whole time they are there – minimum 4 weeks, maximum 1 year. Applicants must be graduates, undergraduates or gap-year students and must be native English speakers.

AGE RANGE:
18+
NUMBERS PASSING THROUGH:
360 in Ukraine, 210 in Moldavia, 90 in Romania
HOW TO CONTACT:
Telephone, write or fax for further information
COSTS/WAITING LISTS:
£545 for all travel out and back, a home and all meals with a local family. Groups go out in January, March, July and October each year

TEACHING ENGLISH ABROAD
(publication)
Vacation Work Publications
9 Park End Street
Oxford OX1 1HJ
Tel: 0865 241978 Fax: 0865 790885

Guide to short- and long-term opportunities for both trained and untrained teachers in the booming field of teaching English as a Foreign Language. The book contains chapters on over 20 countries where EFL is a major industry including Spain, Greece, Eastern Europe, Turkey, Japan, Taiwan etc., plus surveys of the range of possibilities in Africa and Latin America. Each country chapter discusses the ways in which native speakers of English can find work, the red tape involved, contracts and salaries, plus a list of language schools which hire English teachers. The introduction covers general topics such as how to become qualified in EFL, the role of recruitment agencies, and the possible risks and how to avoid them.
ISBN 1 85458 107 4. Available through libraries, bookshops (price £9.95), or direct from the above address (price £11.45 inc. p&p).

TEENAGERS' VACATION GUIDE TO WORK, STUDY AND ADVENTURE
(publication)
Vacation Work Publications
9 Park End Street
Oxford OX1 1HJ
Tel: 0865 241978 Fax: 0865 790885

Information on the wide range of jobs, study courses and adventure holidays that are available for teenagers in Britain and abroad during the school holidays. Lists hundreds of employers – language schools and other educational establishments, adventure holiday and multi-activity companies and non-profit-making youth organisations which arrange courses, expeditions, home stays, exchanges and term stays in Britain, Europe and worldwide. Provides information on youth travel, health, money and red tape etc., plus practical advice on choosing a project.
ISBN 1 85458 044 2. Available through libraries, bookshops (price £6.95), or direct from the above address (price £8.45 inc. p&p).

THEATRE WORKSHOP EDINBURGH (TW)
34 Hamilton Place
Edinburgh EH3 5AX
Tel: 031 225 7942 (Administration),
031 226 5425 (Box Office & minicom)
Fax: 031 220 0112

TW run two youth theatre groups which meet on a weekly basis throughout the year. They operate a Theatre in Education programme which they take out to schools and youth groups. They put on youth productions which go out on tour and they can offer vocational training opportunities for a small number of young people each year.

AGE RANGE:
Any
HOW TO CONTACT:
Telephone or letter for further information
REGIONS SERVICED:
Scotland
SPECIAL NEEDS PROVISION:
All projects are designed to be accessible to people with special needs. Two members of staff work specifically in this area. The workshop regularly employs performers with special needs
COSTS/WAITING LISTS:
£2 per session to participate in youth theatre activities. May be waiting lists

THISTLE CAMPS
see National Trust for Scotland Conservation Volunteers

TOC H
1 Forest Close
Wendover
Aylesbury
Buckinghamshire HP22 6BT
Tel: 0296 623911 Fax: 0296 696137

Toc H runs short-term residential projects throughout the year in the UK and Germany, usually from a weekend up to 3 weeks in duration. Project work undertaken can include work with people with different disabilities; work with children in need; play schemes and camps; conservation and manual work; study and/or discussion sessions. These projects provide those who take part with opportunities to learn more about themselves and the world we live in.

REGIONAL ADDRESSES:
Eight regional offices, details from Head Office
AGE RANGE:
Any
NUMBERS PASSING THROUGH:
500+
HOW TO CONTACT:
Contact Regional Co-ordinators or Head Office
REGIONS SERVICED:
UK
SPECIAL NEEDS PROVISION:
Dependent on the physical limitations

imposed by each individual project
COSTS/WAITING LISTS:
£5 registration fee to cover administration
costs. Toc H raises money to enable
volunteers to pay as little as possible. Places
are offered on a first come, first served basis.
Contact can be maintained at any time. A
continuous update of vacancies is maintained

TRADES UNION CONGRESS (TUC)
Congress House
Great Russell Street
London WC1B 3LS
Tel: 071 636 4030 Fax: 071 636 0632

The TUC provides an information service for
young people at school or college wishing to
know more about trade unions, either as part of
their studies or when considering employment.
The TUC can also help individual schools to
twin with local union branches as part of the
TUC Adopt a School scheme. This can lead to
work experience, work shadowing and trade
unions taking part in projects. In addition,
many trade unions provide special services for
young people who join them. This can range
from special advice on training and education
to special conferences on youth issues. The
TUC itself has an advisory committee and
conference bringing together young trade
unionists.

REGIONAL ADDRESSES:
Details available from Head Office
AGE RANGE:
14+
HOW TO CONTACT:
By letter for information about trade unions
e.g. for school projects or for those leaving
school considering joining a union,
information about government training
schemes and their rights
REGIONS SERVICED:
UK
SPECIAL NEEDS PROVISION:
Most information is generally suitable for all
young people
COSTS/WAITING LISTS:
There is no charge for using the information
service

TRAINING AND ENTERPRISE COUNCILS
(TECs)
Contact through nearest Jobcentre or Careers
Office

Training and Enterprise Councils are responsible
for schemes and opportunities such as youth
training, employment training and training for
business enterprise. TECs operate on a local
basis which enables them to structure training
to suit their own area. For the address of your
local TEC look in the phone book under
'Training'.

TRANS-EUROPEAN EXCHANGE AND
TRANSFER CONSORTIUM (TEXT)
University of Derby
Kedleston Road
Derby DE3 1GB
Tel: 0332 47181 Fax: 0332 203221

TEXT arranges academic places in Europe for students in higher education. The scheme is open to students attending one of 60 TEXT member institutions throughout Europe.

AGE RANGE:
No specific age range
NUMBERS PASSING THROUGH:
c 50
HOW TO CONTACT:
Direct contact with TEXT office or through the TEXT co-ordinator in your institution
REGIONS SERVICED:
Europe
SPECIAL NEEDS PROVISION:
Dealt with on an individual basis
COSTS/WAITING LISTS:
TEXT member institutions are approached on behalf of the student in order to assist in finding an appropriate placement. Costs are negotiated directly between the student and the institution where they will study. Apply at least 6 months in advance

TRANS-EUROPEAN MOBILITY PROGRAMME FOR UNIVERSITY STUDIES (TEMPUS)
British Council
Medlock Street
Manchester M15 4PR

TEMPUS offers financial support for joint European projects which link enterprises and/or universities in central or Eastern European countries with partners in at least two EC countries. It gives mobility grants for HE staff and students and support for youth exchanges. Applications may involve Albania, the Baltic states, Bulgaria, Croatia, the Czech and Slovak states, Hungary, Poland, Romania and Slovenia. Contact the above address for more details.

TRAVELLERS' SURVIVAL KIT series (publications)
Vacation Work Publications
9 Park End Street
Oxford OX1 1HJ
Tel: 0865 241978 Fax: 0865 790885

A range of books covering various countries for both the independent traveller and package tourists and containing the latest information on all aspects of travel from finding the best value accommodation, public transport and food and drink to health precautions, personal safety and border crossings in some of the less accessible

areas covered as well as background information
on the people, culture, history and language.

Current titles available in the series are:
South America (672pp) – £12.95
ISBN 1 85458 069 8
Europe (288pp) – £6.95
ISBN 1 85458 033 7
Soviet Union and Eastern Europe (544pp) –
£8.95 ISBN 1 85458 010 8
The East (for travellers between Turkey and
Indonesia) (448pp) – £6.95
ISBN 1 85458 031 0
Australia and New Zealand (512pp) – £9.95
ISBN 1 85458 065 5
USA and Canada (416pp) – £9.95
ISBN1 85458 089 2
Central America (480pp) – £8.95
ISBN 1 85458 052 3
Cuba (286pp) – £9.95
ISBN 1 85458 091 4
Eastern Europe (360pp) – £9.95
ISBN 1 85458 113 9

All available in libraries, bookshops or direct
from the above address (add £1 for p&p).

UK COUNCIL FOR MUSIC EDUCATION AND TRAINING

Institute of Education
Unversity of London
20 Bedford Way
London WC1H 0AL
Tel: 071 612 6740

Although the UK Council for Music Education and Training cannot offer specific careers advice, they can deal with general enquiries, usually by pointing enquirers in the direction of relevant reference books through which they can pursue their own particular interests.

AGE RANGE:
Any
HOW TO CONTACT:
Letter
REGIONS SERVICED:
UK
SPECIAL NEEDS PROVISION:
Enquiries welcome
COSTS/WAITING LISTS:
None for general information

UK LINGUA UNIT
Central Bureau for Educational Visits and
Exchanges
Seymour Mews House
Seymour Mews
London W1H 9PE
Tel: 071 224 1477

Lingua is the European Community Programme for the Promotion of the Teaching and Learning of Foreign Languages within the Community. Its aims are to improve the quality and amount of language teaching in the EC by helping trainee language teachers, students and young people to take part in exchanges or to train or study abroad as well as encouraging language-learning in industry.

AGE RANGE:
No specific age range
HOW TO CONTACT:
Write to above address for further information
REGIONS SERVICED:
UK

UK ONE WORLD LINKING ASSOCIATION (UKOWLA)
c/o Town Hall
Chesterfield S40 1LP

UKOWLA organises conferences, publishes newsletters and handbooks, and supports and advises generally on all aspects linking young people from the UK with their counterparts in countries throughout the world.

UK SKILLS
76 Portland Place
London W1N 4AA
Tel: 071 753 5222 Fax: 071 436 7630

UK Skills is an independent organisation with charitable status whose main aim is to promote world-class standards of vocational skills through competitions. Co-ordinating the UK entry for the biennial International Youth Skill Olympics is its key task. The next Skill Olympics take place in October 1995 at Lyons, where competitors from some 30 countries will be taking part. A top priority is to develop a national framework of skills competitions in the UK across all industry sectors to increase the opportunities for young people to take part at local, regional and national level. Established skills competitions cover engineering/ manufacturing skills, building trades, motor vehicles, fabrication and welding, electrical

installation, hairdressing, cookery and waiting,
jewellery making, electronics, IT and others are
being developed.

AGE RANGE:
Under 25 (in 1995)
HOW TO CONTACT:
Write for further details of skills competitions in
the UK

ULSTER UNIONIST PARTY
3 Glengall Street
Belfast BT12 5AE
Tel: 0232 324601

UNDER 26
52 Grosvenor Gardens
London SW1W 0AG
Tel: 071 823 5363

Under 26 is a new scheme covering England
and Wales which is open to all young people
under the age of 26. For an annual subscription
of £6 you will receive the Under 26 card. This
card can save you money on travel, holidays,
eating out, clothes, records and sports goods.
When you apply for a card you will receive the
Under 26 Discount Directory, which lists all the
places that offer discounts on production of the
card. The card is also valid in over 150,000
places throughout Europe, where it is very
popular. At present some 3.5 million young

Europeans are carrying the card. As well as discounts, cardholders will receive a regular magazine with features on current issues, plus news of the latest discounts, offers and competitions open to members, and information about the large number of exchange trips, projects and events organised for cardholders. Membership of Under 26 also gives you access to a 24-hour legal advice line whereby you can speak to a trained legal adviser at any time.

REGIONAL ADDRESSES:
Under 26 Cymru, 5 Washington Chambers, Stanwell Road, Penarth, South Glamorgan CF6 2AF Tel: 0222 705611
REGIONS SERVICED:
England and Wales
COSTS/WAITING LISTS:
£6 per year

UNDERSTANDING INDUSTRY (UI)
Enterprise House
59-65 Upper Ground
London SE1 9PQ
Tel: 071 620 0735 Fax: 071 928 0578

UI is a national education/industry partnership organisation which specialises in bringing business people into the classroom to work with young people as part of the school timetable. It aims to give students a greater understanding of how interesting and exciting business and industry can be. UI courses are different, active, and fun, and quite often involve visits to companies to gain first-hand experience. They usually take about 11 hours, broken into nine different sessions covering marketing, design, people at work and management. They take place at school or college during normal hours, so your approach should be through your school/college.

AGE RANGE:
16-19
NUMBERS PASSING THROUGH:
c 25,000
HOW TO CONTACT:
Through teacher
REGIONS SERVICED:
UK
SPECIAL NEEDS PROVISION:
Enquiries welcome

UNITED NATIONS ASSOCIATION (WALES) INTERNATIONAL YOUTH SERVICE
Welsh Centre for International Affairs
The Temple of Peace
Cathays Park
Cardiff CF1 3AP
Tel: 0222 220388 Fax: 0222 665557

UNA (Wales) IYS is concerned with promoting the ideals of the United Nations Charter through the medium of short-term International Voluntary Projects.   These are split into the standard exchange programme running in Europe, North

America, North Africa, Japan and Australia, with projects lasting between 2 and 3 weeks with no skills required; the 'North-South' programme for volunteers wishing to attend a project in Sub-Saharan Africa or India, with projects lasting from 4 weeks up to 6 months, attendance at an IYS Orientation Weekend being compulsory and, for some organisations, relevant skills being required; and the Wales programme, which requires volunteers to act as 'leaders' (co-ordinators) for the groups of international volunteers coming to Wales.

AGE RANGE:
16-18+ (varies according to country)
HOW TO CONTACT:
Write to the above address with an SAE. The list of International Projects comes out in March/April annually, North-South orientation days in February and October.Leaders training begins in April
REGIONS SERVICED:
UK
SPECIAL NEEDS PROVISION:
Enquiries welcome
COSTS/WAITING LISTS:
Standard exchange projects cost between £50-£85 each. This will include accommodation and food while on the project

UNITED WORLD COLLEGES (UWC)
London House
Mecklenburgh Square
London WC1N 2AB
Tel: 071 833 2626 Fax: 071 837 3102

United World Colleges offer students of all races and creeds the opportunity of developing international understanding through combining high quality, internationally orientated academic study with activities which encourage a sense of adventure and social responsibility. Colleges in the UK, Swaziland, USA, Canada, Singapore, Italy, Venezuela and Hong Kong offer broad-based curricula for students drawn from the widest possible variety of national and social backgrounds. Study programmes include full secondary education, the International Baccalaureate Diploma, and vocational training. Selection for places, usually following a strong recommendation from a head teacher or similar, is based on ability, academic achievement prior to entry, and a strong personal desire to further the aims of UWC.

AGE RANGE:
16-18
COSTS/WAITING LISTS:
Most students will be awarded of scholarships for which high academic and personal qualifications are required. Further details from UWC

UNIVERSITIES AND COLLEGES
ADMISSIONS SERVICE
Fulton House
Jessop Avenue
Cheltenham
Gloucester GL50 3SH
Tel: 0242 222444 Fax: 0242 221622

UCAS processes applications to all UK universities and most colleges.

AGE RANGE:
Any
NUMBERS PASSING THROUGH:
400,000 applicants
HOW TO CONTACT:
Telephone or letter to Enquiries
REGIONS SERVICED:
All applications from the UK and overseas to UK institutions
COSTS/WAITING LISTS:
It is best to apply early. The deadline date for receipt of application forms is 15 December of the year preceding entry. There is a £12 application fee which should accompany the form

VACATION WORK PUBLICATIONS
9 Park End Street
Oxford OX1 1HJ
Tel: 0865 241978 Fax: 0865 790885

Vacation Work publications produce a wide range of books covering jobs at home and abroad, travel and adventure. Their comprehensive list covers topics such as summer jobs in Britain and abroad, working your way around the world, teaching English as a second language, international voluntary work and studying abroad. They also publish the *Travellers' Survival Kit* range of books, offering up-to-date information on travel in Central America, Cuba, USA and Canada, Australia and New Zealand, Europe, Eastern Europe and Asia. Contact Vacation Work for a list of publications.

VENTURE SCOTLAND
10 Randolph Crescent
Edinburgh EH3 7TU
Tel: 031 220 4026

A challenging programme of outdoor activities, problem-solving and practical conservation which incorporates weekend and week-long residential courses in remote parts of Scotland. There are opportunities for young people to participate in activities or lead them as volunteers.

AGE RANGE:
15-25
NUMBERS PASSING THROUGH:
150 participants; 70 volunteers
HOW TO CONTACT:
Telephone or letter for information on current

activities and how to get involved
REGIONS SERVICED:
Strathclyde region, predominantly around
Glasgow; Lothian Region, within Edinburgh
SPECIAL NEEDS PROVISION:
Limited provision
COSTS/WAITING LISTS:
Weekend residential course fee is £5; week-
long residential course fee is £25. Ideally,
apply 2 months in advance

VISA SHOP LTD
1 Charing Cross Underground
London WC2
Tel: 071 379 0419 Fax: 071 497 2590

Visa Shop offers a comprehensive service of
visas and passports including information on
requirements for world travel as well as work
permits for students and details of working
holidays.

AGE RANGE:
Any
NUMBERS PASSING THROUGH:
200 per week
HOW TO CONTACT:
Telephone, letter, fax or in person for
information and advice plus visa or passport
forms if appropriate
REGIONS SERVICED:
UK

COSTS/WAITING LISTS:
Information is free. There is a general charge
of £14 for most visas or passports

VOLUNTARY SERVICE BELFAST (VSB)
70-72 Lisburn Road
Belfast BT9 6AF
Tel: 0232 329499 Fax: 0232 321797

VSB provide opportunities for voluntary work
placements with children, the elderly and
disabled and those most in need, as well as
opportunities to take part in challenging
conservation and practical tasks. VSB also
provide vocational skills training for 18-25 year-
olds in areas such as horticulture, working with
children, computing, job search etc.

AGE RANGE:
16+

NUMBERS PASSING THROUGH:
400 volunteers

HOW TO CONTACT:
Telephone, letter or in person for further
information and an application form

REGIONS SERVICED:
Mainly serves the Belfast area but anyone
willing to travel there at their own expense
can apply

SPECIAL NEEDS PROVISION:
Staff are available to provide support

COSTS/WAITING LISTS:
Apply about 4 weeks in advance

THE VOLUNTEER CENTRE UK
29 Lower King's Road
Berkhamsted
Hertfordshire HP4 2AB
Tel: 0442 873311 Fax: 0442 870852

The Volunteer Centre is a resource centre for anyone involved or wanting to become involved in volunteer work at any level of participation. They can provide information on opportunities for volunteering as well as information about matters relating to voluntary work e.g. welfare benefits, expenses, insurance etc. A selection of volunteering opportunities is shown weekly on BBC2 Ceefax. The Signposts service can provide would-be volunteers with a list, available free on request, of organisations in their local area which involve volunteers in their work. The centre produces a wide range of publications and information sheets – write to the above address for further information.

AGE RANGE:
Any
HOW TO CONTACT:
By letter (with SAE) to the Advisory Team for further information on volunteering
REGIONS SERVICED:
UK
SPECIAL NEEDS PROVISION:
Provision varies – depends on the individual volunteering opportunity

COSTS/WAITING LISTS:
Costs of publications vary

VOLUNTEER DEVELOPMENT SCOTLAND
(VDS)
80 Murray Place
Stirling
FK8 2BX
Tel: 0786 479593

VDS is the national resource and development agency on volunteering in Scotland. It mainly provides support services to agencies and individuals who work with volunteers. It also holds information about volunteer bureaux in Scotland so although it is unable to advise on individual placements it can point potential volunteers in the right direction.

AGE RANGE:
Any
HOW TO CONTACT:
Telephone or letter for general information
REGIONS SERVICED:
Scotland
SPECIAL NEEDS PROVISION:
Enquiries welcome within the limit of the available service
COSTS/WAITING LISTS:
There are no costs for information

VOLUNTEER WORK (publication)
Central Bureau for Educational Visits and
Exchanges
Seymour Mews House
Seymour Mews
London W1H 9PE
Tel: 071 486 5101 Fax: 071 935 5741
Tel: 071 725 9402 (credit card orders)

A period of voluntary work can be enriching,
involving you in improving the quality of
community life and environment. Opportunities
exist in developed and developing countries,
and *Volunteer Work* gives information on those
recruiting and placing volunteers for medium
and long-term service in Britain and abroad.
Agency profiles, countries of operation and
projects are given together with the qualifications
and skills required of volunteers, terms of service,
briefing and relevant literature; development
workers and returned volunteers offer valuable
insights through their experiences. The guide
encourages volunteers to consider their
motivation and commitment, and offers practical
advice on preparation and training,
understanding development, travel, health and
insurance.
ISBN 0 900087 92 7. Price £7.99. Available
through bookshops, or direct from the above
address (price £9.49 inc. p&p).

WALES CO-OPERATIVE CENTRE
Llandaff Court
Fairwater Road
Cardiff CF5 2XP
Tel: 0222 554955

This agency gives information and help to groups in Wales planning to set up in business together as a co-operative.

WAR ON WANT
37-39 Great Guildford Street
London SE1 0ES
Tel: 071 620 1111 Fax: 071 261 9291

War on Want, the campaign against world poverty, tackles poverty at its roots, funding practical long-term development projects. Aiming to change attitudes in the richer nations and conditions in the poorer ones, War on Want supports people seeking change in their own localities. Young people who wish to help can volunteer at the Head Office in London, or collect used stamps and send them to War on Want.

WATCH TRUST FOR ENVIRONMENTAL EDUCATION LTD (WATCH)
The Green
Witham Park
Waterside South
Lincoln LN5 7JR
Tel: 0522 544400 Fax: 0522 511616

Watch is the junior wing of the Wildlife Trusts and an environment club that gets you involved. Once you are a member you receive the club magazine, *Watchword,* three times per year plus your local newsletter, which gives you details of activities and groups in your area. You also have the opportunity to take part in national projects.

AGE RANGE:
7+
NUMBERS PASSING THROUGH:
33,000 members – 150,000 taking part in activities
HOW TO CONTACT:
SAE to above address for information
REGIONS SERVICED:
UK
SPECIAL NEEDS PROVISION:
No special provision
COSTS/WAITING LISTS:
Annual membership is £5 per year. Local group costs vary – typically 50p per session

WATERWAY RECOVERY GROUP (WRG)
114 Regent's Park Road
London NW1 8UQ
Tel: 071 722 7217 Fax: 071 722 7213

WRG is the national organisation which arranges restoration and conservation work throughout Britain's canals and waterways. Young people are welcome to join in on week-long, weekends or single-day work parties and events held along the waterway system. WRG provide working holidays throughout the year for minimal charges.

REGIONAL ADDRESSES:
London: Lesley McFadyen, 35 Sylvester Road, East Dulwich, London SE22 9PB Tel: 081 693 3266
North-west: Roger Evans, 45 Hattons Lane, Liverpool L16 7QR Tel: 051 722 6216
North-east: Martin Johnson, 38 Wesley Garth, Beeston, Leeds LS11 8RF Tel: 0532 711215
Midlands: Jonathan Smith, 4a Walford Street, Tividale, Warley, West Midlands B69 2LB Tel: 021 557 2353
South: Tim Lewis, 5 Herongate Road, London E12 5EJ Tel: 081 530 7926
AGE RANGE:
16+
NUMBERS PASSING THROUGH:
1,000-2,000
HOW TO CONTACT:
For general enquiries contact main address

above for an information pack covering all activities of the group

REGIONS SERVICED:
UK

SPECIAL NEEDS PROVISION:
No special provision

COSTS/WAITING LISTS:
Annual subscription to magazine *Navvies* is a minimum of £1.50. A working holiday costs about £30 per week, which covers food and accommodation

---

WATERWAYS FOR YOUTH (WFY)
Inland Waterways Association
114 Regent's Park Road
London NW1 8UQ
Tel: 071 586 2510/2556 Fax: 071 722 7213

Waterways for Youth campaign to encourage greater participation by young people in a variety of leisure and educational activities based on inland waterways. They provide free activity experience at many major events throughout the country. These include canoeing, sailing, rowing, sailboarding, ecology, water safety, knot-tying, painting, nature trails, digger and dredger driving, angling, restoration and conservation (see also Waterway Recovery Group).

CONTACT:
Chairman: Ivor Caplan, 152 Castle Road, Cookley, Kidderminster DY10 3TB Tel: 0562 851256

Vice-chairman: Marion Waters, 5 Harpenden
Road, Wanstead E12 5HJ Tel: 081 530 4767
AGE RANGE:
Up to 17
NUMBERS PASSING THROUGH:
5,000
HOW TO CONTACT:
By telephone or letter to Ivor Caplan (address
above), or the London office for details of
current and future events
REGIONS SERVICED:
UK
SPECIAL NEEDS PROVISION:
Some WFY activities are easily available and
in some instances specially adapted
equipment can be provided
COSTS/WAITING LISTS:
Cost to be negotiated with event organisers
towards expenses for providing Waterways
for Youth activities

WEEKEND ARTS COLLEGE (WAC)
Dalby Street
Kentish Town
London NW5 3NG
Tel: 071 267 9421

The main aim of WAC is to provide professional
training for young people who are seriously
thinking about a career in the performing arts.
WAC runs classes for young people to teach
them basic skills and techniques necessary to
gain further full-time training. Classes are held

in dance, drama and music. Young people have
the opportunity to participate in creative sessions,
perform, receive advice and help with auditions
and interviews and gain experience in different
styles of work.

AGE RANGE:
6-26
NUMBERS PASSING THROUGH:
c 500
HOW TO CONTACT:
Telephone or letter for advice, information
and a prospectus
REGIONS SERVICED:
UK
SPECIAL NEEDS PROVISION:
Young people with special needs can partake
of all the activities at the college
COSTS/WAITING LISTS:
There is a waiting list for courses and it is
advisable to apply as early as possible

WELSH ARTS COUNCIL
Holst House
Museum Place
Cardiff CF1 3NX
Tel: 0222 394711

See separate Arts Council entry

**WELSH COLLEGE OF MUSIC AND DRAMA
(WCMD)**
Castle Grounds
Cathays Park
Cardiff CF1 3ER
Tel: 0222 342854 Fax: 0222 237639

College for professional training in the performing arts. Higher Education Diploma and degree courses offered range from acting, music (all instruments and voice) – all styles, stage management and stage design. Also offers training for those wishing to work as music or drama teachers, or in Theatre in Education. Excellent facilities include two theatres, recital rooms, electronic music studios and design workshops.

AGE RANGE:
Any
NUMBERS PASSING THROUGH:
c 700 students at present
HOW TO CONTACT:
Telephone, letter or fax to above address for information about courses
REGIONS SERVICED:
UK and overseas
SPECIAL NEEDS PROVISION:
If college is informed in advance of special needs requirements they can usually accommodate
COSTS/WAITING LISTS:
Full list of course fees available from the

college. The college has a number of scholarships and prizes on offer to cover course fees. Also, some LEAs give grants for certain courses. Further details available in college prospectus. Auditions held between October and April for entry on to full-time courses the following September.
Applications for part-time courses dealt with as they arrive

THE WESTON SPIRIT
2 Roscoe Place
Bold Street
Liverpool L1 4HF
Tel: 051 709 6620 Fax: 051 707 0577

The Weston Spirit is an organisation that offers its members the opportunity to learn how to live and work together, to respect other peoples' views but to gain the confidence to challenge them and to express their own point of view. Members take part in voluntary work in their own areas and away in residential centres with disabled people. The Weston Spirit offers 'drop-in' facilities and a programme of social, educational and personal development opportunities. It is about gaining self-confidence and control of your own life.

REGIONAL ADDRESSES:
South Glamorgan: Shand House, 20 Newport Road, Cardiff CF2 1BD Tel: 0222 462992
Tyneside: Tyne Theatre and Opera House,

Westgate Road, Newcastle-upon-Tyne
Tel: 091 232 1322
AGE RANGE:
16 or 17 at recruitment
NUMBERS PASSING THROUGH:
1,000
HOW TO CONTACT:
Telephone or letter to your local office
REGIONS SERVICED:
Merseyside, South Glamorgan and Tyneside
SPECIAL NEEDS PROVISION:
The Weston Spirit would like to make itself
accessible to all. However, due to some
access/transport difficulties not all disabilities
can be catered for at present, but enquiries
are welcome
COSTS/WAITING LISTS:
There are no costs or waiting lists

WH SMITH INTERACT
Education Department
Royal National Theatre
South Bank
London SE1 9PX
Tel: 071 928 5214

WH Smith Interact is a scheme where
professionals from the National Theatre visit
schools and colleges to give workshops based
on a subject of your choice covering any aspect
of theatre. Groups of any age, level or experience
can benefit from an Interact session.

AGE RANGE:
Any
HOW TO CONTACT:
Write or telephone for further information
REGIONS SERVICED:
UK
SPECIAL NEEDS PROVISION:
Special needs groups welcome
COSTS/WAITING LISTS:
Preferably contact at least 10 weeks before
you want to have your workshop

WHITBREAD YOUNG VOLUNTEER AWARDS
Freepost (BS6647)
Bristol BS1 4YU
Tel: 0272 252000

The Whitbread Volunteer Action Award Scheme is designed to recognise and reward young people who give up their own time for the benefit of others, especially those disadvantaged by disability, sickness, situation or age. There are two categories in the Award, one for individual volunteers and one for volunteering groups, with a prize of £1,000 for each category.

AGE RANGE:
Under 25
NUMBERS PASSING THROUGH:
Over 200 entries in 1993
HOW TO CONTACT:
Write or telephone for a nomination form

REGIONS SERVICED:
UK (excluding Northern Ireland)
SPECIAL NEEDS PROVISION:
No special provision but applications
welcome
COSTS/WAITING LISTS:
No costs or waiting lists. The Award Scheme
is usually launched in April each year and the
winners are announced in November

WILDFOWL & WETLANDS TRUST (W&WT)
Slimbridge
Gloucester GL2 7BT
Tel: 0453 890333 Fax: 0453 890827

The Wildfowl & Wetlands Trust is an
environmental organisation which can offer
opportunities for young people to gain
experience in various aspects of conservation.
On the practical side you could help with
weeding, hedge-trimming, clearing silt etc. –
messy but absolutely vital! On the administrative
side, you might help with cataloguing of press
cuttings, photocopying, stuffing appeals
envelopes and so on. Or on the 'people' side of
conservation you may help to staff the
Information Desk, help with preparation of
graphic displays/teaching aids, or just generally
help the public with their enquiries.

REGIONAL ADDRESSES:
Regional Centres in Lancashire, West Sussex,

Cambridgeshire, Dyfed, Tyne and Wear, Dumfriesshire and Co. Down. Contact the National Centre at Slimbridge for full details

AGE RANGE:
Varies according to the work

HOW TO CONTACT:
Letter plus SAE to National Centre for further information and leaflets

REGIONS SERVICED:
Enquiries welcome from throughout the UK but most of the work of the Trust takes place in the areas surrounding its Centres

SPECIAL NEEDS PROVISION:
Enquiries welcome

COSTS/WAITING LISTS:
If applicable, costs will be explained. There are no waiting lists

---

WINANT CLAYTON VOLUNTEER ASSOCIATION (WCVA)
38 Newark Street
London E1 2AA
Tel: 071 375 0547 Fax: 071 377 2437

WCVA provides an opportunity for people of all ages and backgrounds to experience another culture and people, by working within it for a period of 3 months from June to September each summer. Placements vary and examples include: working with deprived inner-city kids; working with AIDS patients; helping in a children's home; working in an adult psychiatric rehabilitation centre. All placements are on the east coast of America. Some voluntary experience in the UK would be useful but maturity and keenness are more important.

AGE RANGE:
18+
NUMBERS PASSING THROUGH:
c 20 aged 19-45
HOW TO CONTACT:
Letter or telephone for information
REGIONS SERVICED:
UK
SPECIAL NEEDS PROVISION:
No special provision but has an equal opportunities policy
COSTS/WAITING LISTS:
Volunteers usually need £500 to pay for air fare and insurance and a further £500 to finance their 3-week holiday at the end of their placement. Individuals often fund-raise locally or apply to charities such as the Rotary Club, Round Table, Prince's Trust etc. Volunteers should apply from September to January before the summer they wish to travel

---

WINDSOR FELLOWSHIP
47 Hackney Road
London E2 7NX
Tel: 071 613 0373 Fax: 071 613 0377

The Windsor Fellowship is a 3-year personal development and basic management skills training programme for minority ethnic undergraduates. It is recognised that certain barriers exist in the area of employment, particularly for young black and Asian people. Established in 1986, the Fellowship aims to overcome these by encouraging, supporting and preparing undergraduates for management careers in industry, commerce and public administration. A 2-year programme and a Law Bursary will be offered in 1994. Contact office for details.

AGE RANGE:
16-27
NUMBERS PASSING THROUGH:
190
HOW TO CONTACT:
By telephone, letter, fax or in person for further information
REGIONS SERVICED:
UK
COSTS/WAITING LISTS:
No costs. Application forms must be returned to the Fellowship by the end of March in the year of application to university or college

---

WINGED FELLOWSHIP TRUST
Angel House
20-32 Pentonville Road
London N1 9XD
Tel: 071 833 2594 Fax: 071 278 0370

Volunteers are required for a week or two at five holiday centres for severely physically disabled people. Duties may include lifting, washing, dressing, feeding and pushing wheelchairs. Some domestic work is required of each helper as well as helping on daily outings and helping to entertain guests during their stay. Volunteers need to be fairly fit, cheerful and enthusiastic. Hard work and some late hours are involved in the job. Overseas and touring holidays are also arranged.

AGE RANGE:
17-75
NUMBERS PASSING THROUGH:
6,000 volunteers looking after 5,000 disabled people
HOW TO CONTACT:
Telephone, letter or fax for a booklet on what to expect, an application form and brochure
REGIONS SERVICED:
UK
SPECIAL NEEDS PROVISION:
Usually take on one or two people with disabilities to help as volunteers in the centres by special arrangement with the centre manager
COSTS/WAITING LISTS:
Volunteers should apply at least 1 month in advance

WINSTON CHURCHILL MEMORIAL TRUST
15 Queen's Gate Terrace
London SW7 5PR
Tel: 071 584 9315

Travelling fellowships given to UK citizens to travel overseas with air fares and all expenses paid for projects which will benefit you and your country on your return (awards do not cover courses or academic studies).

AGE RANGE:
Any
NUMBERS PASSING THROUGH:
100 fellowships are given each year
HOW TO CONTACT:
Telephone or letter (with SAE) for information on how to apply
REGIONS SERVICED:
UK
SPECIAL NEEDS PROVISION:
Enquiries welcome
COSTS/WAITING LISTS:
Apply from July to October to travel the following year

WOMEN AND MANUAL TRADES (WAMT)
52-54 Featherstone Street
London EC1Y 8RT
Tel: 071 251 9192/251 9193

Women and Manual Trades was set up in 1970

by women carpenters, plumbers, electricians – women in all the skilled trades – to provide information on training available in these trades for young women, and provide support to help young women handle working in male-dominated occupations. If you're interested in learning more about the exciting work to be done in the manual trades – what it's like, both good and bad – WAMT will send you information, written by women who've done it. WAMT work mainly through schools, producing exercises, videos, cartoon stories, posters etc., but they also answer individual enquiries.

AGE RANGE:
Any
NUMBERS PASSING THROUGH:
c 250 individual enquiries; c 500 through school talks and careers conventions
HOW TO CONTACT:
Letter or telephone
REGIONS SERVICED:
UK
SPECIAL NEEDS PROVISION:
No specific provision. Enquiries are dealt with on an individual basis
COSTS/WAITING LISTS:
No costs involved

WOMEN'S ENVIRONMENTAL NETWORK
(WEN)
Aberdeen Studios
22 Highbury Grove
London N5 2EA
Tel: 071 354 8823

WEN is a non-profit-making organisation which educates, informs and empowers women who care about the environment. It runs seminars, workshops and public meetings, and researches and produces a range of action packs and leaflets on all aspects of environmental issues. It relies on memberships and donations for its survival. Membership entitles you to receive newsletters, briefings and notice of public events, plus information on playing an active role. WEN encourages both men and women to join, but looks at environment issues from women's perspective.

AGE RANGE:
Any
HOW TO CONTACT:
Letter or telephone to above address
REGIONS SERVICED:
UK
SPECIAL NEEDS PROVISION:
Enquiries welcome
COSTS/WAITING LISTS:
Membership rates vary between £7 and £20

WOODCRAFT FOLK
13 Ritherdon Road
London SW17 8QE
Tel: 081 672 6031 Fax: 081 767 2457

The Woodcraft Folk is an educational movement for children and young people designed to develop self-confidence and activity in society with the aim of building a world based on equality, friendship, peace and co-operation. Weekly meetings take place and other activities include international exchanges, non-competitive games, outdoor activities and environmental work.

REGIONAL ADDRESSES:
Midlands: Birmingham and Midland Institute, Margaret Street, Birmingham B3 3BS
Tel: 021 236 4361
North: 252 York Road, Leeds LS9 9DN
Tel: 0532 498359
Scotland: Co-op Union, 95 Morrison Street, Glasgow Tel: 041 429 0952
South-west: Friary House, 15 Colston Street, Bristol BS1 5AP Tel: 0272 227967
Wales: Manora, Cwmystwyth, Dyfed SY23 4AF Tel: 097 422437
AGE RANGE:
No specific age range
NUMBERS PASSING THROUGH:
25,000+ members
HOW TO CONTACT:
Phone or letter for information on activities

REGIONS SERVICED:
UK
SPECIAL NEEDS PROVISION:
All groups encourage full participation by all members of the community
COSTS/WAITING LISTS:
Weekly subscription up to 16 is 40-50p.
16+ annual subscription is £10 waged,
£4 unwaged

WOODLARKS CAMP SITE TRUST
Tilford Road
Farnham
Surrey GU10 3RN
Tel: 0252 716279

Woodlarks Camp is a camp site for physically handicapped people with facilities specially designed for their needs. Enquiries are welcome from people interested in helping for a week. Individuals are invited to write in giving details of their age and interests. They will then be put in touch with the leader of a week's camp where extra help is needed.

AGE RANGE:
Any
NUMBERS PASSING THROUGH:
c 500 volunteers
HOW TO CONTACT:
SAE to above address for more information and a list of camps where extra help may be needed

REGIONS SERVICED:
UK
SPECIAL NEEDS PROVISION:
See above
COSTS/WAITING LISTS:
Costs vary from camp to camp – usually
between £25-£50. Camps run from May to
September. Contact in the New Year for
details of camps

WOOLWICH YOUNG RADIO
PLAYWRIGHTS' FESTIVAL
see Independent Radio Drama Productions

WORK YOUR WAY AROUND THE WORLD
(publication)
Vacation Work Publications
9 Park End Street
Oxford OX1 1HJ
Tel: 0865 241978 Fax: 0865 790885

A guide for the working traveller which includes
hundreds of recent first-hand accounts and offers
authoritative advice on how to find work around
the world, either in advance or on the spot.
Includes sections on teaching English in Eastern
Europe, work in Greek tourism and agriculture,
a summer job programme in Jamaica, au pairing
throughout Europe and Canada, grape-picking
in France and Australia and more. Gives up-to-
date information on how to travel free by working
a passage, dates and details of harvests, and

how to survive when the money runs low. Realistic advice on how to become a barman/ woman, kiwi fruit-picker, ski guide, jackaroo, teacher, fish-packer etc.

ISBN 1 85458 074 4. Available through libraries, bookshops (price £9.95), or direct from the above address (price £11.45 inc. p&p).

WORKING HOLIDAYS 1994 (publication)
Central Bureau for Educational Visits and
Exchanges
Seymour Mews House
Seymour Mews
London W1H 9PE
Tel: 071 486 5101 Fax: 071 935 5741
Tel: 071 725 9402 (credit card orders)

Holiday jobs are excellent ways of experiencing life in other countries and, if you are prepared for a complete change, seasonal work can take you almost anywhere in the world. You could for example pick pears in Australia, teach on a summer camp in North America, cut trails through a rain cloud forest in Costa Rica, be a holiday courier in Spain, pick grapes in France, work on a steam railway in Britain or crew a yacht in the Mediterranean. Well researched and revised annually, *Working Holidays* has over 300 pages of information on over 99,000 paid and voluntary seasonal work opportunities in 70 countries including Britain. Full information for each job is given together with details on work/residence permits, travel,

insurance, accommodation and further sources
of information.
ISBN 0 900087 91 9. Price £7.95. Available
from bookshops, or direct from the above address
(price £9.45 inc. p&p).

WORKING IN SKI RESORTS – EUROPE
(publication)
Vacation Work Publications
9 Park End Street
Oxford OX1 1HJ
Tel: 0865 241978 Fax: 0865 790885

Guide which contains information on how to
find work as a ski instructor, chalet girl, teacher,
au pair, shop assistant, courier, disc jockey,
snow cleaner, ski technician, office worker or
resort representative in a ski resort. The first part
of the book – 'A Job Before You Go' – describes
how to pre-arrange work with over 90 British ski
tour operators, school ski party organisers and
other organisations. The second part – 'Finding
a Job on the Spot', gives reports on over 40
resorts, explaining where the jobs are and how
to get them, plus information on accommodation
and nightlife.
ISBN 1 85458 109 0. Available through libraries,
bookshops (price £8.95), or direct from the
above address (price £10.45 inc. p&p).

WORKNET
Twin Spires
155 Northumberland Street
Belfast BT13 2JF
Tel: 0232 246211 Fax: 0232 320898

Worknet is a community-based employment and training organisation established to develop the potential of the human resource in the Belfast area by means of a series of inter-related programmes. It aims to improve the employment prospects of its client base via training, counselling, employer placement and job-finding. Aimed mainly at the unemployed, Worknet employs 48 staff and is a registered charity.

AGE RANGE:
18-65
NUMBERS PASSING THROUGH:
600+
COSTS/WAITING LISTS:
There are no costs. All interested individuals are immediately interviewed

WORLD CHALLENGE EXPEDITIONS
Soane House
305-315 Latimer Road
London W10 6RA
Tel: 071 964 1331 Fax: 071 964 5298

WCE plans and runs expeditions, lasting approximately 1 month, to far-flung destinations including India, Borneo, Ecuador and Venezuela for school groups mainly and individual applicants. An average team comprises 16-20 members, with fully trained, qualified leaders at a ratio of one leader to eight team members. As well as the leadership training we adopt educational aims including cultural exchange and physical challenge, all at an acceptable, fully inclusive price.

AGE RANGE:
16-20
NUMBERS PASSING THROUGH:
c 250
HOW TO CONTACT:
By telephone or letter for a brochure and application form, either individually or through school
REGIONS SERVICED:
UK
SPECIAL NEEDS PROVISION:
No provision
COSTS/WAITING LISTS:
Expeditions cost approx £2,000 for individuals. Similar price bracket for school groups but varies according to numbers and destination

WWOOF (Working for Organic Growers)
19 Bradford Road
Lewes
Sussex BN7 1RB
Tel: 0273 476286

The aims of WWOOF are to give you first hand experience of organic farming and growing, to help the organic movement, which is often labour intensive, and to make contact with other people in the organic movement. WWOOF is an exchange; in return for working on organic farms, gardens and smallholdings (full-time and quite hard) you will receive meals, somewhere for your sleeping bag and, if necessary, transport to and from the local station. Members receive a newsletter every 2 months which lists details of places needing help each weekend. The newsletter also gives details of events, developments, training and job opportunities in the organic movement and contributions from members.

REGIONAL ADDRESSES:
Contact main office for details
AGE RANGE:
16+
NUMBERS PASSING THROUGH:
2,000 members of which about half are 18-25
HOW TO CONTACT:
SAE to main office for brochure and application form

REGIONS SERVICED:
UK and parts of Europe
SPECIAL NEEDS PROVISION:
No provision
COSTS/WAITING LISTS:
Annual membership is £8

A YEAR BETWEEN (publication)
Central Bureau for Educational Visits and
Exchanges
Seymour Mews House
Seymour Mews
London W1H 9PE
Tel: 071 486 5101 Fax: 071 935 5741
Tel: 071 725 9402 (credit card orders)

A complete guide for those taking a year out
between school and higher education or work,
or higher education and a career. A year out is
a rare chance to stand back, assess where life
has brought you so far, and seize the freedom
offered to learn new skills and develop existing
ones. *A Year Between* provides full details of
over 100 organisations offering placements in
industry, research, business, teaching,
community/social service and youth work in
Britain and overseas as well as opportunities for
discovery, leadership, conservation projects and
further study. Authoritative advice and
information is included together with practical
hints, discussion of the pros and cons, and details
on planning and preparation. *A Year Between*
will help you make the most of a year out.

ISBN 0 900087 88 9. Price £7.99. Available through bookshops, or direct from the above address (price £9.49 inc. p&p).

YEAR IN INDUSTRY
Simon Building
University of Manchester
Oxford Road
Manchester M13 9PL
Tel: 061 275 4396 Fax: 061 275 3844

A scheme offering students a pre-degree taste of industry – paid, challenging work in a company, backed by comprehensive 'off the job' training. The scheme, designed to stimulate students' interest in industry and to help companies spot future graduate talent, is open to students of any discipline but is particularly suited to those interested in any branch of engineering, science, computing, mathematics etc. – acknowledged shortage skills. If you are expecting, or already have an offer of a place on a degree course, Year in Industry can put you in contact with participating companies – the companies choose who they will interview/employ – and you will spend up to a year gaining experience and learning skills in your chosen discipline. At the end you may be offered sponsorship to do your degree course, or you may be offered future employment or summer vacation work with the company. If your placement involves living or working away from home Year in Industry can provide advice and support. 85% of graduates from the pilot scheme returned to industry on completing their degree course – 26% with Firsts, 40% Upper Seconds. Most Admissions Tutors readily support deferred entry.

REGIONAL ADDRESSES:
Year in Industry has 11 regional offices – contact Head Office at above address for your local details
AGE RANGE:
Usually 17-20
NUMBERS PASSING THROUGH:
300+
HOW TO CONTACT:
Phone, letter or fax
REGIONS SERVICED:
UK
COSTS/WAITING LISTS:
No costs. Contact during upper sixth year, 6-12 months before pre-degree starts

---

YOUNG ARCHAEOLOGISTS CLUB (YAC)
Bowes Morrell House
111 Walmgate
York YO1 2UA
Tel: 0904 671417

The YAC is the only national club of its kind for anyone between the ages of 9 and 18. Membership includes a pin badge and membership card which will entitle you to free discounted entry to centres around the country. You will also receive the Club's exciting quarterly magazine *Young Archaeologist.* YAC members can join local branches who organise regular activity-based events. Contact the Club Co-ordinator, Juliet Mather, at the above address for further details.

REGIONAL ADDRESSES:
Contact through address above
AGE RANGE:
9-18
NUMBERS PASSING THROUGH:
2,410 members
HOW TO CONTACT:
Write to above address
REGIONS SERVICED:
UK
SPECIAL NEEDS PROVISION:
No provision
COSTS/WAITING LISTS:
Membership is £5 per year

**YOUNG BRITISH ESPERANTISTS
(JUNULARO ESPERANTISTA BRITA) (JEB)**
Esperanto Centre
140 Holland Park Avenue
London W11 4UF
Tel: 071 727 7821 Fax: 071 229 5784
(office hours only)

Esperanto is the international language created in 1887 and which now has an estimated 8 million speakers around the world. It avoids most of the difficulties which make other languages hard to learn and thus eases international communication. The JEB is the youth section of the Esperanto Association of Britain and the British section of the Worldwide Youth Esperanto Organisation, which holds its annual congress in places as far afield as Korea, Cuba and Canada. JEB organises regular weekend events around Britain, has its own magazine, *Saluton!*, runs a worldwide pen-pal service for its members and can teach you the language by post through a free correspondence course. It also provides a list of 1,000 Esperanto speakers around the world who offer free accommodation in their homes to others who speak the language. JEB also enjoys links with an independent charitable trust which offers grants for trips abroad to international Esperanto events.

AGE RANGE:
Up to 30
HOW TO CONTACT:
Write to the above address or telephone for further information.
REGIONS SERVICED:
UK
COSTS/WAITING LISTS:
Annual membership costs are: 18-30: £5; Unemployed/student: £3; Under 18s: free

YOUNG CONCERT ARTISTS TRUST (YCAT)
23 Garrick Street
London WC2E 9AX
Tel: 071 379 8477 Fax: 071 379 8467

YCAT is a unique charity set up to discover and launch the careers of outstanding young musicians. YCAT selects these musicians through a series of auditions held each year in London. YCAT selects only those musicians considered to possess the vital qualities needed for a major career. YCAT acts as agent to these musicians for an initial period of 3 years. YCAT depends entirely on sponsorship and contributions from trusts, foundations and individuals concerned with the artistic life of this country.

AGE RANGE:
Under 28 for instrumentalists, under 32 for singers on 1 January of each year
NUMBERS PASSING THROUGH:
No specific numbers
HOW TO CONTACT:
Telephone, letter or fax
REGIONS SERVICED:
Worldwide but principally UK
SPECIAL NEEDS PROVISION:
No special provision
COSTS/WAITING LISTS:
£25 entry fee for auditions. YCAT artists are subject to commission on engagements

YOUNG DIG
Unit 5 Archway Business Centre
19-23 Wedmore Street
London N19 4RZ
Tel: 071 263 3981

Young DIG is the young people's section of uhe Disablement Income Group. It is concerned with ensuring the financial welfare and independence of young disabled people through promoting independent living, providing training in benefits, developing self-advocacy skills and producing written material specifically tailored to their needs.

AGE RANGE:
16-25
NUMBERS PASSING THROUGH:
Young DIG has only just been formed
HOW TO CONTACT:
By letter
REGIONS SERVICED:
England, Wales and Northern Ireland
SPECIAL NEEDS PROVISION:
See above
COSTS/WAITING LISTS:
Membership fee £2.50

YOUNG ENTERPRISE (YE)
Ewert Place
Summertown
Oxford OX2 7BZ
Tel: 0865 311180 Fax: 0865 310979

Young Enterprise provides young people with the opportunity to learn about the world of work and business by running their own company while still in full-time education, usually through school or college. Companies are formed producing a very diverse range of products and services. Most important is the support of volunteer advisers from local business. There is also a voluntary examination which recognises the valuable skills acquired, helpful in job interviews or for college and university entrance. Together with Skill (National Bureau for Students with Disabilities), Young Enterprise has developed Team Enterprise, which offers an alternative approach to the Company Programme for students who require greater support.

REGIONAL ADDRESSES:
Scotland: see Young Enterprise Scotland
Northern Ireland: c/o NISTRO, University of Ulster, Shore Road, Newtonabbey, Co. Antrim, BT37 0QB Tel: 0232 365131 (ext. 2682) Fax: 0232 362804
Wales: The Lodge, 21 Bryn-y-Bia Road, Llandudno, Gwynedd LL30 3AS Tel: 0492 545983 Fax: 0492 546603

AGE RANGE:
14-19
NUMBERS PASSING THROUGH:
30,000
HOW TO CONTACT:
Programme arranged through school/college
REGIONS SERVICED:
UK – European and worldwide links
SPECIAL NEEDS PROVISION:
Team Enterprise, the special needs version of
the programme, is available
COSTS/WAITING LISTS:
Each YE company pays a registration fee,
usually from company income, and the
voluntary examination costs about £6, which
is often paid by the school

YOUNG ENTERPRISE SCOTLAND (YES)
123 Dysart Road
Kirkaldy KY1 2BB
Tel: 0592 651597 Fax: 0592 655708

YES offers young people between the ages of 15
and 19 the chance to develop their enterprise
skills, and assists you in making the difficult
transition from school to work or further study.
It does this by providing the opportunity for you
to set up and run your own company. YES issues
a business kit containing advice and all the
office records required. You will have the help
of some of the 700 advisers from industry who
will act as consultants, but you have to make the
decisions and tackle the real problems of

production, selling, personnel, cash flow etc. There are over 250 YES companies each year and you have the option of taking part in the examination, Company Competition and training events. YES is a combination of fun, stimulation and learning. Provision is made for those with special needs, usually through the Team Enterprise programme.

AGE RANGE:
15-19
NUMBERS PASSING THROUGH:
Over 3,500 per annum
HOW TO CONTACT:
Letter, telephone or fax
REGIONS SERVICED:
All regions in Scotland
SPECIAL NEEDS PROVISION:
Available through Team Enterprise

YOUNG EUROPEAN MOVEMENT (YEM)
158 Buckingham Palace Road
London SW1W 9TR
Tel: 071 730 5291 Fax: 071 730 5168

The YEM is an organisation of young people, brought together by a common belief in a united Europe, who wish to understand what is going on and to make the most of the opportunities available. YEM organises seminars, study visits and conferences on political, social and cultural subjects, as well as on career and study opportunities abroad. It publishes a newsletter three times a year, together with information about events all over Europe which its members can attend. It is also part of the international Jeunesse Européene Fédéraliste (JEF), so that everyone who joins YEM also becomes part of a youth organisation with members in over 20 countries throughout Europe.

REGIONAL ADDRESSES:
Scotland: Glasgow University YEM, c/o Glasgow University Union, 32 University Avenue, Glasgow
Wales: Mudiad Ieuenctid Ewrop, c/o Student Union, St David's University College, Lampeter, Dyfed SA48 7ED
AGE RANGE:
16-35
NUMBERS PASSING THROUGH:
c 2,000 members
HOW TO CONTACT:
Telephone, letter or fax to London office for leaflets and further information as appropriate
REGIONS SERVICED:
UK
SPECIAL NEEDS PROVISION:
No special provision at this time
COSTS/WAITING LISTS:
Membership is £5 per year. Study visits cost about £100, summer schools about £50 and an international seminar about £200. Some travel subsidies are available and business sponsorship can help towards covering costs

YOUNG EXPLORERS' TRUST (YET)
c/o The Royal Geographical Society
1 Kensington Gore
London SW7 2AR
Tel: 0623 861027

YET is an advisory body concerned with youth expeditions. It provides advice and contacts for groups and individuals planning expeditions, mainly abroad. Whilst YET does not plan expeditions itself, it can put individuals in touch with those who do. YET also runs an approval and grant aid scheme for youth expeditions (groups not individuals) to remote areas overseas.

REGIONAL ADDRESSES:
Extensive network of local contacts but initial contact should be made through main office
AGE RANGE:
The lower age limit is 14 and the majority of expedition members should be under 20, although there is some flexibility
NUMBERS PASSING THROUGH:
Over 1,000 enquiries
HOW TO CONTACT:
By letter to the London office or by phoning the number above for general advice and information as well as personal contacts with local expertise where appropriate
REGIONS SERVICED:
UK
SPECIAL NEEDS PROVISION:
Advice and contacts available

COSTS/WAITING LISTS:
There are no costs for using YET services

**YOUNG FRIENDS GENERAL MEETING
(Young Quakers)**
Friends Meeting House
Meeting House Lane
Lancaster LA1 1TX
Tel: 0524 849470

YFGM is the co-ordinating body of British Young
Friends (Quakers). It endeavours to represent
Young Friends' interests and concerns both
inside and outside the Society of Friends. It
meets in February, May and October in different
parts of the country and organises various
weekend meetings on particular themes or for
particular activities. Non-friends with an interest
in Quakerism are very welcome. It sends
representatives to many other Quaker
committees and other youth groups.

REGIONAL ADDRESSES:
For local groups contact the Outreach Group,
c/o YFGM at the above address
AGE RANGE:
18-30
NUMBERS PASSING THROUGH:
100-200 at conferences, about 500 on
national address list
HOW TO CONTACT:
By letter or telephone to the above address

REGIONS SERVICED:
England, Scotland and Wales
SPECIAL NEEDS PROVISION:
Disabilities and special dietary requirements
can usually be accommodated with prior notice
COSTS/WAITING LISTS:
Weekend conferences cost from £7 to £12.
Costs vary for other weekend discussions and
trips, and for overseas opportunities for
mixing with other young Quakers. Numbers
are sometimes limited, but this is rare

YOUNG HUMANISTS (YH)
14 Lamb's Conduit Passage
London WC1R 4RH
Tel: 071 430 0908 Fax: 071 430 1271

Young Humanists is a network of young people
committed to the Humanist idea of 'doing it
without God' – exploring ideas and ethics,
supporting ethical projects and working towards
a free, open society without religious dogma.
As well as working to protect and promote
Humanist values, YH have frequent local and
national social meetings and events and produce
a newsletter, *Share*. The YH are part of the
International Humanist and Ethical Youth
Organisation (IHEYO), and all YH members
receive the IHEYO newsletter. As well as an
annual week-long international conference,
IHEYO organises many international exchange
visits where members stay in the homes of local

Humanists who arrange sightseeing and social events.

REGIONAL ADDRESSES:
Contact through Head Office
AGE RANGE:
30 and under
NUMBERS PASSING THROUGH:
c 100
HOW TO CONTACT:
By letter (with SAE) or telephone to Head Office for general information, leaflets etc. and a sample newsletter
REGIONS SERVICED:
UK
SPECIAL NEEDS PROVISION:
Enquiries welcome
COSTS/WAITING LISTS:
Annual subscription fee is £1 for under-18s, £2 for 18 and over

---

YOUNG MEN'S CHRISTIAN ASSOCIATION (YMCA)
National Council of YMCAs
640 Forest Road
London E17 3DZ

The YMCA provides a range of services and activities, including housing for the homeless, vocational training, recreation, sporting activities, drug and alcohol counselling and advice, and much more. There are over 200

YMCAs across the UK and they are open to people of any religious faith.

AGE RANGE:
The emphasis is on young people but anyone is welcome
NUMBERS PASSING THROUGH:
1.5 million each year in England
HOW TO CONTACT:
Check telephone directory or contact the National Council for your nearest centre and contact direct for details of services available
REGIONS SERVICED:
UK and worldwide
SPECIAL NEEDS PROVISION:
Contact your local centre for details
COSTS/WAITING LISTS:
Small charge for some activities; charges for membership and accommodation vary from association to association

---

**YOUNG NADFAS (NATIONAL
ASSOCIATION OF DECORATIVE AND FINE
ARTS SOCIETIES)**
8a Lower Grosvenor Place
London SW1W 0EN
Tel: 071 233 5433

Young NADFAS welcomes all young people between the ages of 8 and 18 years to share in the enjoyment of the visual and performing arts. Throughout the country enthusiastic young are looking into local history, visiting museums and galleries, creating works of art, making music, acting, studying wildlife or participating in numerous other interesting projects geared to particular age groups. Events are arranged during the school holidays and breaks by enlightened organisers, the accent being placed on participation wherever possible.

HOW TO CONTACT:
Letter only to above address
REGIONS SERVICED:
UK

YOUNG ORNITHOLOGISTS' CLUB (YOC)
c/o RSPB
The Lodge
Sandy
Bedfordshire SG19 2DL
Tel: 0767 680551 Fax: 0767 692365

Bi-monthly colour magazines; competitions with exciting prizes; projects which help the RSPB protect wildlife; over 1,500 local groups in schools and the community; exciting 1-day activities at over 200 centres; a touring team which brings activities to many towns in Britain each year; over 50 holidays both in the UK and abroad. Advice is available on careers in conservation.

REGIONAL ADDRESSES:
Scotland: 17 Regent Terrace, Edinburgh, EH7 5BN Tel: 031 556 5624/9042
North: Brookfoot House, Brookfoot Mills,

Eland Road, Brighouse, West Yorkshire
AGE RANGE:
5-18
NUMBERS PASSING THROUGH:
125,000 members
HOW TO CONTACT:
Write to Head Office for information and
membership details
REGIONS SERVICED:
UK
SPECIAL NEEDS PROVISION:
Participation in both residential and non-
residential activities is encouraged
COSTS/WAITING LISTS:
£7 annual subscription, £2 for careers advice
booklet

YOUNG PEOPLE'S TRUST FOR THE
ENVIRONMENT AND NATURE
CONSERVATION (YPTE)
95 Woodbridge Road
Guildford
Surrey GU1 4PY
Tel: 0483 39600 Fax: 0483 301992

The YPTE provides an information service on
endangered species, environmental and
conservation matters and will answer specific
questions on any of these topics. They also
provide a school lecture service, one-day field
trips and residential 'environmental discovery'
courses for schools and individuals.

REGIONAL ADDRESSES:
Contact through Guildford office
AGE RANGE:
Up to 18
NUMBERS PASSING THROUGH:
YPTE reached about 96,000 young people in
1992 through its various services
HOW TO CONTACT:
By letter (with SAE) to above address
REGIONS SERVICED:
UK
SPECIAL NEEDS PROVISION:
No special provision
COSTS/WAITING LISTS:
Residential field courses cost about £138 per
week. Funding is usually from schools or
parents

YOUNG SCOT (publication)
Scottish Community Education Council
(SCEC)
Rosebery House
9 Haymarket Terrace
Edinburgh EH12 5EZ
Tel: 031 313 2488 Fax: 031 313 68007

Young Scot has now been going 12 years. An
annual subscription of £6 entitles you to: 1) the
Young Scot Information Handbook, which is
packed with essential and useful information on
life after school and beyond; 2) the Young Scot
Euro Under 26 Card which entitles you to
savings on travel, eating out, theatre, fashion,

music, driving lessons, bikes, hairdressers, insurance, cars, sports gear etc. at over 2,000 outlets in Scotland and a further 100,000 in another 19 European countries; 3) the Young Scot 24-hour Helpline which offers you access to a team of qualified and friendly lawyers at any time of the year, and any time of the day or night; 4) the *Young Scot* magazine – sent to your home address at least four times a year – giving you up-to-date and topical information on areas such as travel, health, the arts, music, fashion, sport etc.

AGE RANGE:
15-26
HOW TO CONTACT:
Letter, telephone or fax to SCEC
REGIONS SERVICED:
Scotland
COSTS/WAITING LISTS:
£6 annual subscription for full membership or £1 for a copy of the *Young Scot Information Handbook*. Young Scot membership can also be bought at Youth Information Centres, most theatres, and at Scottish City Link coach stations in Glasgow and Edinburgh

---

YOUNG VISITORS (publications)
c/o ERYICA
101 Quai Branly
75740 Paris

The *Young Visitors* series are pocket guides giving up-to-date information for young people living, studying, on holiday or working in another country. They are published by ERYICA, the European Youth Information and Counselling Association, and are available from the Central Bureau. Guides are available for Britain, France, Germany, Hungary, Ireland, Italy, Luxembourg, Netherlands, Portugal and Spain and provide information on travel, accommodation, leisure activities, welfare, passports, visas, insurance and other topics relevant to young travellers. Some are more comprehensive than others so it is advisable to look for the one you need in your local library before ordering.

YOUNG WILDLIFE PHOTOGRAPHER OF THE YEAR COMPETITION
c/o BBC *Wildlife* Magazine
Broadcasting House
Whiteladies Road
Bristol BS8 2LR
Tel: 0272 238166 Fax: 0272 467075

Young Wildlife Photographer of the Year is the junior section of the international Wildlife Photographer of the Year competition, and is open to people aged 17 years and under. The competition is judged in three age categories and all entries must be photographs of wild animals or wild places. The main competition includes the Eric Hosking Award for the best portfolio of wildlife photographs by a photographer aged 26 years or under. The Award includes a holiday for two people to an exotic location. The winning entries from the junior and main competition are published in the BBC *Wildlife* magazine and are included in an exhibition at the Natural History Museum, London and on tour around the UK and overseas.

AGE RANGE:
17 and under, 26 and under for the Eric Hosking Award
HOW TO CONTACT:
Telephone, fax or letter to above address for application forms and further information about the current competition
REGIONS SERVICED:
Worldwide
SPECIAL NEEDS PROVISION:
Enquiries welcome
COSTS/WAITING LISTS:
None for entering

YOUNG WOMEN'S CHRISTIAN ASSOCIATION (YWCA)
Clarendon House
52 Cornmarket Street
Oxford OX1 3EJ
Tel: 0865 726110 Fax: 0865 204805

The YWCA runs clubs and community centres and provides affordable, safe, non-dormitory accommodation. Youth participation is encouraged in management of all Houses and Youth Centres. Many further education courses are available through the YWCA as well as

special provision such as drug counselling,
support for single parents etc. – contact YWCA
above for further details.

AGE RANGE:
Any
NUMBERS PASSING THROUGH:
c 35,000 under 25
HOW TO CONTACT:
By letter to Head Office, or in person to your
nearest centre
SPECIAL NEEDS PROVISION:
Special accommodation units (although most
centres consider applications). Some special
club provisions
COSTS/WAITING LISTS:
Annual membership is £6. Accommodation
is subsidised and therefore cheaper than
equivalent in the private sector. Charges for
courses are often met by employers

YOUTH ADVENTURE
Malden Hall
Herbert Street
London NW5 4HD
Tel: 071 267 3286 Fax: 071 267 2215

Youth Adventure's mission is to assist young
individuals to achieve personal growth through
the pursuit of new initiatives and opportunities
for personal growth. They provide
encouragement, advice and financial assistance
to 13-21 year-olds resident in the UK who are

showing a personal commitment to their own
idea of adventure or challenge. Grants range
from £20 to £250 with the current average being
£80. Priority is given to the disabled, homeless,
unemployed, refugee and at risk young people.

AGE RANGE:
13-21
NUMBERS PASSING THROUGH:
c 1,000 projected in 1994/95
HOW TO CONTACT:
By phone or letter for an application form.
While all applications must be from the
individual young person in his/her own
words, supporting material is welcomed. All
questions on the form must be answered but
applications can be received on audio or
video tape or in braille
REGIONS SERVICED:
UK
SPECIAL NEEDS PROVISION:
Wheelchair accessible offices; disabled
community represented on grants committee
and young people with special needs
prioritised; large print guidlines and forms on
request
COSTS/WAITING LISTS:
Monthly meetings; decisions within 10 weeks
maximum

YOUTH AND MUSIC
28 Charing Cross Road
London WC2H 0DB
Tel: 071 379 6722 Fax: 071 497 0345

Youth and Music run a nationwide ticket concessionary scheme, Stage Pass, which can enable you to get up to 50% off tickets to performances at venues all round the country, details of which are contained in a monthly magazine sent to all members. Youth and Music are also the British section of the Fédération Internationale des Jeunesses Musicales and are responsible for recruitment of British musicians and singers for the Fédération's worldwide activities including the World Orchestra and World Choir. They also promote their own concerts targeted for young audiences new to music, and are in the process of developing an educational programme.

REGIONAL ADDRESSES:
Youth and Music, 9 Black Swan Court, 67 Westgate Road, Newcastle-upon-Tyne NE1 1SG Tel: 091 230 1130
Yorkshire Youth and Music, Dean Clough Industrial Park, Halifax HX3 5AX
Tel: 0422 345631 Fax: 0422 321823
AGE RANGE:
14-30
NUMBERS PASSING THROUGH:
23,000 members

HOW TO CONTACT:
For advice on musical careers etc. contact the
London office by letter, telephone or fax. For
all other matters contact either London or
regional offices
REGIONS SERVICED:
UK
SPECIAL NEEDS PROVISION:
Access depends on individual venues
COSTS/WAITING LISTS:
Stage Pass costs: £14 for London and Home
Counties, £7.50 outside this area. Stage Pass
entitles you to buy two discounted tickets

YOUTH ARTS DIRECTORY (publication)
Sales Department
National Youth Agency
17-23 Albion Street
Leicester LE1 6GD
Tel: 0533 471200 Fax: 0533 471043

Want to know who is doing what in your
locality? Want to know who is doing dance,
drama or video in your or any other part of the
country? The *Youth Arts Directory* gives details
of over 250 projects in England and Wales,
covering some 30 art forms. The entries are
indexed by art form, and arranged
geographically.
ISBN 0 86155 136 2. Available through libraries,
or direct from the above address (price £5.50,
post free).

YOUTH CAMPAIGN FOR NUCLEAR
DISARMAMENT (YCND)

162 Holloway Road
London N7 8DQ
Tel: 071 607 3616/700 2393
Fax: 071 700 2357 E-mail: cnd@gn.apc.org.

Youth CND is an organisation run by young people for young people. Members receive a copy of the magazine *CND Today* four times per year, as well as Youth CND publications and campaign materials (posters, stickers etc.). It also runs a popular School Speaking Service with a government-funded group called Peace Through NATO, as well as producing education packs useful for school projects.

REGIONAL ADDRESSES:
Scottish CND: 6 Dalcross Pass, Glasgow G11 5RE Tel: 041 339 4844
CND Cymru: 9 Idris Terrace, Swansea/ Abertawe SA9 0JY Tel: 0792 774687
Both of these are national offices rather than regional contacts and should be the first point of contact in Scotland and Wales

AGE RANGE:
22 and under

NUMBERS PASSING THROUGH:
c 4,000-5,000

HOW TO CONTACT:
By telephone, letter or fax to the National Office for information pack, advice and campaign materials

REGIONS SERVICED:
UK, but see Scottish and Welsh offices above
SPECIAL NEEDS PROVISION:
No special provision
COSTS/WAITING LISTS:
Membership is approx £4 per year

YOUTH CLUBS UK
11 St Bride Street
London EC4A 4AS
Tel: 071 353 2366 Fax: 071 353 2369

Youth Clubs UK supports a national network of youth clubs throughout the UK, through 41 local associations and three divisions in Scotland, Northern Ireland and Wales. Youth Clubs UK organises a wide range of leisure activities and innovative community projects. Young people in the clubs have the opportunity to join the National Members Group, which represents young people's views in the management of Youth Clubs UK and gives opportunities for involvement in many community projects, representation of Youth Clubs UK abroad etc. Residential centre in the New Forest offers vacation courses with leisure activities and sports options.

AGE RANGE:
8-25
NUMBERS PASSING THROUGH:
715,000 in membership of clubs

HOW TO CONTACT:
Through your local association – the number can be obtained from YCUK by phone
REGIONS SERVICED:
UK

YOUTH EXCHANGE CENTRE (YEC)
The British Council
10 Spring Gardens
London SW1H 9PE
Tel: 071 389 4030 Fax: 071 389 4033

The YEC, a department of the British Council, promotes international youth exchanges through the provision of advice, information, training and grants. The YEC is the UK national agency for the European Community-funded programme Youth for Europe, which promotes youth exchanges between the EC Member States. Priority is given to groups of young people who would not normally have the opportunity for such an international experience. The YEC provides grant aid to groups of young people aged 15-25. Support is available for exchanges with EC Member States, the rest of Europe, Central and East European countries, the USA and Japan. All groups of young people are eligible for support, provided they meet the YEC's basic criteria. To support its work, the YEC produces a series of Information Kits, setting out the step-by-step organisation of a youth exchange, *Help!? Guidelines on International Youth Exchanges*, a handbook for exchange organisers, and a quarterly newsletter, *Youth Exchange News*.

REGIONAL ADDRESSES:
12 regional committees – details available from above
AGE RANGE:
15-25
NUMBERS PASSING THROUGH:
19,000 young people took part in youth exchanges in 1992/93
HOW TO CONTACT:
Telephone or letter to Head Office or regional contacts for advice/information pack
REGIONS SERVICED:
UK
SPECIAL NEEDS PROVISION:
Special consideration given to groups containing young people with special needs
COSTS/WAITING LISTS:
There are no costs for using the services of the YEC

YOUTH EXCHANGE PROGRAMME (YEP)
Central Bureau for Educational Visits and
Exchanges
Seymour Mews House
Seymour Mews
London W1H 9PE
Tel: 071 486 5101

The Youth Exchange Programme aims to promote out-of-school exchanges to all young people, no matter what their occupation. The programme promotes short cultural exchanges between groups in two or more EC countries. You would have to find a similar group in one or more other EC countries, perhaps through a twin town. You would then need to plan a series of exchange activities which have a clear European dimension. Normally, each group must visit the other, within a 2-year period, for between 1 and 3 weeks. The groups must be independent of, say, school, college, sporting or political activities.

AGE RANGE:
15-25
HOW TO CONTACT:
Letter or telephone to above address for more information
REGIONS SERVICED:
UK

YOUTH HOSTELS ASSOCIATION (England and Wales) (YHA)
Trevelyan House
8 St Stephens Hill
St Albans
Hertfordshire AL1 2DY
Tel: 0727 855215 Fax: 0727 844126

YHA is a registered charity. Its aim is 'to help all, especially young people of limited means, to a greater knowledge, love and care of the countryside, particularly by providing hostels or other simple accommodation for them in their travels, and thus promote their health, rest and education'. YHA has over 240 Youth Hostels throughout England and Wales and over 5,000 worldwide. Great Escape activity holidays are of particular interest to young people and include walking, cycling, riding and mountain sports and take place at home or abroad.

REGIONAL ADDRESSES:
North and Midlands: PO Box 11, Matlock, Derbyshire, DE4 2XA Tel: 0629 825850
South: 11b York Street, Salisbury, Wiltshire SP2 7AP Tel: 0722 337515
Wales: 1 Cathedral Road, Cardiff CF1 9HA Tel: 0222 396766

AGE RANGE:
Any

NUMBERS PASSING THROUGH:
320,000

HOW TO CONTACT:
By telephone to the Information Department (Tel: 0727 855215/845047) for general information, leaflets and advice

REGIONS SERVICED:
UK

SPECIAL NEEDS PROVISION:
Many hostels are accessible by wheelchair. Activity holidays can be attended by anyone

COSTS/WAITING LISTS:
Membership costs: Under 18: £3; Over 18: £9; Family: £18; Life membership: £120.

Overnight fees range from £3.50 up to £16.50 per night depending on the grade of Youth Hostel. There are no waiting lists but all accommodation is subject to availability and booking in advance is recommended, especially during the busy summer months

---

YOUTH INFORMATION SHOPS
c/o National Youth Agency
17-23 Albion Street
Leicester LE1 6GD
Tel: 0533 471200 Fax: 0533 471043

Youth Information Shops are a new development introduced by the National Youth Agency. They are high street shops where young people are able to get information about all sorts of topics (from accommodation to recycling) and in all sorts of forms (from individual counselling to computer print-outs). At present there are two shops up and running – in Bradford and Nottingham – with plans well advanced for many more throughout the country: Rochdale, Liverpool, Coventry, Gloucester, Mansfield, Sheffield, Horsham, Chatham, Huddersfield, Accrington etc. To find out more about the Information Shops, and to find out when there may be one opening in your area (perhaps you could help set one up?) contact the National Youth Agency at the above address.

YOUTH TRAINING (YT)

Youth Training is an alternative to full-time education and offers you the chance to undertake some form of work-based training as the first stage in a particular job or career or even as the first step towards a university or college course. Young people under 18 not in a job or full-time education are guaranteed an offer of a suitable training place but you can still apply if you are over 18. You can also apply if you have a job – training can be done in your own time through open learning etc., or it is possible your employer will include some form of training as part of your work. Training is available in almost any type of job or career and is structured to your specific needs. Participants have the opportunity to gain vocational qualifications which are recognised by employers nationally and can lead to further training and improve career prospects. Your local Careers Office or Jobcentre can give you more information about the opportunities available in your area.

YOUTHACTION NORTHERN IRELAND
Hampton
Glenmachan Park
Belfast BT4 2PJ
Tel: 0232 760067 Fax: 0232 768799

Youthaction run various events and activities in sport, competitions and a wide range of personal development programmes in Hampton, a residential and conference centre, or in Encounter, a cottage in the Mournes. They run training courses in youth and community work as well as conferences, seminars and workshops on issues of interest to young people and much more. Any enquiries from young people are welcome.

AGE RANGE:
No specific age range, mainly 17-25
NUMBERS PASSING THROUGH:
40,000 through affiliated groups
HOW TO CONTACT:
Letter, telephone or fax for advice and information
REGIONS SERVICED:
Northern Ireland
SPECIAL NEEDS PROVISION:
Enquiries welcome
COSTS/WAITING LISTS:
Examples of costs are 25p per member of an affiliated youth club; £15 for young adult conference (all costs included – food, travel etc.); £2 entry to certain competitions. Places may be limited on individual programmes

---

YOUTHAID
409 Brixton Road
London SW9 7DQ
Tel: 071 737 8068

Information about rights and opportunities for young people in training, education and employment.

Part Three

WHAT TO GO FOR AND HOW TO APPLY

INTRODUCTION

This section is designed to introduce CVs, application forms, job search and interview techniques. The information is aimed at giving **you** the edge in today's job market. Although careers are mentioned throughout this section, the techniques described are equally valid for college, university, and vocational training schemes.

Before looking for work it is essential that you 'know yourself' so that you can decide on the type of job and the industry that you want to work in. The next few pages encourage self-assessment aimed at helping you focus your thoughts more clearly on what you want out of life and from your future career.

Skills Check

What's a skills check?

Your skills check will help you focus your thoughts more clearly when thinking about your future career and what direction you want to take. It looks at what you have done and what you feel are your strengths.

Put a tick against all the things that you can do to whatever degree – remember to tick things that you have experienced outside work as well as at work. Also put a tick against the things that you feel particularly good at (don't be shy!).

What are my skills?

	What can I do?	What am I good at?
Verbal Communication	❏	❏
Selling	❏	❏
Public speaking	❏	❏
Telephone	❏	❏
Answering queries	❏	❏
Teaching	❏	❏
Written Communication		
Writing letters or reports	❏	❏
Understanding written reports	❏	❏
Minute- or note-taking	❏	❏
Correcting mistakes	❏	❏

	What can I do?	What am I good at?
Technical		
Machine-operating	❑	❑
Fault-finding	❑	❑
Maintenance	❑	❑
Repairs	❑	❑
Practical		
Building	❑	❑
Woodwork	❑	❑
Decorating	❑	❑
Making things	❑	❑
Administration		
Keeping files	❑	❑
Organising systems	❑	❑
Organising people	❑	❑
Dealing with letters	❑	❑
Numeracy		
Accounts	❑	❑
Cash-handling	❑	❑
Using maths	❑	
Working out measurements or quantities	❑	❑
Mental Ability		
Problem-solving	❑	❑
Thinking of new ideas	❑	❑
Figures	❑	❑

Other
Write down any other skills you feel you have
that are not covered by these.

What's next?

Look over what you've ticked. It shows the areas
and skills that you already have which will be
useful to future employers. It also shows areas
that you may want to get involved in or improve.

For any job or area of work that you are interested
in try to identify the skills that you think may be
needed. Write them down and see how they
compare with what you have already

> Try it in your spare time
> Do it on a voluntary basis
> Start to get training

then:-

Write action plans to get information from:

> Your local reference library
> Your Careers Office/Jobcentre
> Talking to people you know

Work Style

What's my work style?

Everybody has their own opinion of what gives job satisfaction. For example, some people prefer security – although this often means comparatively low pay. Others prefer higher-risk types of work, where there isn't as much security and where pay can be much higher. Most of us tend to choose a compromise between the two.

If you can find out as much about what you want from work as possible, it will help you identify what areas of yourself and your career to work on.

What do I want from work?

Answer all the following questions using the following key:-

    Y (for yes) if this is what you do want

or **N** (for no) if you do not mind.

Remember, be honest with yourself – there aren't any right or wrong answers.

PAY	YES	NO
Enough to live on	Y	N
High wages	Y	N
Paid by performance	Y	N
Regular wages	Y	N

HOURS	YES	NO
Fixed hours	Y	N
Overtime	Y	N
Flexible hours	Y	N
PROSPECTS		
Promotion chances	Y	N
Security	Y	N
LOCATION		
Work near home	Y	N
Work anywhere	Y	N
Based near home but working away	Y	N
Travelling long distances	Y	N
CONDITIONS		
Hot	Y	N
Cool	Y	N
Outdoors	Y	N
Clean workplace	Y	N
OTHER PEOPLE		
Prefer working alone	Y	N
Prefer working in a group	Y	N
Like dealing with the public	Y	N
MANAGEMENT		
Use own initiative	Y	N
Be supervised	Y	N
Manager available if needed	Y	N
DEPTH OF INVOLVEMENT		
Like to develop your abilities	Y	N
See end result	Y	N
OTHER THINGS YOU MAY WANT		
Status	Y	N
To help others	Y	N
To get recognition from others	Y	N

Forming a picture of your working style

Look over the question sheet again. Start to ask yourself questions about some of the answers you have given.

> How do your work style answers reflect your life at the moment?
> How do they match the areas of work you may be interested in?
> What sort of changes in work style would you make to get the right job?
> What would you not change at all no matter what the job?
> Why would you be unprepared to change these?

The next steps

Having given careful consideration to the previous pages you should now have a clearer idea of what you can offer an employer and also what you want.

Now identify the type of work that you want to research in more depth and compare what you **can** do with what you **want** to do.

Using the information you have recorded about yourself, ask yourself the following:-

- What are my current skills?
- Which new skills could I learn?
- Qualifications/training I have or could obtain
- What are my physical attributes?
- What physical conditions do I want to avoid?
- What situations am I comfortable in/wish to avoid?
- What do I want from my job?
- Any personal interests I would like my job to incorporate

Having researched the job you think you would like, ask yourself the following and compare with your personal requirements:-

- Which skills does the job require?
- Which skills would need to be learned?
- Which qualifications/training will be required?
- Which physical qualities are required?
- What does the job give me?
- Which of my interests are incorporated?

Job Search

No one can just walk out and get a job. You need to know yourself so that you can choose the right type of job and industry to suit you. You need to have researched that job so that you can develop the skills necessary. Finally you need to be **committed** to finding a job.

Do not just react to advertised vacancies as everybody else will also be applying. Try to be productive and create your own vacancy by using the speculative approach or personal contacts.

Finding a vacancy

The first step to getting a job is finding a vacancy. Below are listed a few methods of finding vacancies:-

1. Personal contact
Many vacancies found like this will not have been advertised so there is less competition

2. Speculative
Again, these vacancies will not have been advertised. 10% chance of being interviewed using this approach

3. Agencies
Check agency is experienced in your type of

work and that they usually have vacancies not advertised elsewhere

4. Newspapers
Local newspapers usually have a specific day for job vacancies

National newspapers – check with your team adviser or employment co-ordinator for the best newspapers for your type of work

5. Specialist magazines
Many national publications. Often locally published recruiting newspapers/magazines

6. Jobcentres
Vary from area to area

Correct tools

Finding a job is a job in itself and must be approached as such.

You will need the correct tools:-

- A quiet place to work
- Relevant notes from this course
- A copy of your CV
- Scrap paper
- Good quality paper
- Envelopes
- Stamps

- Pens
- A ruler
- A dictionary

Put time aside and send a set number of applications each week. Sending the odd application and waiting for a reply is wasting time.

If you hear nothing after one week telephone to ensure your application has been received. Keep a record of all employers contacted.

Doing My Application Form

The first contact

The application form is usually your first contact with an employer so, to make the most of every opportunity, you'll want to create a good impression. Here's a checklist of some of the things you should do:-

Before starting

- Carefully read **all** the instructions
- If there is anything you aren't sure of **ask someone**

Completing the form

- Do a test version on a photocopy or blank piece of paper
- Use a good, black pen
- Write clearly and neatly
- Make sure the spelling is correct
- If you do make a mistake on the final version, use Tippex rather than crossing out (wait for it to dry as well)
- Keep your answers short and relevant
- Decide what skills the employer is looking for and reflect those skills on the form

After completing it

- Check it carefully
- Make sure dates are correct and that they make sense
- Is it clear which job you are applying for?
- Make a copy of the form – you will need to read it before your interview
- Don't cram the form into a small envelope
- Post the form as soon as possible

REMEMBER: Many people do not complete their forms properly. Because of this they are not selected for interview. There is no need for you to be in that position – give yourself the best chance by taking time and trouble over it.

How do I request an application form?

If an advertisement asks you to write for an application form, do that and no more.

Example to request an application form

The Personnel Manager
Pearson Perambulators
Nirvana Industrial Complex
Guppy
Essex GU5 1XB
(their address)

27 Squat View Terrace
Stickleback
Near Troutville
Surrey SM99 4BU
Tel: 0324 123456
(your address)

1 January 1994

Reference Number
(if given in advert)

Dear Sirs,

Sales Assistant

Please forward an application form for the above position as
advertised in The Chronicle on 28th December 1992 and, if
possible, a job description.

Yours faithfully

Your Signature

S Snurd
(print your name underneath)

Telephone Techniques

Checklist for telephone usage

* **Smile**

* Give all your attention to the call

* Use the person's name

* Prepare a script of your main points

* **Listen** to what the other person says

* Vary the tone and emphasis of your voice

* Be clear and concise

* Do not be frightened of pausing

Dial a smile – don't phone a groan!

Notes On Your Technique

Interview Techniques

Preparation

Arrive on time
- Check how long the journey takes
- Make sure you know which department to go to

Do your homework
- Know as much as possible about the organisation
- Find out as much as possible about the job

Know yourself
- Can you outline your life and career clearly?
- Think of examples of your successes and achievements
- Show a positive attitude towards previous employers

What do you want from the interview
- List the information that you want to know

The interview

Initial impressions
- Dress smartly and conventionally
- Find out the interviewer's name from the receptionist
- When entering the room smile, bid them good day and use the interviewer's name
- Do **not** smoke unless the interviewer does

Conversation
- A good interview is a two-way conversation

- Be normal
- Concentrate on what the interviewer is saying

Using the interview to your advantage

- Use every opportunity to speak positively about your past and current work/training
- You should be talking for 60% of the time
- Never answer just 'yes' or 'no'. Expand your answers
- Be clear and precise
- Be positive

After the interview

- If you have heard nothing after one week, telephone
- If unsuccessful try to find out why
- All unsuccessful interviews are practice for the next one – you will eventually be successful

REMEMBER

Enthusiasm
Energy
Experience relevant to the job
Knowledge of the company

Responding to interview questions

a) What did you do in your last job?

Explain what your last job involved and include
the following points:-

- Duties that are relevant to the job you are
  applying for
- Skills used in the job
- Types of people you dealt with
- Reasons for any promotion
- Areas of responsibility
- Machines and equipment used

b) Why did you leave your last job?

Mention only the reasons that make you look
good. If your health was a factor then do not
discuss in depth but stress that you are now fit
and able to do everything required by the new
job.

Many reasons are acceptable to an employer,
such as:-

- The job was temporary or seasonal
- Part-time
- Deciding to change direction
- Low pay
- Redundancy
- Too much travel
- Unsociable hours

c) Have you ever done this type of work?

Always try to answer positively and explain any experience that shows knowledge and ability. If you have limited or no experience then tell the interviewer about anything else that demonstrates how quickly you can learn. Stress how keen you are to learn.

d) What machines/equipment can you use?

This question applies to all jobs. Mention the following:–

- All equipment and experience that would be used in the job applied for. Be precise and use the name and type of equipment if possible
- Experience of any other machines that may be relevant. Again, be precise
- Any relevant machinery used for your hobbies

e) What wage/salary are you looking for?

You will usually be informed of the salary offered. However, this is sometimes negotiable, which can be awkward. If you ask too high a figure you may 'price yourself out'; too low and you could be 'underselling yourself'. Here are some ideas on how to respond:–

- Do not specify a figure

- Be a little vague, i.e. a fair day's pay for a fair day's work; standard rate for the job is fine; the company has a good reputation so I'm sure the wage/salary will be suitable

If possible, after the interview find out what other workers doing the same job are paid. If you are then offered the job you at least have an idea and will be able to negotiate.

f) Why do you want to work for this company?

You must give positive reasons which suggest you will be loyal to the company. It also provides the opportunity for you to demonstrate that you have researched well prior to the interview – impressive.

g) Did you have much time off during your last job?

If you had very little time off then state that fact in a positive way. If you had a lot of time off then explain the reasons and state why it would not happen in this job.

h) Why should we take you on?

Answer quickly and positively. List your positive attributes, even if this means repeating yourself. Make sure you demonstrate that you are reliable, loyal, efficient, hard-working and capable of doing the job.

i) Do you have good health?

The interviewer is looking for two things here –
your fitness for the particular job and your
general health.

Try to set his/her mind at rest on both issues:–

- If you are in good health, then say so positively
- If you have entered any health information
  on your application form discuss this but
  assure the interviewer it will have no
  detrimental effect on the job applied for and
  that your general health is good
- Refer to examples that demonstrate you have
  overcome any disability

j) What are your strengths?

Yet another chance to list your positive qualities.
Cover the following:–

- Skills
- Pride in doing a good job
- Enthusiasm for the job
- Experience
- Ability to get on well with others
- Interest
- Reliability
- Efficiency

k) What are your weaknesses?

Never admit to any weaknesses. It is possible to respond as follows:–

- I have none that prevent me from being a good worker
- None in relation to this job

l) Tell me more about yourself

This gives you a chance to expand aspects of your personal life. You should demonstrate that you have outside interests; have links between these interests and the job; have normal domestic circumstances.

Mention the following:–

- Hobbies/leisure activities
- Clubs of which you are a member
- Position held in any club, etc.
- Past job experience
- Your family
- Brief personal history

m) What did your last employer think of you?

Give a positive answer, mentioning jobs for which you received praise. Stress your efficiency, reliability, punctuality, etc. If you have an open reference from your last employer, then show that. Never criticise previous employers as this

give the impression you may criticise this
employer in the future.

n) How old are you?

If you are asked this question then the employer
may be worried you are too young or too old for
the job. Don't just give your age but point out
the advantages and discuss any disadvantages.

Curriculum Vitae

Your CV should be aimed at getting an interview and is your selling document.

It should get the employer's:–
> **A**ttention
> **I**nterest
> **D**esire
> **A**ction

Although a standard example is included in this book, there are alternative methods and various books are available in reference libraries. However, whichever format you use remember that this is often the only contact that the employer will have had with you, so make it count.

Things to do when writing it

- Use your **skills check** list
- Use **short** sentences containing facts.
- Start with **action** words. For example:
  'Developed a stock control system...'
  'Gained driving licence...'
  'Organised work schedules ...'
  Don't start with things like
  'My duties consisted of ...'
- Use **positive** words – see below
- **Any** negative information and you will fail to get an interview

Making it sound positive

Some words to use:

Achieved	Effective	Outgoing
Administered	Efficient	Participated
Advised people	Expanded	Positive
Analysed	Experienced	Productive
Arranged events	Guided	Proficient
Benefit	Implemented	Qualified
Built	Improved	Reliable
Capable	Initiated	Repaired
Competent	Involved	Resourceful
Controlled	Led	Specialised
Created	Liaised	Successful
Designed	Maintained	Supervised
Detailed	Managed	Stable
Developed	Monitored	Versatile
Directed	Organised	

These words may help you when writing about your personal skills – i.e. things you believe you are good at, or qualities that you have:

Active	Inspecting
Calculating data	Interpreting data
Checking accuracy	Interviewing people
Classifying	Maintaining records
Coaching people	Mediating
Compiling	Motivating staff
Constructing	Organising people
Co-ordinating events	Operating equipment
Correspondence	Persuading people
Counselling people	Planning
Delegating	Preparing charts
Dispensing information	Programming computers
Drafting reports	Promoting events
Editing	Protecting
Handling complaints	Raising funds

Example of CV

PERSONAL DETAILS:

NAME: Andrew Craddock

DATE OF BIRTH: 5 June 1973

ADDRESS: 12, Keats Avenue
                Anytown
                AT1 2BU

MARITAL STATUS:
Married with one child aged 2.

TELEPHONE: 0728 97532

GENERAL HEALTH: Good

EDUCATION:

Sept.ember 1983 – June1989

St Mary's Comprehensive School, Anytown.

TRAINING:

July 1989 – June 1991

2 years' apprenticeship in Engineering with A. Grease & Co Ltd. Attended Lastown Technical College on day release and evening classes.

Gained Part 1 of City & Guilds Mechanical Engineering. Awarded Technical College prize for Best Project 1990.

WORK HISTORY:

July 1989 – June 1991

Apprentice Engineer, A. Grease & Co Ltd, Lastown.

Duties

Working on all aspects of Mechanical Engineering in a large contract toolroom.

Equipment Used

Centre Lathe, Capstan, Jig Borer, Hand Press.

July 1991– January 1992

Unemployed as a result of moving to a new area.

February 1992 – September1992

Capstan Setter Operator, Blank Engineering Co, Anytown.

Duties

Setting and operating CNC machines.

October 1992 – February 1993

Unemployed due to redundancy.

February 1993 – October 1993

Waiter, Rose Garden Tea Rooms, Anytown.

Duties:

Reception of diners, taking orders, waiting on table, dealing with complaints, accepting payment for meals.

October 1993 – March 1994

Participant on a Drive For Youth programme devised to test and develop through a series of difficult scenarios.

Showed a particular ability to get on with others and persuade them to undertake tasks with the minimum of friction.

SPARE TIME ACTIVITIES:

Member of Anytown five-a-side football team.

Volunteer youth worker at Leasowes Youth Club.

Hill walking.

ADDITIONAL INFORMATION:

Clean driving licence

REFERENCES:

Mr K. Fu
Supervisor
A. Grease & Co Ltd
China Street
Lastown LT1 2TL

Tel: 0428 87654

Mr V. Young
Youth & Community Worker
Leasowes Youth Club
Leasowes Avenue
Anytown AT1 2BZ

Tel: 0728 25791

Miss A. Trouble
Minister
56 Vicarage Way
Anytown AT1 4ZB

Tel: 0728 665598

Covering Letters

To cover a CV

Your Ref: UT 168

FAO: Personnel Manager

13 North Street
Newbridge
Essex OD2 9PZ

Tel: 0968 446966

15 April 1994

Dear Sir/Madam

PRODUCTION ASSISTANT POST

I was very interested to see your advertisement in the Sunday Times.

I feel positive that my previous work experience and training make me a suitable candidate for the position currently offered. During my five months training on the Drive For Youth Development Programme I have worked hard with a team making me more aware of the needs and sensitivities of others. I have also developed my organisational and planning abilities.

The full breadth of my training and experience is shown in the enclosed CV.

I would be grateful for an interview at your earliest opportunity.

Thank you for your time and attention.

Yours faithfully,

J. Jones

When applying without any previous advertisement

13 North Street
Newbridge
Essex
OD2 9PZ

The Personnel Manager

Tel 0968 446966

15th April 1994

Dear Sir/Madam

PRODUCTION ASSISTANT

I am applying for any vacancies in your production department.

During the past five months I have been on the Drive For Youth Development Training Programme. Over this period I have been improving my teamwork, planning, organisation and communication skills. I am very enthusiastic and keen about my work and I believe I have a very approachable character with my work colleagues. I am also very tactful and sensitive to the needs of others which I feel could be useful when dealing with customers at a time of their bereavement.

I enclose my CV and look forward to your reply regarding any current or future vacancies that you feel I may be suited for.

Thank you for your time and attention.

Yours faithfully,

J. Jones

To cover an application form

Your Ref: UT 168/SMB/jh   13 North Street
Newbridge
Mr C.J. Jameson,   Essex
Personnel Manager   OD2 9PZ

Tel: 0968 446966

15th April 1994

Dear Mr Jameson

PRODUCTION ASSISTANT POST

Please find enclosed my completed application form for the above position as advertised in the Sunday Times.

I am very interested in this position and I am confident that I have the necessary drive and self-motivating approach to my work that you are looking for. I have been developing my interpersonal and organisational skills during my training over the last five months and I am keen and enthusiastic to learn new approaches and develop my abilities.

I am looking forward to meeting you at any interview you may arrange.

Thank you for your time and attention.

Yours sincerely,

J. Jones

Part Four

HELP!

AL-ANON & ALATEEN
61 Great Dover Street
London SE1 4YF
Tel: 071 403 0888
(Northern Ireland 0232 243489)
24-hour hotlines

Help for relatives and close friends of people with drinking problems. (Alateen provides support for young people aged 12-20 who have a relative with a drinking problem.) Check telephone directory under 'Alcoholics', or contact above for a local group.

ALCOHOL CONCERN
305 Gray's Inn Road
London WC1X 8QF
Tel: 071 833 3471

Scotland: 137-145 Sauchiehall Street, Glasgow G2 3EW Tel: 041 333 9677

Wales: PO Box 2010, Cardiff Tel: 0222 398791

Northern Ireland: Northern Ireland Council on Alcohol, 40 Elmwood Avenue, Belfast BT9 6AZ Tel: 0232 664434

All these addresses can put you in touch with a local contact for advice if you think you or someone you know is drinking too much.

BRITISH PREGNANCY ADVISORY SERVICE (BPAS)
7 Belgrave Road
London SW1V 1QB
Tel: 071 222 0985

Counselling and advice on contraception, pregnancy and abortion.

BROOK ADVISORY CENTRES
153a East Street
London SE17 2SD
Tel: 071 708 1234

Counselling and advice on contraception, pregnancy and abortion. Centres based around the country – contact above for nearest one.

CHILDLINE
Freepost 1111
London EC4B 4BB
Tel: 0800 1111

Free 24-hour service for children and young people in danger or in trouble.

CITIZENS ADVICE BUREAUX

Can provide help and advice on a wide range of issues such as housing, benefits, debt, the law, employment rights etc.

Check in Yellow Pages for your nearest CAB or contact: National Association of Citizens Advice Bureaux (NACAB), 115 Pentonville Road, London, N1 9LZ Tel: 071 833 2181

COMMISSION FOR RACIAL EQUALITY
10-12 Allingham Street
London SW1E 5EH
Tel: 071 828 7022

Help and advice in cases of racial discrimination.

EATING DISORDERS ASSOCIATION
Tel: 0494 793 223

Support for anyone with anorexia or bullimia. Can put you in touch with a local group.

EQUAL OPPORTUNITIES COMMISSION
Overseas House, Quay Street
Manchester M3 3HN
Tel: 061 833 9244

FAMILY PLANNING ASSOCIATION
27-35 Mortimer Street
London W1N 7RJ
Tel: 071 636 7866

Free contraceptive advice. Check telephone directory under 'Family' for nearest clinic or contact above between 10am and 3pm.

FREELINE SOCIAL SECURITY
England, Scotland and Wales:
Tel: 0800 666555
Northern Ireland: Tel: 0800 616757

Free telephone enquiry service offering information on all aspects of welfare benefits.

Other languages: Tel: 0800 289188 (Urdu); 0800 521360 (Punjabi); 0800 252451 (Chinese); 0800 289011 (Welsh)
Disability Information:
Tel: 0800 882200 (voice); 0800 243355 (minicom)

GAMBLERS ANONYMOUS
Tel: 071 384 3040
24-hour helpline for for people with problems with gambling.

GLAD - GAY AND LESBIAN LEGAL ADVICE
Tel: 071 976 0840
Monday to Friday 7pm-9.30pm.

LAW CENTRES

Can provide free legal help and advice. Details of your nearest centre in telephone directory under 'Law Centres' or contact Law Centres Federation, Duchess House, Warren Street, London W1P 5DA Tel: 071 387 8570.

MAC HELPLINE
Tel: O800 591028

The MAC helpline has been set up by the cancer care charity Cancer Relief Macmillan Fund. It's your line if you want to talk about cancer. The MAC helpline is a completely free, confidential service for young people and those close to them. You can call to talk right away, or you can leave a phone number where you can be called back when you know you won't be disturbed, or when you've had time to sort out the questions you really want to ask. The people you will talk to know about cancer. More important, they know what worries young people about cancer. They may be able to put you in touch with local groups or professionals who may be able to help. MAC is open 9.30am – 5pm on weekdays (and to 7pm on Mondays and Thursdays) and at any other time if you want to leave a message on the answerphone.

MIND
Granta House
15-19 Broadway
Stratford E15 4BQ
Tel: 081 519 2122

Information and advice on all aspects of mental health. Referral to local groups.

NATIONAL AIDS HELPLINE
Tel: 0800 567123
Minicom: 0800 521361

24-hour free and confidential helpline.

Other languages:
Asian languages (Bengali, Gujarati, Hindi,
Punjabi and Urdu): Tel: 0800 282445
Cantonese: Tel: 0800 282446
Arabic: Tel: 0800 282447

NATIONAL DEBTLINE
Tel: 021 359 8501
10am-4pm Monday and Thursday,
2pm-7pm Tuesday and Wednesday

Helpline for people with debt problems.

NATIONAL MISSING PERSONS HELPLINE
Tel: 081 392 2000
24-hour helpline

Anyone who has left home and wants to contact
their family, or needs help or advice van ring the
number above.

NCH ACTION FOR CHILDREN
85 Highbury Park
London N5 1UD
Tel: 071 226 2033

Counselling helpline for children, young people and families.

NETWORK FOR THE HANDICAPPED
16 Princeton Street
London WC1R 4BB
Tel: 071 831 8031/7740

Provide legal advice and assistance to people with disabilities.

RAPE CRISIS CENTRES
PO Box 69
London WC1X 9NJ
Tel: 071 837 1600 (24 hours)

Offer free counselling for women and girls who have been raped or sexually assaulted in any way. Check telephone directory under 'R' for the nearest centre or phone above number

RELEASE
388 Old Street
London EC1V 9LT
Tel: 071 729 9904
(Advice line, Monday to Friday 10am-6pm)

Tel: 071 603 8654
(Emergency line)

Information, advice and counselling on drug use and legal problems.

SAMARITANS

24-hour confidential helpline. Check telephone directory under 'S' for local number or ask the operator (dial 100) to put you through directly.

SHELTER - National Campaign for the Homeless
88 Old Street
London EC1V 9HU
Tel: 071 253 0202

Campaigns for the homeless and has a national network of advice centres.

SURVIVORS
38 Mount Pleasant
London WC1X 0AN
Tel: 071 833 3737
7pm-10pm, Tuesday, Wednesday and Thursday

Helpline for any man or boy who has been sexually assaulted by another man.

UNITED RESPONSE
162-164 Upper Richmond Road
Putney
London SW15 2SL
Tel: 081 780 9686 Fax: 081 780 9538

United Response is a national charity helping an increasing number of young people with learning disabilities and/or mental health problems. It specialises in support for people who live at home, and the development of a network of residential and day services in the community.

VICTIM SUPPORT
Cranmer House
39 Brixton Road
London SW9 6DD
Tel: 071 735 9166

Help and support for victims of crime. Can put you in touch with a local group.

YOUTH ACCESS
Magazine Business Centre
11 Newarke Street
Leicester LE1 5SS
Tel: 0533 558763

Confidential counselling service for young people. Contact above for details of your nearest service.

INDEX

NOTE

This index can be used as a supplement to the main categories in Part One. If you are unable to identify your interests with any of the categories listed on page 17, you may find what you are looking for by browsing through this index. You will also find here a listing for every organisation or publication with an entry in Parts Two and Four and a reference to many other organisations, activities and publications mentioned in those entries.

Additional copies
of *Go for it!*

If you would like to order more copies of this book for whatever reason, whether you are a private individual, a school, college or any other organisation or business, please contact the address below by letter or by phone. If you prefer you can complete the order form on this page or copy the information required onto a postcard or letter.

Please send me ..... copy/copies of *Go for it!* at £7.99 (postage included)

Name ....

Address ....

....

....

I wish to pay by Access(Mastercard)/Visa/ cheque the total amount of £.............

Card no ☐☐☐☐☐☐☐☐☐☐☐☐☐☐☐☐

Card expiry date ....

Cardholder's signature ....

All cheques payable to Lennard Associates

Telephone credit card orders accepted on 0582 715866.

Send orders to: Lennard Associates Ltd, Windmill Cottage, Mackerye End, Harpenden, Herts AL5 5DR